The Expression of Modality

W
DE
G

The Expression of Cognitive Categories

ECC 1

Editors

Wolfgang Klein
Stephen Levinson

Mouton de Gruyter
Berlin · New York

The Expression of Modality

edited by
William Frawley

with the assistance of
Erin Eschenroeder
Sarah Mills
and Thao Nguyen

Mouton de Gruyter
Berlin · New York

Mouton de Gruyter (formerly Mouton, The Hague)
is a Division of Walter de Gruyter GmbH & Co. KG, Berlin.

♾ Printed on acid-free paper which falls within the guidelines
of the ANSI to ensure permanence and durability.

Library of Congress Cataloging-in-Publication Data

The expression of modality / edited by William Frawley.
    p. cm. − (The expression of cognitive categories ; 1)
    Includes bibliographical references and index.
    ISBN-13: 978-3-11-018435-8 (cloth : alk. paper)
    ISBN-10: 3-11-018435-4 (cloth : alk. paper)
    ISBN-13: 978-3-11-018436-5 (pbk. : alk. paper)
    ISBN-10: 3-11-018436-2 (pbk. : alk. paper)
    1. Modality (Linguistics)   I. Frawley, William, 1953−   .
II. Series.
    P299.M6E97   2005
    415'.6−dc22

                                                    2005034176

Bibliographic information published by Die Deutsche Bibliothek

Die Deutsche Bibliothek lists this publication in the Deutsche Nationalbibliografie;
detailed bibliographic data is available in the Internet at <http://dnb.ddb.de>.

ISBN-13: 978-3-11-018435-8 hb
ISBN-10: 3-11-018435-4 hb
ISBN-13: 978-3-11-018436-5 pb
ISBN-10: 3-11-018436-2 pb

Preface

The papers that constitute *The Expression of Modality* provide a picture of the core issues in modality, the latest advances, and prospects for future work. As such, this book is not a handbook or state-of the art per se, but more like a comprehensive tutorial on how notions of possibility, probability, necessity, belief, and confidence are expressed and learned in human language and how to analyze and explain such notions. Not only are foundational ideas discussed – e.g., differences across root, deontic, and epistemic modality – but so are leading-edge ideas (such as new views of the logic of possibility) and illustrations of the variety of the manifestations of modality in languages not often treated in the canon of modality studies (e.g., ASL). *The Expression of Modality* is therefore designed as a kind of working text, something which stands between the settled ideas of modality and the future of research in the area.

Jan Nuyts, in *Modality: Overview and linguistic issues*, lays out the basics for any understanding of modality by covering all the essential concepts and terms, differentiating ideas where past studies gave conflated notions and converging others where previous work has made unproductive splits. Important lessons from his paper are the need to identify the locus of modal force and effect and the significance of scales vs. categorical notions. Nuyts' paper is in many ways a primer to modality as a whole.

Ferdinand de Haan, in *Typological approaches to modality*, takes the ideas that Nuyts so nicely explicates and applies them to a broad typological analysis of modality. He shows how typology has an essentially conceptual motivation, clarifies the modes of modal expression in the world's languages, and elucidates the ways modality interacts with mood, realis-irrealis, and other categories. One might take de Haan's paper as a kind of handbook for the field: when you go out to study a language in situ, keep these ideas and distinctions at the ready.

In *Formal approaches to modality*, Stefan Kaufmann, Cleo Condoravdi, and Valentina Harizanov outline systems of propositional logic and the nature and function of modal logic within such systems. They then offer a new picture of modality in terms of modal bases and accessibility relations across worlds. In addition to the admirable clarity and completeness of the formal exposition, one significant lesson inferable from their paper – not argued by them but an implication – is that discrete, abstract frameworks can work with the kind of scalar data and "realism assumptions" of empirical and typological linguistics. (This is nicely seen in their consideration of "settledness," e.g.) *Formal approaches to modality* might thus be understood not only as a logical counterpart to de Haan's work – a kind of handbook for the "field modal-logician" – but also as a statement about where and how logical and data-driven linguistics might work together with some hard thought in all camps.

Elizabeth Traugott provides a comprehensive picture of the historical development of modals in *Historical aspects of modality*. Important ideas here are considerations of the nature of historical change, the varied trajectories of formal changes, and, especially, the ever-present *counter-data* that fine tune accepted notions about such claims as unidirectionality, paths of grammaticalization, and the superiority of formal over functional, or functional over formal, explanations. If de Haan's paper is a kind of fieldguide to modality, and if Kaufmann, Condoravdi, and Harizanov's paper is a fieldguide for the modal logician, then Traugott's paper is a fieldguide for the linguistic archivist. Her work clearly shows the need for close attention to data so that nuanced claims about the causes and direction of historical change can be properly advanced.

Soonja Choi, in *Acquisition of modality*, takes us through the landscape of the acquisition of notions of possibility, necessity, and evidence. She offers important crosslinguistic data on the learning of modals, showing that children at a very early age are sensitive to the subtlety of meanings and range of forms in the languages to which they are exposed. Moreover, not all of children's behavior is traceable to features of input. Her paper is a good example of how empirical work on acquisition cuts the fine line between frequentist and nativist accounts and between purely formal explanations and explanations with syntactic and semantic-pragmatic interactions.

Munro's *Modal expression in Valley Zapotec* and Wilcox and Shaffer's *Modality in American Sign Language* are designed to illustrate how much of the foregoing finds illustration in two languages that not only are infrequently used in studies of modality, but also have maximally different grammaticalization possibilities. In her study of modality in Valley Zapotec, Pamela Munro describes the range of distinct grammatical expressions for modal notions in the language, and she shows how regularities in modality in Valley Zapotec both converge with universal patterns (e.g., with deontic and epistemic differentiated) and diverge from them (e.g., no core modality in the usual sense). ASL has a similar pattern: with trends in development analogous to what Traugott describes, ASL follows universal tendencies, but modality in ASL also interacts with intensification and so manifests some alternate routes of development. These two papers can be read as invitations for those working in the data-intensive side of linguistics to look closely and thoroughly at more languages for modal patterns.

The book closes with the *Topical outline*, put together by my research assistants, Erin Eschenroeder, Sarah Mills, and Thao Nguyen. This outline is designed as an accompaniment to reading or a way for a user of this book to go back and check ideas. The *Topical outline* is a critical part of the book's function as a tutorial.

I have assembled *The Expression of Modality* for a purpose larger than just to aggregate ideas on modal notions in the world's languages. I would hope that a book like this would stand a small test of time and serve as a very modest first step in trying to unify claims in critical areas of linguistics. A useful strategy would be to read the papers in this book – and hence modality in general – against the backdrop of current theoretical oppositions: scalar vs. categorical, functional vs. formal, frequentist vs. nativist, modular interfaces vs. multiply interactive distributive models, cognitive vs. noncognitive accounts, etc. If work in modality can enlighten these oppositions, perhaps more of such work in other areas can help us advance our field as a whole.

I wish to thank the following publishers for their kind permission to reprint illustrations: Cambridge University Press, Langue de Signes Éditions Publications, University of Chicago Press, and TJ Publishers.

William Frawley   Washington, DC, November, 2005

Contents

Modality: Overview and linguistic issues[1]

Jan Nuyts

1. Introduction

The notion of *modality* has been used in different ways in the literature. It is occasionally used in a very broad sense, such as to refer to any kind of speaker modification of a state of affairs, even including dimensions such as tense and aspect. This use is most common in philosophy (see Perkins 1983: 6; Palmer 1986: 9), but it occasionally also occurs in linguistics (e.g., Ransom 1977, 1986; Dietrich 1992). So used, the term is synonymous with what others would call (in more grammatical terminology) *tense-aspect-modality* (TAM) categories (e.g., Givón 1984, 1990), or, in more semantic terminology, *qualifications of states of affairs* (cf. Nuyts 2001a, 2005). In this chapter I will use the latter terms to refer to this wider domain.

The notion of modality in the present chapter is the more common, narrower one, referring to a semantic subfield of the wider domain of TAM categories or qualifications, one which is complementary to semantic domains such as tense/time and aspect. This is a vague characterization, and purposefully so, reflecting the problem encountered time and again by researchers in the field that, unlike the categories of time and aspect, which, in spite of disputes, can be defined in straightforward and coherent semantic terms, modality turns out to be very hard to delineate in simple, positive terms. In fact, as Bybee et al. (1994: 176) put it, "it may be impossible to come up with a succinct characterization of the notional domain of modality." Instead, the domain is usually characterized by referring to a set of more specific notions, each of which is defined separately, and which may be taken to share certain features motivating their grouping together under the label *modality*, but which differ in many other respects. As such, the notion of modality is best viewed as a supercategory (Nuyts 2005), which is much more loosely structured – and in fact probably belongs at a higher level of abstraction – than categories such as time and (types of) aspect. There is, however, also no unanimity among scholars as to how the set of modal categories should be characterized, either in terms of its outer borders – i.e., which semantic notions or dimensions do and which do not belong to it (cf., e.g., the disputes over the status of evidentiality) – or in terms of its internal organization – i.e., how the field should be divided up in distinct categories and what their precise boundaries are. Behind these disputes is also a difference in opinion about which features motivate the grouping of categories under the modal umbrella. The purpose of this chapter is to survey the different notions, positions and problems in this regard. Given my longstanding concern with the subject matter, however, I cannot avoid a certain influence of my own perspective and views on these matters (Nuyts 2001a, 2005).

This chapter first introduces and defines the three notions traditionally most commonly mentioned as the modal categories – *dynamic*, *deontic*, and *epistemic* – and presents a number of alternative ways proposed in the literature to divide the semantic space occupied by these. We then survey a series of notions at the margins of the set of modal notions, in that some scholars do, but others do not, include them in the category (e.g., alethic modality, boulomaic modality/attitude, and evidentiality). The chapter then turns to dimensions proposed in the literature for further subdividing or determining the usage possibilities of some of the modal categories, i.e., subjectivity vs. objectivity or intersubjectivity, and performativity vs. descriptivity. Further discussion concerns elements presented as the common thread which binds together different modal categories, and as such offers a perspective on the identity of modality as a semantic group. The chapter closes, briefly, with discussion of the situation of the modal categories among the TAM or qualificational categories in general.

2.   The basic categories

There is no unanimity among scholars regarding the list of categories to be called *modal*, but in one traditional version, modality comprises three basic semantic dimensions: *dynamic*, *deontic* and *epistemic*. These three meanings are also found in alternative views regarding the composition of the list, but often hidden behind other labels. We first define the three traditional categories, and then turn to the alternative views/divisions of the field.

2.1. Dynamic modality

Dynamic modality (Palmer 1979, 1983, 2001; Perkins 1983), sometimes also called *facultative modality* (Goossens 1985) or *inherent modality* (Hengeveld

1988), is traditionally characterized as an ascription of a capacity to the subject-participant of the clause (the subject is able to perform the action expressed by the main verb in the clause), of the kind expressed in the modal auxiliary in (1a), or the predicative adjective in (1b):

(1)   a.   That kid **can** sing like Frank Sinatra.
      b.   Pete is perfectly **able** to solve this problem if he wants to.

This definition needs at least three modifications.

First, it may be better to define dynamic modality in terms of a property of the first argument of the predicate, or of the controlling participant in the state of affairs (usually the agent). In passives, such as (2), the (implicit) controlling participant, rather than the grammatical subject, carries the capacity:[2]

(2)   The door has a key lock now, so that it **can** be opened and closed from both sides.

Second, as observed by Palmer (1979: 91ff), the category is not restricted to ability alone, but also covers the indication of a need or necessity for the first-argument participant, as expressed by the modal auxiliary in (3a) and the auxiliary-like predicate in (3b):[3]

(3)   a.   I **must** find a solution for this problem soon now or I'll go crazy.
      b.   Excuse me for a minute. I **have to** go to the bathroom urgently.

Third, the category not only covers capacities/abilities/potentials and needs/necessities which are fully inherent to the first-argument participant (henceforth called *participant-inherent dynamic*). It also covers abilities/ potentials and needs/necessities which are determined by the local circumstances (and which may thus be partly beyond the power and control) of that participant (we will call this *participant-imposed dynamic*). Thus, in examples (1) and (3), the preferred reading is that the property is exclusively due to the first-argument participant, but in (4) and (5) (as in (2)), the property is conditioned by external factors, explicitly mentioned in the utterance, as in (4a) and (5a), or implicit in the situation described in the utterance, as in (4b) and (5b):

(4)   a.   I've unlocked the back door, so you **can** enter the house there.
      b.   John will be **able** to participate in the debates starting next week.

(5)   a. To open that door you **must** turn the key and lift the latch simulta-
          neously.
      b. I'll be home in half an hour or so but I **need to** get fuel first.

Dynamic modality possibly needs to be extended even further to cover cases
which go beyond abilities/potentials or needs/necessities of any participant
in the state of affairs, and rather characterize a potential or a necessity/in-
evitability inherent in the situation described in the clause as a whole (to be
called *situational (dynamic)*). The clearest instances of this appear in expressions in which there simply is no participant, as in (6a), but it can also
appear in cases with inanimate first-argument participants, such as (6b) and
(6c), and even with animate (including human) first-argument participants,
as in (6d) and (6e), or in (6f), in which the first-argument participant is left
implicit:

(6)   a. In winter it **can** even snow in this hot desert.
      b. In winter temperatures **can** sink well below zero here.
      c. The book **need** not be in the library. It **can** also be on my desk.
      d. John **cannot** be in Spain. I've just seen him in the grocery store.
      e. We all **have to** die someday.
      f. It is **possible** to enter the cave if one manages to climb the steep
          wall below it.

While there is no unanimity as to whether cases of the situational type
should be considered part of the dynamic modal category, one argument in
favor of grouping all the cases in (1)–(6) together is that they all basically
express the same meaning of inherent potential or inherent necessity/in-
evitability. The difference among them resides in the entity to which the
potential or necessity is ascribed – an individual, a situation, or a mixture of
both (Nuyts 2005).[4]

2.2. Deontic modality

Deontic modality is traditionally defined in terms of permission and obligation (Kratzer 1978: 111; Palmer 1986: 96–97). In more general terms, however, it may be defined as an indication of the degree of moral desirability of
the state of affairs expressed in the utterance, typically, but not necessarily,
on behalf of the speaker (speakers can report on others' deontic assess-

ments – see performativity vs. descriptivity, below). The notion of morality involved should be defined widely since it can relate to societal norms and to strictly personal ethical criteria of the individual responsible for the deontic assessment: a gangster can deontically assess some state of affairs in quite positive terms while the average person would assess the same state of affairs as morally unacceptable (and the gangster can obviously be perfectly aware of this clash). The notion of degree in the definition may be taken to suggest that this semantic category involves a gradual scale going from absolute moral necessity via degrees of desirability to acceptability, and – if one assumes that the category also includes a dimension of polarity – further on to the negative values of undesirability and absolute moral unacceptability. Not everyone subscribes to this scalar view, however: especially in logic, there is a strong trend to analyze all modal categories – hence also deontic modality – in terms of discrete values (usually only possibility and necessity), and to consider negation a separate operator interacting with the modal operator (Kratzer 1978).

This semantic category is rendered in the most direct or straightforward way by expressions such as the modal auxiliaries in (7a), expressing respectively moral desirability and necessity, and the predicative adjective in (7b), expressing moral desirability.[5] It is represented in a more complex way by expressions of permission and obligation for the first-argument participant in the clause, as involved in the modal auxiliary in (7c) and the speech act verb in (7d):

(7)   a. We **should** be thankful for what he has done for us, so we **must** find a way to show our gratitude to him.
      b. (It is) **Good** that they've warned us for this tricky part of the trip.
      c. You **may** come in now.
      d. I **demand** that you come in immediately.

Expressions of permission, obligation and interdiction can be considered more complex because they not only involve an assessment of the degree of moral acceptability of a state of affairs, but also a translation of this assessment into (non-verbal) action terms. Specifically they involve an intention to instigate or (not) hinder another person's actions or positions (usually the addressee's, who can, but need not figure as the clausal subject, cf. Lakoff 1972) pertaining to the state of affairs, in view of the judgment of its degree of acceptability.[6]

2.3. Epistemic modality

The third traditional modal subcategory is *epistemic modality*. The core definition of this category is relatively noncontroversial: it concerns an indication of the estimation, typically, but not necessarily, by the speaker, of the chances that the state of affairs expressed in the clause applies in the world. In other words, it expresses the degree of probability of the state of affairs, as indicated by the modal auxiliary *will* in (8a) or the modal adverb *maybe* in (8b):

(8)   a. Someone is knocking at the door. That **will** be John.
      b. This manuscript is damned hard to read. **Maybe** some more light
         can help.

As in deontic modality, this dimension can be construed as a scale – from absolute certainty via probability to fairly neutral possibility that the state of affairs is real. Moreover, if one assumes that the category also involves polarity, the scale even continues further on to the negative side, via improbability of the state of affairs to absolute certainty that it is not real. The scalar view is probably quite noncontroversial in functional linguistics, but most formal semanticists will not accept it (Kratzer 1978): as mentioned above, the latter strongly tend to consider modality (epistemic and other) a matter of discrete categories, with negation functioning as a separate operator. (This trend is not limited to formal semantic approaches, though: e.g., van der Auwera and Plungian 1998 adopt this perspective as well, at least in practice, although they admit – pp. 82–83 – that one could make further refinements in this division.)

2.4. Alternative divisions of the semantic domain

Several scholars have proposed different organizations of the conceptual semantic domain of modality in order to emphasize certain (other) semantic relations among categories or to give a different perspective on the issue, such as a focus on properties of the linguistic forms expressing modal categories. In most of these alternatives, the notion of epistemic modality remains basically untouched, but reorganization is to be found in dynamic and deontic modality.

Some scholars consider what we have called *situational (dynamic)* not to belong to the category of dynamic modal meanings at all. Van der Auwera and Plungian (1998), e.g., call this category *participant-external modality*, as opposed to *participant-internal modality* (i.e., our participant-inherent and participant-imposed dynamic categories). Moreover, they consider this participant-external category to be very closely related to deontic modality – indeed, they consider deontic modality to be a special case of participant-external modality, with the difference that in the latter, the possibility or necessity is purely inherent in the physical circumstances of the state of affairs, whereas in the former they are imposed by a person (the speaker or someone else) or an institution (see also Goossens 1983, 1999). In other words, this alternative view takes *ascription to the first-argument participant* to be the dividing criterion, whereas the above view draws the line where *moral imposition by a subject outside the state of affairs* comes in.

Root modality involves a more drastic reorganization. Especially in the Anglo-American literature, this notion is very frequently used as the only counterpart for epistemic modality. It is sometimes explicitly related to deontic modality (Steele 1975a; Talmy 1988; and Sweetser 1990). But in practice Sweetser's and probably also Talmy's use of it turns out to be wider, also including (at least part of) dynamic modality. Hofmann (1976) and Coates (1983) even explicitly use root modality as a cover term for deontic and dynamic modality. In the same vein, Palmer (2001) covers deontic and dynamic modality under the label *event modality* (as opposed to *propositional modality*, covering epistemic modality and evidentiality).

Yet another classification is that of Bybee and colleagues (Bybee 1985; Bybee et al. 1994; Bybee and Fleischman 1995). Next to epistemic modality, they distinguish between *agent-oriented modality* and *speaker-oriented modality*. The former covers meanings which "predicate conditions on an agent [i.e., the first-argument participant in our earlier terminology – JN] with regard to the completion of an action referred to by the main predicate, e.g., obligation, desire, ability, permission and root possibility" (Bybee and Fleischman 1995: 6). Speaker-oriented modality covers "markers of directives, such as imperatives, optatives or permissives, which represent speech acts through which a speaker attempts to move an addressee to action" (Bybee and Fleischman 1995: 6). If one considers the latter moods to be part of deontic modality (as Bybee and colleagues do), then this classification crosscuts the category of deontic modality, grouping part of it with the dynamic modal meanings as defined above (including situational (dynamic) modality) and part of it in a separate category. But if one excludes mood categories from the domain of (deontic) modality (hence rejects speaker-oriented modality as a modal category), then this proposal is essentially identical to the one distinguishing epistemic modality and root modality. Bybee et al. (1994) moreover distinguish a category of *subordinating modality*, but this is basically a formal category covering modalities (or moods) in subordinate clauses.

3.   Categories on the margins of modality

We have surveyed the traditional core notions of modality. Beyond these, there are other, more controversial notions which some scholars have proposed as modal categories, but which others exclude.

3.1. Mood

Mood is used in a number of different ways in the literature, most importantly to refer to the inventory of basic utterance types in a language, such as declarative, interrogative, imperative, optative, etc., and to capture distinctions such as indicative vs. subjunctive or realis vs. irrealis. Clearly, both these phenomena show relations to the traditional modal categories, but there are different views as to how to see them. Bybee et al. (1994) essentially include both these categories in the domain of modality, assigning separate modal subcategories to each (see above). Palmer (2001) takes a comparable position. Others exclude them from the modal territory, assigning the issue of utterance types to the domain of illocutions (e.g., van der Auwera and Plungian 1998), and considering notions such as indicative vs. subjunctive or realis vs. irrealis as formal categories of grammatical expressions of modal notions, along with other expressive devices, such as auxiliaries, adverbials, etc. (see de Haan this volume). In the latter view modality is a semantic notion, but mood is a grammatical one.

3.2. Alethic modality

Alethic modality is a notion which was originally proposed in the context of modal logic (von Wright 1951), and which sometimes also figures in formal semantic approaches to modality (Lyons 1977: 791; Palmer 1979: 2–3, 1986: 10–11). In those frameworks, the notion is close to, yet distinct from, epistemic modality: according to definition, alethic modality concerns the necessary or contingent truth of propositions (i.e., *modes of truth*), whereas epistemic modality concerns the state of a proposition in terms of knowledge and belief (i.e., *modes of knowing*). In linguistic semantic analyses of modality, however, the notion is hardly ever used. This might be a terminological matter: the distinction between alethic and epistemic modality shows some similarity to that between objective and subjective epistemic modality often made in linguistic semantics (on this link, see Lyons 1977); and one can also detect certain similarities to the distinction between epistemic modality and situational (dynamic) modality. On the other hand, to the extent that the distinction raises the suggestion that one should distinguish between types of likelihood in terms of something like *truth in the world* vs. *truth in an individual's mind*, it has been explicitly criticized by Palmer (1986: 11), who states: "there is no distinction between [...] what is logically true and what the speaker believes, as a matter of fact, to be true" and "there is no formal grammatical distinction in English, and, perhaps, in no other language either, between alethic and epistemic modality."

3.3. Volition/intention

There is no unanimity among scholars regarding how to handle the notions of *volition*, as expressed by the auxiliary-like predicate in (9a), and *intention*, as expressed by the auxiliary in (9b):

(9)   a. I **want** you to tell me truth.
      b. I promise I **will** never lie to you again.

Some authors count volition as a subcategory of deontic modality (e.g., Palmer 1986). Others rather include it in the category of dynamic modality (e.g., Goossens 1983; Palmer 2001). Still others simply exclude it from the set of modal categories (e.g., van der Auwera and Plungian 1998). Similarly, Palmer (2001) does include *commissives* – a category close to if not identical with intention – in deontic modality, whereas most other authors do not mention intention, hence probably exclude it from deontic modality. Conceptually, the notion of intention does show some relation to the concepts of obligation and permission: like the latter, it relates to action terms, the difference being that in this case it relates to the actions of the assessor him/herself. Volition, on the other hand, is less clearly related to action plans, but instead appears to primarily refer to desires. The question is whether that still counts as a modal notion, and if so, in which modal subcategory it falls (see also the discussion of boulomaic modality below).

3.4. Evidentiality

Another matter of dispute – a very complex one – concerns *evidentiality*, which can be characterized as an indication of the nature of the sources of information which the speaker (or somebody else) has to assume or accept the existence of in the state of affairs expressed in the clause (Chafe and Nichols 1986; Willett 1988). That is, it involves a characterization of the origins of the knowledge about the state of affairs, or of the compatibility of the (postulated) state of affairs with the general epistemological background of the issuer. Evidentiality is usually taken to cover a number of different subcategories of information source:

- Directly perceived through the issuer's own sense organs (often called *experiential*), as, e.g., expressed by the main predicate in (10a).
- Indirectly deduced on the basis of other, directly perceived information (*inferential*), as expressed in the adverb in (10b), or derived from or compatible with other general background knowledge (what one might call *reasoned*), as expressed by the predicative adjective in (10c).
- Received from others (*hearsay* or *reportative*), as expressed by the main predicate in (10d).

(10) a. I've **noticed** that he's quite down lately.
     b. **Apparently** he's in his office – at least, his coat is hanging here and I hear voices inside.
     c. Your explanation sounds very **plausible**.
     d. I **hear** he's won the class competition this year.

The category of evidentiality has traditionally been defined to cover only grammatical expressions of these meanings. English has hardly any such forms, however. (The modal auxiliary *must* is a possible, though not uncontroversial, exception. Coates 1983: 41, e.g., calls it epistemic but admits that it also has an inferential meaning component. Palmer 2001: 8–9 calls it deductive, i.e., inferential, but handles it together with the epistemic forms. Bybee et al. 1994: 180 list it under the epistemic meanings but label it as expressing inferred certainty.) Hence the examples in (10) feature lexical expressions.[7]

    There are different opinions as to whether evidentiality is distinct from epistemic modality, and if so, as to whether it is even a modal notion at all.

That the relation between evidentiality and epistemic modality should be problematic is not surprising, of course: there is a logical connection between them in the sense that epistemic judgments are conceptually based on evidence, and evidentials refer to types of the latter. In line with this, evidential categories often suggest or imply a certain degree of probability of the state of affairs. For example, hearsay evidence tends to be considered less reliable than direct visual perception. Hence the former often suggests lower probability of the state of affairs than the latter, which normally implies certainty (see also Givón 1982 on relations between epistemic values and the use of evidential markers). Nevertheless, authors interpret the relations between these categories differently.

Thus, some authors do include evidentiality in the category of epistemic modality (e.g., Bybee 1985; Palmer 1986). Some do not directly do so, but do closely associate the two categories by adjoining them under one modal supercategory (cf. Hengeveld's 1989 *epistemological modality*, or Palmer's 2001 *propositional modality*). Others see them as two related but separate categories, although both count as modal (cf. Nuyts 2004a, who prefers the notion *attitudinal* over *modal* to label these categories). Still others simply exclude evidentials from the set of modal categories (e.g., Anderson 1986; Bybee et al. 1994 – see also de Haan this volume). Quite a few authors differentiate subtypes of evidentiality, however, in terms of the tightness of their link to epistemic modality or in terms of their inclusion as a modal notion. Inference is often considered to be much more closely tied to epistemic modality than hearsay or experientiality (e.g., Palmer 2001; Nuyts 2005), and van der Auwera and Plungian (1998) even include inference in epistemic modality but exclude the other evidential categories entirely from the modal categories. In fact, inference (including reasoned, see above) shares at least one property with epistemic modality which the other evidential categories do not – it also involves degrees (viz. in the reliability of the inference): there are strong forms (e.g., *clearly, obviously, logical*), moderate forms (e.g., *appear, plausible, presumably*), and weak forms (e.g., *seem(ingly)*). Degrees are not the case for hearsay or experientiality (in the latter, languages may mark differences between types of sense organs – visual, acoustic, tactile, etc., cf. Willett 1988 – but that is not a matter of degrees of experientiality). Moreover, while the epistemic implications of a hearsay or experiential marker can be cancelled quite easily (e.g., although a hearsay marker often signals reduced reliability, if it is used when citing the words of an expert it has the opposite effect), this appears much more difficult in the case of inferential markers: degrees of strength of inference quite strongly correlate with suggestions of degrees of epistemic likelihood. Apparently, evidentiality is semantically not a very tight category.

3.5. Boulomaic modality/attitude

A category which is only sporadically mentioned, let alone thoroughly ana-lyzed, is *boulomaic modality* or *attitude* (also called *emotional attitude* – Nuyts 2001a; see also Kratzer 1978; Hengeveld 1989; Nuyts 2005). This category indicates the degree of the speaker's (or someone else's) liking or disliking of the state of affairs, as expressed by the predicative adjective in (11a), the adverb in (11b), or the main verb in (11c):

(11)   a.   A: I'll be joining you guys to Paris – B: (That's) **Wonderful.**

      b.   **Unfortunately**, I won't be able to join you guys on your trip to Paris.

      c.   I **love** it that we'll be in Paris all together.

Why this category has not been systematically analyzed in the work on modal notions is unclear. Maybe it is because this meaning is hardly pre-sent in the system of modal auxiliaries in the West European languages, which has strongly dominated the analysis of modality. There are plenty of lexical expressions with this kind of meaning in these languages, however, and the category has properties which make it quite comparable to uncon-troversially modal notions. Like deontic and epistemic modality, it can be analyzed as scalar, with a positive and a negative pole, and it is clearly atti-tudinal (see below). *Volition* may also belong to this type. It will not always be easy to draw a precise line between this category and deontic modality, however, a problem which no doubt extends beyond the issue of the status of volition. Still, (dis)liking something is not the same thing as (dis)approving of something.

4. Dimensions subcategorizing (expressions of) modal categories

In the literature one not only finds reference to different types of modal categories, but also to dimensions which further subdivide (some of) them. These dimensions are meant to account for differences in individual usages of modal expressions or for different usage properties of modal expression types. Modality across languages can be expressed by a range of linguistic form types (see de Haan, this volume, for an overview). But, as already suggested above, in most languages even each modal category individually can be expressed by a range of devices: in European languages, e.g., most modality types typically have grammatical, adverbial, adjectival and verbal forms. For instance, English expresses epistemic modality through auxiliaries such as *may* or *could*, adverbs such as *maybe* or *surely*, adjectives such as *probable* or *certain*, and full verbs such as *think* or *believe*. Semantic dimensions are then often invoked to differentiate across these alternatives or some of their usage types.[8]

4.1. Subjectivity vs. objectivity/intersubjectivity

One dimension often brought up is the distinction between *subjective* and *objective* modal categories – see, e.g., Lyons (1977), Coates (1983), Palmer (1986). This distinction is usually introduced in discussions of epistemic modality, but it has also been brought to bear on deontic modality (e.g., by Lyons 1977). Most authors use the notions *subjective* and *objective* in a quite intuitive way, without formally defining them. Lyons (1977: 797ff), however, does define them, as follows: objective epistemic modality expresses an objectively measurable chance that the state of affairs under consideration is true or not, while subjective epistemic modality involves a purely subjective guess regarding its truth. Thus, when uttering a sentence like *Alfred may be unmarried*, the speaker can either indicate that (s)he is simply uncertain about the (hypothetical) fact that Alfred is unmarried – i.e., subjective modality – or (s)he may mean to indicate that there is a mathematically computable chance that Alfred is unmarried, for example because (s)he knows that Alfred belongs to a community of ninety people, of which there are thirty unmarried, hence one chance in three that he is unmarried – i.e., objective modality. Some authors consider this a matter of two different semantic categories of (epistemic or deontic) modality (e.g., Hengeveld 1988, and probably also Lyons 1977); other authors are less clear as to the status of this dimension. Most or all authors do attempt to relate this dimension to different expression types, but there is no unanimity about which meaning-form correlations actually hold (witness the quite different analyses of the modal auxiliaries in Lyons 1977; Palmer 1979; Coates 1983; or of modal expressions in general in Perkins 1983; Kiefer 1984; Watts 1984; and Hengeveld 1988).

Lyons' definition of subjectivity vs. objectivity draws on differences in the quality of the evidence leading to the judgment. An alternative way to define the intuitively appealing distinction between more and less subjective modal expressions is in terms of who is responsible for the modal evaluation. This distinction can be termed *subjectivity* vs. *intersubjectivity*, and it can be defined as follows (cf. Nuyts 1992, 2001a: 33, 2001b): an evaluation is subjective if the issuer presents it as being strictly his/her own responsibility; it is intersubjective if (s)he indicates that (s)he shares it with a wider group of people, possibly including the hearer (not to be confused with a *descriptive* use of modal forms). In other words, it might be a matter of whether the modal judgment is common ground between the speaker and the hearer or others. This dimension appears structurally present in deontic and epistemic modality, and also in inferentiality and boulomaic attitude, but not in dynamic modality (i.e., only in *attitudinal* categories – Nuyts 2005). But it is not present in all individual expressions of these semantic categories. Corpus research (cf. Nuyts 2001b) indicates that in epistemic forms (but the situation is no doubt similar in the other attitudinal categories) expression of the dimension depends on the possibility to code the issuer of the evaluation – i.e., it is only present in predicative (verbal or adjectival) expressions, but not in grammatical or adverbial ones. A first person subject then codes subjectivity, and an impersonal subject codes intersubjectivity:

(12) a. **I think** they have forgotten to take the key.   = subjective

     b. **It is quite probable** that they have forgotten to take the key.

                                                  = intersubjective

     c. **Probably** they have forgotten to take the key.   = neutral

The fact that not all modal expressions carry this feature might at once be an argument to assume that this is an independent semantic category akin to similar categories proposed in the literature, such as DeLancey's (1997) *mirativity* or Slobin and Aksu's (1982; Aksu-Koç and Slobin 1986) *prepared vs. unprepared minds* (see, e.g., DeLancey 1986; Nichols 1986; Woodbury 1986; Lee 1993; Choi 1995 for other related categories – cf. Nuyts 2001b for discussion). This category is semantically close to evidentiality (cf. Nuyts 2001b), but in line with DeLancey's arguments concerning mirativity, there are reasons not to include it among the evidential dimensions as such, but to consider it something separate (Nuyts 2005).

There is of course an intricate – and not always obvious – relationship between the notion of subjectivity in modal categories, and notions of subjectivity elsewhere in the literature, including the notion of subjectification in diachronic change (see Traugott 1989, 1995; Traugott and Dasher 2002: 19; Traugott this volume), and the notion of subjectivity as defined by Langacker (1990; see also Nuyts 2001a, 2001b).

4.2. Performativity vs. descriptivity

Another dimension structurally at work in modal categories (specifically, in all attitudinal ones) concerns the question of whether the speaker is committed to the evaluation, i.e., the issue of *performativity* vs. *descriptivity* (cf. Nuyts 2001a: 39). A performative expression marks an attitude to which the speaker is fully committed at the moment of speech. In a descriptive use, the speaker is not committed, but is only reporting on an attitude regarding some state of affairs held by someone else, or by the speaker at some point in time other than the moment of speech, or as a hypothetical possibility. This concept is related to yet distinct from speech act performativity: both involve the performance of something here and now, and in both this performance is expressed on the spot by means of the utterance, but in speech act performativity this concerns a linguistic act towards a hearer, while modal performativity concerns an evaluation of a state of affairs in terms of some criterion. Again, in epistemic modality in the West Germanic languages (Nuyts 2001a), the expression of a descriptive evaluation requires the possibility to code the issuer: it is restricted to predicative (verbal and adjectival) epistemic expressions, which allow the speaker to alter the grammatical subject or the tense (from first person and present for performativity to non-first person and/or non-present for descriptivity). Epistemic adverbs and auxiliaries can thus only be used performatively. The situation is no doubt comparable in the other attitudinal categories.[9]

5. Dimensions relating modal categories

The modal categories surveyed herein clearly involve a set of quite divergent semantic notions. The question is, then: what motivates the linking together of some or all of these under the umbrella of the supercategory of modality? Several elements have been proposed in the literature.

5.1. Meanings of the modal auxiliaries and their developmental relations

A first element – probably the major one for most functionalist linguists – is the empirical fact that there is a significant cross-linguistic trend for languages to have a category of grammatical forms – the modal auxiliaries – which expresses precisely the set of meanings introduced earlier, and, even more importantly, that there is, again crosslinguistically, a systematic developmental relationship between these meanings in these forms (cf. Traugott this volume): they evolve along a quite fixed path which runs from dynamic to deontic to epistemic. This path applies in diachrony and ontogenesis (Goossens 1982; Shepherd 1993; Bybee and Pagliuca 1985; Stephany 1986, 1993). In diachrony the path is traditionally assumed to be linear from dynamic via deontic to epistemic, but there are now reasons to question the universality of the strictly linear view, since there are quite a few cases which clearly show a parallel – though not necessarily temporally simultaneous – development from dynamic into deontic and from dynamic into epistemic (Bybee 1988; Bybee et al. 1994 on *may*; Goossens 1999 on *must*; Nuyts 2001a: 232–233; Van Ostaeyen and Nuyts 2004 on Dutch *kunnen* 'can, may').

This factor is specifically tied to the system of modal auxiliaries: forms of the alternative modal expression types do not usually feature the same range of meanings as the modal auxiliaries, nor does the meaning development typical of the modal auxiliaries apply in the same way to these other expressive devices. Nevertheless, the tie of this element to the meanings of the modal auxiliaries may explain at least in part why meanings such as evidentiality and boulomaic attitude are so often excluded from the modal categories, since these are only minimally present in the system of auxiliaries.

5.2. Shared semantic characteristics

A second factor motivating the grouping of semantic categories under modality is that they all share some fundamental semantic property. There are a few different formulations of what this might involve.

The most common one – typically associated with scholars analyzing these domains in terms of discrete values – characterizes all modal categories in terms of possibility and necessity (Kratzer 1978; van der Auwera and Plungian 1998). In terms of a scalar view, this is equal to saying that all categories involved have at least a strong and a weak value. According to this principle, also volition/intention, boulomaic attitude, and inferential evidentiality would be modal categories since they, too, have this property. Hearsay and experiential evidentiality would be excluded, however. If the presence of a scale were to be taken as the common property, then dynamic modality would be excluded as well, since it is strictly binary.

The semantic correspondences between the modal categories have been formulated in yet other ways. For example, Talmy (1988) has argued that each of these categories can be seen in terms of force-dynamics (see also Sweetser 1990). Kratzer (1978) and Perkins (1983) characterize them as resulting from relating a state of affairs to specific domains of knowledge, in Perkins' terms natural laws, social rules and conventions, or rational principles.

5.3. Shared status as attitudinal categories

Yet another way to motivate the grouping of the semantic categories is through their status as *attitudinal* categories (Nuyts 2005): they all indicate – each in a different way – to what extent the speaker (or another person, in descriptive cases) is committed to the state of affairs. This characterization obviously does not apply to categories such as time and aspect, which merely situate or specify the state of affairs in the world.

In terms of the traditional modal notions, this characterization clearly does include deontic and epistemic modality (which indicate the degree of moral and existential commitment), but not dynamic modality (not even situational dynamic modality: when a speaker states that *it can rain here in summer*, i.e., that there is a potential for rain, (s)he is merely describing a fact). On the other hand, this characterization does include boulomaic attitude (which expresses the degree of affective commitment). And it probably even includes evidentiality, or at least some subtypes. By addressing the issue of information sources, evidentials signal that the existential status of the state of affairs is not obvious. The fact that inferentiality even involves an indication of the degree of confidence with which the existence of the state of affairs can be concluded from the evidence is perfectly in line with this analysis. Of course, the characterization of the category of modal meanings in terms of degrees of commitment strongly suggests that this definition is coextensive with the characterization of the category as involving scalar meanings – but if so, the fact that hearsay and experiential evidentiality are not scalar casts some doubt on their status. A similar point holds for the characterization of modal categories as relating a state of affairs to background knowledge. This definition is essentially in accordance with the characterization in terms of attitudes (i.e., evaluations of states of affairs drawing on different kinds of general principles which are part of one's knowledge of the world). However, this definition is clearly applicable to inferentiality but not to hearsay, which only requires the words of some other person but no background knowledge, nor to experientiality, which implies that there is no prior knowledge involved at all.

This characterization of the common ground of modal categories explains why they should typically and structurally feature the distinctions above, while other qualificational categories, such as time or aspect (or dynamic modality, for that matter), do not (cf. Nuyts 2001a, 2005): if one is talking about commitments, it is important to be able to make it very clear, in an immediate way, who is making them (performativity vs. descriptivity); and if one is concerned with attitudes, it is often essential to be able to make it clear whether one is alone in one's views, has backing for them (subjectivity vs. intersubjectivity), is neutral, or is subjectively biased in one's assessment (subjectivity vs. objectivity).

6. The relationship of modal categories to other TAM categories

In closing, a few words are in order about the position of the modal categories among the TAM or qualificational categories in general. Typological research (e.g., Foley and Van Valin 1984; Bybee 1985; Hengeveld 1989; Van Valin 1993) has demonstrated that there is a strong tendency for TAM markers to be ordered according to a cross-linguistically recurrent semantic pattern, viz. in terms of their relative extension of semantic scope (for variations, see Bybee 1985; Bhat 1999). One can also observe these scope relations in purely semantic terms, as in (13):

(13) a. I am **probably** going to Paris **tomorrow**.
      b. You **may** go to that soccer game **tomorrow**.

In (13a), the epistemic marker *probably* is clearly not covered by the time marker *tomorrow*: the judgment of probability is valid at the moment of speech, and is not situated tomorrow. The time marker, however, *is* part of the information which is said to be probable, and so the time adverbial is within the semantic scope of the evidential adverbial, but not vice versa. (13b) does not mean that the hearer will receive permission tomorrow to go to a soccer game, but that the hearer has permission (at least) from the moment of the utterance of the sentence onwards, to go to a soccer game tomorrow. So the deontic form has the temporal one within its scope, but not vice versa. Similar observations apply to other combinations of qualificational dimensions. These semantic relations among categories are, moreover, not accidental (in the sense that they would just vary depending on the individual example), but systematic, within and across languages. This systematicity can tentatively be rendered in terms of a hierarchization of the most important qualificational dimensions introduced in this chapter, as in (14) (boulomaic attitude is missing, because its position is not entirely obvious yet – but it probably belongs just above or below deontic modality):

(14) > evidentiality
      > epistemic modality
        > deontic modality
          > time
            > quantificational aspect [frequency]/dynamic modality
              > qualificational aspect [internal phases]
                v (parts of the) STATE OF AFFAIRS

More formalized variants of such a hierarchy have been proposed in the context of functional grammar models (Van Valin 1993; Dik 1997), but the enormous differences between these proposals go to show that the discussion about the precise format of the system, including the precise ordering of categories, is far from settled (cf. Nuyts 2001a for discussion).

There are also many factors which complicate the seemingly simple picture presented in (14). One is performativity vs. descriptivity in the attitudinal categories in the system: the schema in (14) essentially only applies for the performative version of such categories. Another complicating element is the fact that the attitudinal categories appear not to combine in a simple way in an utterance. There appears to be a one-commitment-per-clause principle (Nuyts 2001a: 336, 2004). This is probably the effect of basic cognitive principles underlying the system – in general, the system in (14) may yield not just linguistic dimensions but very basic elements of the way we conceptualize the world (Nuyts 2001a).

What the schema in (14) does show is that the modal categories systematically have a wider semantic scope than categories such as time and types of aspect. It also shows that the juxtaposition of the categories of time, aspect and modality in treatments of TAM marking is somewhat misleading: modality is at a higher level of abstraction than time and aspect, and only specific modal categories can be put on par with these latter qualificational categories.

Notes

1. This research was sponsored by the Fund for Scientific Research – Flanders (VNC-project 1 G.0470.03), and by a collaborative project (*Geconcerteerde Onderzoeksactie*) funded by the Research Council of the University of Antwerp (GOA 2003/4).

2. This formulation is tentative since the capacity is not as clearly tied to the implicit actor in (2) as it is to the explicit actor in (1). Hence (2) might tend towards the participant-external (dynamic) reading to be discussed below. In this connection, also observe that *John is able to open the door* is fine, but *the door is able to be opened* is not. This raises interesting questions in need of further investigation regarding the role of syntactic structure in the meaning of the dynamic uses of these forms.

3. In her analysis of the English modals, Coates (1983) does not – within her category of *root modality* – mention this meaning of *must*, as distinct from what others would call the deontic use of this modal; this is unlike *can*, for which she does distinguish ability, possibility, and permission. Yet the meaning of *must* in (3a) – and (5a) below – cannot be put under the label of moral necessity.

4. There is no doubt, though, that this meaning diachronically constitutes a step from the core dynamic meaning to the deontic and epistemic meanings. But likewise, the participant-imposed meaning constitutes a historical step from the participant-internal to the situational meaning. See Van Ostaeyen and Nuyts (2004) for evidence to this effect on the basis of a detailed diachronic analysis of Dutch *kunnen* 'can, may.'

5. The deontic modals are typically described as expressing permission or obligation, yet at least for some of them, this is only part of the story. In English, e.g., deontic *must* can clearly also be used to express mere moral necessity, without involving an expression of an obligation to do something. One might even argue that in the case of *must* the moral necessity reading is the basic one, and the obligation reading is only triggered in certain specific contexts, i.e., when the first-argument participant is the hearer.

6. Permissions, obligations and interdictions possibly even extend beyond deontic modality, however: it is not unlikely that they can also result from drawing consequences from situational (dynamic) possibilities or necessities. For instance, when an office director orders a collaborator to write such and such a letter, this may have more to do with situational necessities than with deontic assessments. If so, then obligation, permission and interdiction (and 'intention,' see below) would better be considered a completely separate semantic category, which belongs at an entirely different level in a semantic analysis from notions such as dynamic or deontic modality.

7. The precise delimitation of non-grammatical forms expressing this meaning category is far from simple, however, especially for the categories *experiential*

and *hearsay.* Does the normal use of the perception predicates – not only the vague one in (10a), but also more specific ones such as *see, hear, feel,* etc., as used in expressions such as *I've **seen** him enter the grocery store,* or *I've **heard** how he dashed down the stairs* – belong to the category of experientials? Does the normal use of markers of direct or indirect speech reporting – often simple speech act verbs, e.g., as used in vivid narration, *and he **said**, "don't do that" "I will do it" she **answered** "Oh you won't," he **replied*** – belong in the range of hearsay markers? And what of the prepositional phrase in ***according to our lawyer** you don't stand a chance in this trial*? These matters require further consideration in order to clear up the status of the category of evidentiality.

8. Corpus research of the paradigm of epistemic expressions in Dutch, German and English (Nuyts 2001a), further supported by experimental research (Nuyts and Vonk 1999), has shown that there is one more dimension systematically differentiating between the alternative form types, of a more communicative nature – information structure (cf. also Nuyts 2000): can the epistemic expression be focalized or not? Adjectives can and usually are, mental state predicates can but are not often, adverbs and auxiliaries cannot. In general, however, these investigations have also shown that focalization of epistemic expressions is a very exceptional and marked situation (see also Steele 1975b, Plank 1981), which only occurs in situations of contrast. To what extent these observations also apply to other modal categories is a matter for further empirical research – see Langacker 1974, Lötscher 1985 and Chafe 1994 on the special informational status of qualificational expressions in general. (One further but non-systematic factor in the use of individual epistemic expressions is their mitigating or argumentative use – see Nuyts 2001a.)

9. It need not be identical, though. For instance, in deontic modality in Dutch, the modal auxiliaries do allow descriptivity, due to the fact that they have developed a structural possibility to code the issuer, viz. in constructions of the type *je mag niet roken van mama* '(literally) you may not smoke from mama,' i.e., 'mama does not allow you to smoke.'

References

Aksu-Koç, Ayhan and Dan Slobin
    1986   A psychological account of the development and use of evidentials in Turkish. In *Evidentiality*, W. Chafe and J. Nichols (eds.), 159–167. Norwood: Ablex.

Anderson, Lloyd B.
    1986   Evidentials, paths of change, and mental maps: Typologically regular asymmetries. In *Evidentiality*, W. Chafe and J. Nichols (eds.), 273–312. Norwood: Ablex.

Bhat, D. N. S.
1999   *The Prominence of Tense, Aspect and Mood.* Amsterdam: John Benjamins.
Bybee, Joan L.
1985   *Morphology.* Amsterdam: John Benjamins.
1988   Semantic substance vs. contrast in the development of grammatical meaning. *Berkeley Linguistic Society* 14: 247–264.
Bybee, Joan L. and Suzanne Fleischman
1995   Modality in grammar and discourse: An introductory essay. In *Modality in Grammar and Discourse*, J. L. Bybee and S. Fleischman (eds.), 1–14. Amsterdam: John Benjamins.
Bybee, Joan L. and William Pagliuca
1985   Cross-linguistic comparison and the development of grammatical meaning. In *Historical Semantics: Historical Word-Formation*, J. Fisiak (ed.), 59–83. Berlin/New York: Mouton de Gruyter.
Bybee, Joan L., Revere D. Perkins and William Pagliuca
1994   *The Evolution of Grammar: Tense, Aspect and Modality in the Languages of the World.* Chicago: University of Chicago Press.
Chafe, Wallace
1994   *Discourse, Consciousness, and Time.* Chicago: University of Chicago Press.
Chafe, Wallace and Johanna Nichols (eds.)
1986   *Evidentiality.* Norwood: Ablex.
Choi, Soonja
1995   The development of epistemic sentence-ending modal forms and functions in Korean children. In *Modality in Grammar and Discourse*, J. L. Bybee and S. Fleischman (eds.), 165–204. Amsterdam: John Benjamins.
Coates, Jennifer
1983   *The Semantics of the Modal Auxiliaries.* London: Croom Helm.
DeLancey, Scott
1986   Evidentiality and volitionality in Tibetan. In *Evidentiality*, W. Chafe and J. Nichols (eds.), 203–213. Norwood: Ablex.
1997   Mirativity: The grammatical marking of unexpected information. *Linguistic Typology* 1: 33–52.
Dik, Simon C.
1997   *The Theory of Functional Grammar.* Berlin/New York: Mouton de Gruyter.
Dietrich, Rainer
1992   *Modalität im Deutschen.* Opladen: Westdeutscher Verlag.
Foley, William A. and Robert D. Van Valin
1984   *Functional Syntax and Universal Grammar.* Cambridge: Cambridge University Press.

Givón, Talmy
  1982   Evidentiality and epistemic space. *Studies in Language* 6: 23–49.
  1984   *Syntax: A Functional-Typological Introduction, vol. 1*. Amsterdam:
            John Benjamins.
  1990   *Syntax: A Functional-Typological Introduction, vol. 2*. Amsterdam:
            John Benjamins.
Goossens, Louis
  1983   *Can* and *kunnen*: Dutch and English potential compared. In *Een
            spyeghel voor G. Jo Steenbergen*, F. Daems and L. Goossens (eds.),
            147–158. Leuven: Acco.
  1985   Modality and the modals. In *Predicates and Terms in Functional
            Grammar*, M. Bolkestein, C. De Groot and L. Mackenzie (eds.),
            203–217. Dordrecht: Foris.
  1999   Metonymic bridges in modal shifts. In *Metonymy in Language and
            Cognition*, K.-U. Panther and G. Radden (eds.), 193–210. Amster-
            dam: John Benjamins.
Hengeveld, Kees
  1988   Illocution, mood and modality in a functional grammar of Spanish.
            Journal of Semantics 6: 227–269.
  1989   Layers and operators in functional grammar. *Journal of Linguistics*
            25: 127–157.
Hofmann, Thomas R.
  1976   Past tense replacement and the modal system. In *Syntax and seman-
            tics, vol. 7: Notes from the Linguistic Underground*, J. McCawley
            (ed.), 85–100. New York: Academic Press.
Kiefer, Ferenc
  1984   Focus and modality. *Groninger Arbeiten zur Germanistischen Lin-
            guistik* 24: 55–81.
Kratzer, Angelika
  1978   *Semantik der Rede*. Königstein: Scriptor.
Lakoff, Robin T.
  1972   The pragmatics of modality. *Chicago Linguistic Society* 8: 229–246.
Langacker, Ronald
  1974   Movement rules in functional perspective. *Language* 50: 630–664.
  1990   Subjectification. *Cognitive Linguistics* 1: 5–38.
Lee, Hyo Sang
  1993   Cognitive constraints on expressing newly perceived information:
            With reference to epistemic modal suffixes in Korean. *Cognitive
            Linguistics* 4: 135–167.
Lötscher, Andreas
  1985   Akzentuierung und Thematisierbarkeit von Angaben. *Linguistische
            Berichte* 97: 228–251.

Lyons, John
    1977   *Semantics*. Cambridge: Cambridge University Press.
Nichols, Johanna
    1986   The bottom line: Chinese Pidgin Russian. In *Evidentiality*, W. Chafe
              and J. Nichols (eds.), 239–257. Norwood: Ablex.
Nuyts, Jan
    1992   Subjective vs. objective modality: What is the difference? In *Layered
              Structure and Reference in a Functional Perspective*, M. Fortescue,
              P. Harder and L. Kristoffersen (eds.), 73–98. Amsterdam: Benjamins.
    2000   Tensions between discourse structure and conceptual semantics: The
              syntax of epistemic modal expressions. *Studies in Language* 24:
              103–135.
    2001a   *Epistemic Modality, Language and Conceptualization*. Amsterdam:
              John Benjamins.
    2001b   Subjectivity as an evidential dimension in epistemic modal expres-
              sions. *Journal of Pragmatics* 33: 383–400.
    2004   Over de (beperkte) combineerbaarheid van deontische, epistemische
              en evidentiële uitdrukkingen in het Nederlands. *Antwerp Papers in
              Linguistics* 108: 1–136.
    2005   The modal confusion: On terminology and the concepts behind it. In
              Modality: Studies in Form and Function, A. Klinge and H. H. Müller
              (eds.), 5–38. London: Equinox
Nuyts, Jan and Wietske Vonk
    1999   Epistemic modality and focus in Dutch. *Linguistics* 37: 699–737.
Palmer, Frank R.
    1979   *Modality and the English Modals*. London: Longman.
    1983   Semantic explanations for the syntax of the English modals. In
              Linguistic Categories, vol. 2, F. Heny and B. Richards (eds.), 205–
              217. Dordrecht: Reidel.
    1986   *Mood and Modality*. Cambridge: Cambridge University Press.
    2001   *Mood and Modality* (2nd Edition). Cambridge: Cambridge University
              Press.
Perkins, Michael R.
    1983   *Modal Expressions in English*. London: Pinter.
Plank, Frans
    1981   Modalitätsausdruck zwischen Autonomie und Auxiliarität. In *Sprache
              und Pragmatik: Lundner Symposium 1980*, I. Rosengren (ed.), 57–
              71. Lund: CWK Gleerup.
Ransom, Evelyn
    1977   On the representation of modality. *Linguistics and Philosophy* 1:
              357–379.
    1986   *Complementation: Its Meanings and Forms*. Amsterdam: John Ben-
              jamins.

Shepherd, Susan C.
1993   The acquisition of modality in Antiguan Creole. In *Modality in Lan-
         guage Acquisition*, N. Dittmar and A. Reich (eds.), 171–184. Berlin/
         New York: Mouton de Gruyter.

Slobin, Dan and A. Aksu
1982   Tense, aspect, and modality in the use of the Turkish evidential. In
         Tense-Aspect, P. Hopper (ed.), 185–200. Amsterdam: John Benjamins.

Steele, Susan
1975a   Is it possible? *Working Papers on Language Universals* 18: 35–58.
1975b   On some factors that affect and effect word order. In *Word Order
         and Word Order Change*, C. Li (ed.), 197–268. Austin: University of
         Texas Press.

Stephany, Ursula
1986   Modality. In *Language Acquisition*, P. Fletcher, M. Garman (eds.),
         375–400. Cambridge: Cambridge University Press.
1993   Modality in first language acquisition: The state of the art. In *Modal-
         ity in Language Acquisition*, N. Dittmar and A. Reich (eds.), 133–
         144. Berlin/New York: Mouton de Gruyter.

Sweetser, Eve
1990   *From Etymology to Pragmatics*. Cambridge: Cambridge University
         Press.

Talmy, Leonard
1988   Force dynamics in language and cognition. *Cognitive Science* 12:
         49–100.

Traugott, Elizabeth Closs
1989   On the rise of epistemic meanings in English: An example of subjec-
         tification in semantic change. *Language* 65: 31–55.
1995   Subjectification in grammaticalisation. In *Subjectivity and Subjectivi-
         sation*, D. Stein and S. Wright (eds.), 31–54. Cambridge: Cambridge
         University Press.

Traugott, Elizabeth Closs and Richard B. Dasher
2002   *Regularity in Semantic Change.* Cambridge: Cambridge University
         Press.

van der Auwera, Johan and Vladimir A. Plungian
1998   Modality's semantic map. *Linguistic Typology* 2: 79–124.

Van Ostaeyen, Gert and Jan Nuyts
2004   De diachronie van kunnen. *Antwerp Papers in Linguistics* 109: 1–186.

Van Valin, Robert D.
1993   A synopsis of role and reference grammar. In *Advances in Role and
         Reference Grammar*, R. Van Valin (ed.), 1–164. Amsterdam: John
         Benjamins.

von Wright, Georg H.
1951   *An Essay in Modal Logic*. Amsterdam: North-Holland.

Watts, Richard
    1984   An analysis of epistemic possibility and probability. *English Studies*
                65: 129–140.
Willett, Thomas
    1988   A cross-linguistic survey of the grammaticalization of evidentiality.
                Studies in Language 12: 51–97.
Woodbury, Anthony C.
    1986   Interactions of tense and evidentiality: A study of Sherpa and English.
                In *Evidentiality*, W. Chafe and J. Nichols (eds.), 188–202. Norwood:
                Ablex.

Typological approaches to modality

Ferdinand de Haan

1. Introduction

This chapter surveys the typological literature on modality.[1] Studies within the typological tradition place an emphasis on explaining language structures through analyzing their function (hence typology is part of the functionalist approach to linguistics).[2] Typological analyses involve cross-linguistic comparisons and generalizations, for which explanations are sought. Explanations for cross-linguistic generalizations very often are extra-linguistic in nature. That is, explanations can be drawn from language use, cognition, and from sociological factors. In addition, explanations may be drawn from the history of the language (the diachronic dimension). Diachronic explanations play an important role in typological approaches to modality (known as *grammaticalization* studies). However, since they are treated in detail elsewhere (Traugott, this volume), the area of grammaticalization will receive little attention here.

Most of the typological literature on modality is concerned with its semantic aspects. This is in accord with the general philosophy that linguistic form can best be explained from language use. Thus, an analysis of the modal *must* in sentence (1) below could involve taking into account the context in which it occurs, the mode of language (for instance, spoken or written), a comparison with cognate verbs in related languages, a comparison with *must* in earlier stages of English, and possibly even the sociological data of the speaker:

(1)   He told MSPs that a thorough investigation of the cause was needed and lessons *must* be learned for the future. (BBC online, May 13, 2004)

This does not mean that such detail is always required or even rigorously followed where it would be appropriate. It is merely meant to illustrate the range of phenomena that can be taken into account when one takes a typological approach to linguistics.

Within typology, the area of modality has not received the same level of attention that categories like ergativity or causativity have enjoyed. Although there are some good typological studies of modality that are older than 20 years, Palmer (1986) is the first book-length work that takes a typological outlook. Palmer (1986) and (2001) are standard reference works on modality in a typological perspective. Even though Palmer (2001) is nominally the second edition of Palmer (1986), there are enough differences in theoretical outlook between the two books to consider them separate works. There are works on modality in functional-typological frameworks, such as Functional Grammar (e.g., Dik 1997) and Role and Reference Grammar (e.g., Foley and Van Valin 1985), but for reasons of space these will not be discussed in any great detail. Other typological surveys are Chung and Timberlake (1985) and Givón (1984). A very good recent work on epistemic modality in a functional-cognitive framework is Nuyts (2001). There are of course numerous studies and monographs of modality in a single language or language family, and they will be mentioned as is warranted in the general discussion. Much typological work on modality is currently being done at the University of Antwerp by Johan van der Auwera's group, with several papers on modal categories in the *World Atlas of Language Structures* (Haspelmath et al. 2005), e.g., a chapter on Imperative – Hortative systems (Van der Auwera et al. 2005).

Because of the relative youth of typological studies on modality, there is as yet no consensus on the proper terminology for modal meanings. For this reason, a section of the paper is devoted to various proposals for developing a consistent and cross-linguistically valid set of terminology.

The next section is devoted to a survey of the ways in which modality can be expressed. As is the norm for typological studies, an element is considered modal if it has modal meanings (like obligation, permission and prohibition). This means that there are quite a number of formal modal elements besides the familiar (from English) modal verb.

The sections thereafter deal with various topics that are currently in fashion, and that also have relevance for other theoretical frameworks. They are a discussion on the status of the irrealis, and interactions of modality and tense and modality and negation.

Another recent development within typology is that of semantic maps, in which the semantic inventory of a given feature in a given language is mapped on an abstract representation of that feature. This has been done for several features (perfect, evidentiality, indefiniteness) and also for modality.

The chapter closes with some remarks on evidentiality, a category which is very often considered to be modal. It is treated as such in Palmer (1986), for instance.

2. Terminology

Part of the typological literature on modality is concerned with the proper terminology of modality. Over the last couple of decades several different sets of terminology have been proposed in the literature, often with subtle differences in meaning. This section surveys the most important terminological debates in the typological literature. It is not meant to be an exhaustive listing of all terms used in modality, of which there are many. (See Nuyts this volume).

Following the logicians (from von Wright 1951 on), the original division in modality is between *epistemic* and *deontic*. Epistemic modality, as in *John must have been at home*, refers to the degree of certainty the speaker has that what s/he is saying is true. Deontic modality, as in *John must go to school*, deals with the degree of force exerted on the subject of the sentence to perform an action. This force can come from the speaker but also from an unspecified third source. This division is used in such works as Lyons (1977), Palmer (1990 [1979], 2001 [1986]), Frawley (1992), de Haan (1997), van der Auwera and Plungian (1998, but see below), Traugott and Dasher (2002), as well as in various grammatical studies of single languages. Generally, this division requires a separate modality, often referred to as *dynamic* modality, to encode ability (and, depending on the author, often volition as well). An example is the sentence *John can swim*, in which one reading of the modal verb *can* denotes the subject's ability to swim.[3]

While the status of epistemic modality is not in doubt, scholars have proposed new terminology for the deontic side of the spectrum. The most influential proposal is that of *root* modality. This term makes reference to root (or main) clauses and it is somewhat of a misnomer, since it does not only occur in root clauses. The term has been around since the late 1960s (no doubt owing to the rise of generative grammar and its emphasis on syntax), but the first influential study to employ the notion of root modality appears to be Coates' (1983) corpus study on the English modals. She rejects the term *deontic* on the grounds that this term primarily refers to the logical notions of obligation and permission, while modals such as *must* and *may* have other interpretations as well (1983: 20–21). The term *root* covers both deontic and dynamic modality, as defined above. In Coates' model of modality, modal meanings are gradual, without "arbitrary cut-off points," as she says. Her view is that modals have core and peripheral meanings, and the terms *deontic* and *dynamic* refer only to the core meanings, hence her use of a neutral term, *root* modality (but see Palmer 1986: 103–104 for arguments against the term *root*).

There is a clear difference between the terms *deontic* and *root* modality. Unfortunately, this difference is somewhat subtle and in many studies the two terms are used interchangeably. However, in coining and using the term *root* modality, linguists can show that there are aspects of modality that lie outside the traditional domain of modality in logic and lend themselves poorly to descriptions in terms of modal logic. The use of a term such as *root* modality highlights this aspect of modality (Sweetser 1990).

An influential set of terminology is given by Bybee, Perkins and Pagliuca (1994), whose work is based on the premise that, in order to understand the range of modal meanings in a language, one must understand the diachronic developments of modal elements. They propose, therefore, the following division of modality (1994: 177):

- Epistemic
- Subordinating
- Agent-oriented
- Speaker-oriented.

The use of the term *epistemic* is relatively straightforward, since it includes possibility and probability among the meanings. Another epistemic category is *inferred certainty*, which is used when the speaker has good reasons to believe that the statement is true (an example is *There must be some way to get from New York to San Francisco for less than $600*).

Subordinating moods refer to the use of modality in subordinate clauses, such as *concessive* (*although* …) and *purposive* (*so that* …) clauses. One exponent of subordinating moods is the *subjunctive* (see below).

Agent-oriented modality refers to those cases in which the agent of a clause is influenced in some way in performing the action described in the clause: "Agent-oriented modality reports the existence of internal and external conditions on the agent with respect to the completion of the action expressed in the main predicate." (1994: 177). Some types of agent-oriented modality are *obligation* (there exist external factors that compel the agent to complete the action, as in *All students must obtain written permission from the Dean ...*), *necessity* (there exist physical conditions, as in *I need to hear a good loud alarm in the morning to wake up*), *ability* (there exist agent-internal enabling conditions – see above), and *desire* (there are internal volitional conditions). A very important type of agent-oriented modality is *root possibility*, which is related to ability, but also takes external factors into account. An example of root possibility is *I actually* couldn't *finish it because the chap whose shoulder I was reading the book over got out at Leicester Square* (1994: 178, from Coates 1983: 114). The use of the modal *couldn't* does not denote an internal inability, but rather an inability caused by the external factor of someone else's leaving.

Speaker-oriented modality refers to those cases in which the speaker is the "enabling condition," i.e., those cases in which the speaker gives someone an order or gives someone permission. This type of modality includes *directives* (a term from Lyons 1977), *imperatives* (the command mood, see below), *prohibitions, optatives* (see below), *admonitions* (warnings), and *permissions.*

In this framework, agent-oriented and speaker-oriented modality roughly divide the area of root modality, or deontic/dynamic modality. The deciding factor in Bybee et al.'s framework is the enabling factor. If it is the speaker, then we are dealing with speaker-oriented modality; otherwise it is an instance of agent-oriented modality.

Some scholars have sought to refine this framework while keeping the basic structure intact. Hengeveld (2004) uses the term *participant-oriented* modality instead of *agent-oriented* modality. This is done to include those cases in which the subject of the sentence is not actually an agent (as in *John needs to be left in peace today*, in which the subject, John, has the thematic role of patient).

Van der Auwera and Plungian (1998: 80–86) make a distinction between *participant-internal* and *participant-external* modality. Participant-internal modality is more or less identical with dynamic modality as it deals with ability and need (as in *John needs a book*). Participant-external modality is again divided into deontic and non-deontic participant-external modality. In this view, deontic modality is a subtype of participant-external modality. It encompasses permission and obligation (either from the speaker or another source). Non-deontic modality deals with possibility and necessity. It refers to circumstances wholly external to the situation. An example is the sentence *To get to the station, you can take Bus 66* (1998: 80). In this view, there is no need for a special category of subject-oriented modality because it is either subsumed under deontic modality or, in the case of imperatives, optatives, etc., because it is not considered to be part of modality. In addition, volition is in their view not part of modality either. As the authors themselves admit (1998:84), the term *participant*-oriented is perhaps too vague, given that a sentence usually has more than one partici- pant. They consider the term *subject-oriented* as an alternative but reject it on the grounds that it is probably not valid cross-linguistically. They cite the case of the experiencer in Kannada, a Dravidian language, which is not a subject (based on Bhat 1991).

Another distinction frequently made in typological studies is that be- tween real and unreal events, or a realis-irrealis distinction. It has been claimed that there are languages that encode modality this way rather than in a deontic-epistemic way. This is an important observation and a separate section is devoted to this distinction.

3. Expressions of modality

In the typological tradition, categories tend to be defined semantically. Thus, a morpheme is classified as modal if it has a modal meaning (epistemic, deontic, etc.). This means that modal meanings are expressed by various morphological, syntactic, and lexical categories. This section is a survey of the ways in which modality is expressed across languages.

3.1. Modal auxiliary verbs

The best-known means of expression for speakers of English is doubtless the modal verb:

(2)   a. John must go to school.
       b. John must be at school.

The modal verb *must* is used to denote necessity on the subject (deontic modality) and strong conviction of the speaker (epistemic modality). These are examples of strong modality (Palmer 1986). English also has expres- sions for weak modality:

(3)   a. John may go to school
       b. John may be at school.

The modal verb *may* denotes permission (deontic modality) or possibility (epistemic modality).[4]

Thus, modal verbs such as *must* and *may* are ambiguous between epistemic and deontic modality. This is a very frequent cross-linguistic phenomenon. Ambiguity of modal verbs is found, among others, in the Germanic, Slavic, and Romance language families in Europe, as well as in certain languages outside Europe. An example of an African language with modal verbs is Yoruba, in which the verb *lè* is used for weak epistemic and deontic modality, and the verbs *gb.d.* and *ní láti* for strong epistemic and deontic modality (Adewole 1990: 80):

(4)   Ó gbòdó wà nílé.
       'He must be at home.' or 'He must be in.'

3.2. Mood

The category of *mood* is here defined as a morphological verbal category which expresses the modal value of the sentence. Mood is therefore the grammaticalized expression of modality, just as, say, tense is the grammaticalized expression of time. Mood is therefore an obligatory category in those languages that have it.

The most common moods cross-linguistically appear to be the *indicative* and the *subjunctive*. These moods are found in, among others, the classical languages (e.g., Sanskrit, Classical Greek, and Latin) but also in the modern descendants of Latin, in the Slavic languages, and in certain Germanic languages (notably Icelandic and German). It has also been described for Bantu languages like Swahili, Native American languages (for instance, languages from the Algonquian language family), and Australian languages like Gooniyandi and Mangarayi.

As a first approximation, we can say that the indicative is used to describe real, factual events, while the subjunctive is used for unreal, hypothetical events (but see below). This can be illustrated with data from Latin (Hale and Buck 1903). Example (5) shows the use of the Subjunctive[5] in main clauses. Example (5a) shows the potential use of the Subjunctive, while (5b) shows an example of a wish, the optative use (Hale and Buck 1903: 273, 269):

(5) a. cuneo   hoc agmen disici-as
         wedge-ABL this line   split-2SG.SUBJ.PRES
         'With a wedge, one could split this (military) line.'

     b. sint   beati
         be-3PL.SUBJ.PRES happy-PL
         'May they be happy!'

Other uses of the Subjunctive in main clauses in Latin are obligations, hortatives, yes/no questions, and hypotheses.

In subordinate clauses, the Subjunctive is used after main verbs of hoping,
fearing, volition, and surprise, among others. Examples are shown in (6),
from Palmer (2001: 133 with glosses slightly adjusted):

(6) a. Time-o   ne   laborem   auge-am
         fear-1SG.IND.PRES COMP work.ACC increase-1SG.SUBJ.PRES
         'I am afraid that I shall increase my work.'

     b. Ut mihi   aedis aliquas conduc-at   volo
         COMP I.DAT house some   buy-3SG.SUBJ.PRES wish-1SG.PRES.IND
         'I want him to rent a house for me.'

The Indicative in Latin in used for facts (again from Hale and Buck 1903:
293–294):

(7) a. quid tac-es
         why be.silent-2SG.IND.PRES
         'Why are you silent?'

     b. quoad   potu-it,   resist-it
         as.long.as can-3SG.IND.PERF resist-3SG.IND.PERF
         'As long as he could, he resisted.'

Given the data from Latin, it is tempting to equate the indicative-subjunctive distinction with the realis-irrealis distinction alluded to in the section
on terminology. This is a frequently held view, but there are good reasons
for keeping the two sets of terminology distinct. As this problem has attracted some attention in the typological literature, a separate section will
be devoted to it.

One objection that can be raised here is the fact that there are languages
which distinguish other moods besides indicative and subjunctive. One
such mood is the optative, which is frequently used to express the semantic

categories of wishing and hoping. A separate optative mood has been reconstructed for Proto-Indo-European, and is found in such languages like Classical Greek and Sanskrit. In Latin, the old Optative and Subjunctive merged into one Subjunctive mood (Buck 1933: 298–301). An example from Classical Greek can be found in Sophocles, *Ajax* 550, cited in Palmer (2001: 205):

(8)   ó: pai   génoio   patrós   eutuxésteros
      o child become-2SG.OPT.AOR father-GEN luckier
      'O child, may you be luckier than your father.'

Other languages that have a separate optative category are the Athabaskan languages. In Navajo, for instance, it is formed by a verbal prefix *ó-* plus optionally a sentence-final particle, such as *laanaa* 'would that' (Young and Morgan 1987: 162). In Slave, the verbal prefix for the Optative is *ghu-* (Rice 1987: 548). However, the optative has other uses besides wishing. The Navajo Optative has potentiality as a possible interpretation (similar to the Latin example (6a) above). In Slave, the Optative can have additional meanings, such as necessity and even futurity (Rice 2000: 249–51). This suggests that we are dealing with a mood in Athabaskan that is not unlike the Latin Subjunctive and that calling it an Optative may not be accurate. It shows that one cannot always judge the content of a given category by its given label.

A further mood which is found in many, indeed most, languages is the imperative, or the mood which is used to give a direct command. Thus, in Russian, the Imperative of the verb *rabota-t'* work-INF is *rabota-j* 'work-IMP.2SG or, in the plural, *rabota-jte* work-IMP.2PL.

The imperative differs somewhat from the other moods discussed in that it is limited to a certain speech situation, namely when the speaker addresses the hearer directly and gives a direct command.[6] Therefore, it is performative in nature because by uttering the imperative, the speaker gives the command. It is quite different from deontic modality in this respect. While it may seem as though the sentence *You must go to school* is identical in all respects to *Go to school!*, they are in fact different. In the construction with the modal verb the command can come from other sources beside the speaker (e.g., a person not present in the discourse or even abstract objects, in this case the law), and can be used on non-second persons (as in *He must go to school*). With an imperative the "commander" is the speaker and the "commandee" the hearer(s). There are syntactic differences as well which to a degree depend on the language in question. In English, an Imperative cannot be in a subordinate clause (**I said that go to school!*) but a corresponding sentence with a modal verb can (*I said that you must go to school.*). The fact that imperatives are performative has led some scholars to treat them as distinct from modality proper.

Related to imperatives are jussives and hortatives. When the subject of a command is not the addressee, but someone not participating in the speech situation (i.e., 3rd person) or a group to which the speaker belongs (1st person), then we are dealing with jussives or hortatives. This can be illustrated by the English form *let's*, but can be found as part of the verbal paradigm in many languages (Palmer 1986: 109–11; Van der Auwera et al. 2005).

3.3. Modal affixes

In many languages modality is marked by means of affixes on the verb. This is, for instance, the case in Turkic languages, Greenlandic Eskimo, Dravidian languages like Tamil, and many Native American languages. In (9), some examples from various languages are shown:

(9) a. Tamil   (Dravidian: Asher 1979: 170; *-laam* permission)
         avan peeca-laam
         3SG   speak-PERM
         'He is allowed to speak.'

     b. Koasati   (Muskogean: Kimball 1991: 200; *-sahá:wa* probability)
         ó:la-fon   ałí:ya-:sahá:w-ok …
         town-ALL   go-PROB-SS.FOC
         'She must have gone to town [also possibility].'

     c. Turkish   (Turkic: Lewis 1967: 125–7; *-meli* necessitative)
         gel-me-meli-siniz
         come-NEG-OBLIG-2PL
         'You ought not to come.'

The difference between mood and modal affixes is that mood is an obligatory category. That is, a speaker of a language like Italian must choose between the Indicative and Subjunctive, while a speaker of, say, Tamil can choose not to use a modal affix. This is similar to English, where speakers always have the option to use a modal auxiliary or not.

It is not always easy to tell if we are dealing with a mood or with a modal affix. Many grammars do not make a distinction between the two categories and indeed many works on modality do not do so either. Nevertheless, the distinction is worth making because a language can have both moods and modal affixes. Such a language is Turkish, which besides the Necessitative morpheme *meli* also has a Subjunctive mood (Lewis 1967: 132). One way of telling moods and modal affixes apart might be to consider the degree of cohesion. If the morpheme can easily be separated from the rest of the verb (as is the case with the morphemes shown in example (9) above), then we are dealing with an affix. If we are dealing with an inseparable part of the verb (as is the case in the Latin examples (7) above), then we are dealing with a mood. This area needs more research, and it quite likely involves degrees of grammaticalization.

3.4. Lexical means

There are also less grammaticalized (and more lexical) means of expressing modality. These means can, for the most part, be found in English, though some types are better known from other languages.

3.5. Modal adverbs and adjectives

Modality can be expressed by means of adverbs. In English, typical examples are *probably*, *possibly*, *necessarily*, and *maybe*. This list is by no means exhaustive, obviously. Some examples are:

(10) a. John is probably at home.
      b. Maybe John is at home.
      c. John is supposedly at home.

As mentioned in Perkins (1983: 89), modal adverbs in English are primarily epistemic in nature.

In many languages these forms have become more grammaticalized, and sometimes they are the only way to express modal notions. The main ways of expressing strong modality in Russian, for instance, are with adjectives (*dolžen*) and adverbs (*nado* or *nužno*). The former has a subject in the Nominative and declines according on the gender of the subject, while the latter takes a Dative subject and is invariant. An example is shown in (11):

(11) a. ja   dolžen   idti   v voksal
        I-NOM must-MASC go-INF to station-ACC
        'I must go to the station.'

    b. mne   nado idti   v voksal
        I-DAT must go-INF to station-ACC
        'I must go to the station.'

3.6. Modal tags

Epistemic modality, the expression of speaker's confidence, can be expressed with such tags as *I think, I guess,* and *I believe* (Thompson and Mulac 1991). An example is in (12) (1991: 313):

(12) It's just your point of view you know what you like to do in your spare time I think.

While tags like *I think* are derived from pure matrix clauses, they behave more like modal adverbs and they show signs of grammaticalization. Corpus research shows that the complementizer *that* is often omitted (in about 90 % of the cases). They can occur at various places in the sentence (initially, medially, and finally). A further step on this grammaticalization path would be the use of tags like *I think* as a pure adverb. This seems to have happened in certain Creole languages, such as Tok Pisin (Keesing 1988), where this tag has been simplified to *ating* with the meaning 'maybe.'

    Modal tags have not received very much attention in the literature, but it would seem that they are also mostly epistemic in nature. An exception might be volition verbs, like *want.* Although English is not a good example (the verb *want* has a different clause structure), something like this seems to have happened in the history of Greek. The Future particle *tha* in Modern Greek derives ultimately from the construction *thelo na* 'want-1SG that.' Volition is a dynamic modal category, not an epistemic one, but this example shows that matrix clauses with a 1SG subject have a tendency to become tags, and then adverbs or particles.

3.7. Modal particles

Another common means of expression is the modal particle. This is a method not very common in English. Modal particles are rarely found in British English but seem to become more popular in American English. An example is (13), where the words *too* and *so* function as "contrary to what you said/thought" modal particles (from the WWW):

(13) a. Affective is too a word!
      b. There is so a Santa Claus!

Modal particles are well known from Germanic languages like Dutch and German (Abraham 1991), where they are ubiquitous. Two examples from German are shown in (14). As can be seen from the translations, it is not always easy to give an adequate rendering of modal particles in languages that lack them. Sometimes the best solution is to just leave them untranslated, as in (14b), where the particle *doch* can best be translated with a slightly irritated intonation (Abraham 1991: 335, 340):

(14) a. Kommt   er denn
          come-3SG.PRES he MP
          'Will he really come?' or 'Will he come after all?'

      b. Gib   mir   doch den   Löffel
          give-IMP me-DAT   MP   the-ACC spoon
          'Give me the spoon!'

One problem is that it is not always clear whether we are dealing with an adverb or a particle. This is a poorly researched area and it is likely that any distinction between the two must be made on a language-by-language basis. For instance, it has been claimed that modal particles in Dutch can never receive stress, nor can they occupy the first position in a sentence (Geerts et al. 1984: 891). Modal adverbs can have stress and occupy sentence-initial position. However, given the English data shown in (13), in which the particles do have stress, this may not be a cross-linguistically useful diagnostic.

The nebulous status of modal particles is at least partly due to their origins. German and Dutch modal particles can derive from a number of sources: Abraham (1991: 332) lists modal particles that come from adverbs, adjuncts, scalar particles, adjectives and interjections. The typological concern addressed by Abraham is why languages like German and Dutch have a multitude of modal particles while closely related English has none (or at least very few). Abraham's (1991) view is that the peculiar syntax of German and Dutch is responsible. Modal particles occur mainly between the verbal elements of the sentence; the verbs *bracket* the part of the sentence where modal particles typically occur. English (as well as the Romance languages) lack such a sentence part and hence lack the possibility of developing modal particles. There are problems with this analysis, however. Languages like Russian have a number of modal particles, yet word order is very free. The same goes for the older Indo-European languages (like Classical Greek), which teem with modal particles but whose word order is very free, or at least lack a German-type sentence structure.

Because modal particles have the entire sentence in its scope, they are often found at clause boundaries, and very often clause-finally. Cantonese (Matthews and Yip 1994: chapter 18) is an example of a language with a plethora of sentence-final particles, many of which are modal. An example is given in (15), in which the particle marks a polite request (Matthews and Yip 1994: 351):

(15) Léih béi dō   dī   sìhgaan ngóh lā
      you give more some time   me   PRT
      'Give me a bit longer, won't you?'

3.8. Modal case

The Tangkic language family of Northern Australia provides us with a typologically unusual device for marking modality. In Lardil, Yangkaal and Kayardild, modality can be marked on the Noun as a case marker.[7] In Kayardild, (Dench and Evans 1988; Evans 1995, 2003) a (non-subject) noun phrase can have an optional case morpheme, besides a regular case marker, which denotes mood. An example is shown in (16), from Evans (2003: 208):

(16) dangka-a burldi-ju yarbuth-u   thabuju-karra-ngun u
      man-NOM   hit-POT   bird-M.PROP   brother-GEN-INSTR-M.PROP

      wangal-ngun-u
      boomerang-INSTR-M.PROP

      'The man will/can hit the bird with brother's boomerang.'

The morpheme *-u*, which occurs on all non-subject NPs, is called the Modal Proprietive and is used to denote future and potential meanings. This morpheme must co-occur with the Potential suffix *-ju* which is found on the verb.

Besides the modal Proprietive, there are several other modal case morphemes, not all of them used for modal categories as we understand the term here; some have tense meanings (like the modal Ablative which, used together with the Past tense morpheme, denotes anteriority). Evans (1995: chapter 10) is a full discussion of modal case and its development.[8]

4. Realis and irrealis

We now turn to some recent developments in the typological literature on modality. We will start with the realis-irrealis distinction. This distinction divides the world into real and unreal events or situations. It has been claimed that there are languages which encode modality in precisely this way, i.e., there are languages with irrealis morphemes, which mark an action or situation as unreal.

While languages with irrealis morphemes can be found on every continent, they have most prominently been described for New Guinea (Roberts 1990; Bugenhagen 1994). Other languages with irrealis morphemes can be found in North America (Chafe 1995; Mithun 1995). A recent typological study is Elliott (2000).

One of the major problems in discussing irrealis issues is the fact that the term *irrealis* is very vague and can refer to a number of different circumstances (see Palmer 2001: 149). Furthermore, the semantic content of irrealis morphemes differs from language to language (even between languages that are closely related). This makes defining a cross-linguistic category of irrealis very hard.

One example is the future. It can be argued that future is a prototypical irrealis category because it refers to events that have not yet happened and are therefore unreal. In languages like Amele and Muyuw, the future is indeed an irrealis category. However, in others it is treated as a realis category. One such language is the Native American language Caddo (Chafe 1995: 358), shown in (17). The Future morpheme *-ʔaʔ* occurs not with the Irrealis prefix *t'a-/t'i-* but with the Realis prefix *ci-*:

(17) cíìbáw-ʔaʔ / ci-yi=bahw-ʔaʔ
      1SG.AG.REAL-see-FUT
      'I will look at it.'

In yet other languages, the future can be used with either realis or irrealis, depending on the speaker's judgement of likelihood that the event described will actually occur. One such language is Central Pomo, a Californian language (Mithun 1995: 378–80). The same goes for other categories that can be considered part of irrealis, including categories like negation, hypothesis, and imperative.

Given these facts, it appears that *irrealis* is a term that is not comparable from language to language and, consequently, it may be asked whether it is a useful or even valid object for typological research. This problem is examined in Bybee et al. (1994: 236–40) and Bybee (1998). These studies reach the conclusion that the term *irrealis* is too broad to be of real use. This is illustrated with data from the Australian language Maung (Capell and Hinch 1970). In Maung, Irrealis and Realis have the following categories under them:

(18) Realis and Irrealis in Maung

REALIS	PRESENT:	Indicative present, future
	IMPERATIVE:	Negative only
	PAST:	Simple and complete past, imperfect
IRREALIS	PRESENT:	Potential, negative present and future
	PAST:	Negative past, Conditional, Imperative

This can be illustrated with the verb -*udba* 'to put' (Capell and Hinch 1970: 67):[9]

(19) REALIS

ŋi-udba	'I put (pres.)'
ŋi-wan-udba	'I shall put'
juwunji g-udba	'don't put it!'
ŋi-udba-ŋ	'I put it (perfect)'
ŋi-udba-ŋ-u	'I was putting'

IRREALIS

ni-udba-ji	'I can put'
marig ni-udba-ji	'I don'/won't put'
da ŋi-udba-nji	'if I put'
marig ŋi-udba-nji	'I didn't put'
g-udba-nji	'put it!'

The two problematic cases for treating the morpheme *-ji* as an Irrealis morpheme are the Future and the Imperative. The positive Future is a Realis category while the negative Future is an Irrealis one (it is identical to the negative Present). The positive Imperative is Irrealis while the negative Imperative (or Prohibitive) is a Realis one, at least in the analysis of Capell and Hinch (1970). The important point for the present discussion is that, as is the case with the Latin Subjunctive, there is no correspondence between Realis-Irrealis on the one hand, and real and unreal situations on the other.

As a further complication, it is very possible for closely related languages to differ in their treatment of irrealis and realis category. Examples can be found in various Papuan New Guinean languages (Roberts 1990; Bugenhagen 1994). It is cases such as these that have led Bybee (1998) to conclude that these irrealis morphemes actually encompass a range of modal notions, and there is little, if any, consistency between irrealis morphemes in different languages. Morphemes that are analyzed as irrealis morphemes are in fact morphemes that only encode part of the irrealis spectrum. Consequently, the term *irrealis* should not be used, in this view.

According to Palmer (2001: 145) there are two ways in which irrealis can manifest itself. Palmer refers to these types as *joint* and *non-joint systems*. In one type of language, the *joint* type, an irrealis morpheme co-occurs with another morpheme which encodes the actual type of irrealis. An example is (20) from the New Guinean language Amele (Roberts 1990: 372). The Different Subject morpheme *-eb* is used when the main verb has some marker of irrealis modality, in this case the Future morpheme *-an*:

(20) ho bu-busal-eb   age qo-qag-an
      pig SIM-run.out-3SG.DS.IRR 3PL hit-3PL-FUT
      'They will kill the pig as it runs out.'

It might be premature to call this *joint-marking* because the Irrealis morpheme occurs as part of a Different Subject morpheme, which would have to be present in any case. A difference between realis and irrealis DS morphemes only shows up in examples like (20) above, where the action in both clauses is simultaneous. When the action is not simultaneous or when the subjects in both clauses are identical, there is no difference in realis-irrealis marking on these morphemes.

The second type, called *non-joint*, has irrealis morphemes that do not need other morphemes but function all by themselves. An example is (21), from Muyuw (Bugenhagen 1994: 18). The Irrealis morpheme *b(i)-* is used here to denote future. It contrasts with the Realis morpheme *n(i)-*, which is used for realis events. Note that it is not necessary to choose between either morpheme. It is perfectly grammatical to omit the Realis and Irrealis morphemes. In that case the modality of the sentence is determined by other means, for instance by using the particle *bo*, which denotes certainty.

(21) yey b-a-n   Lae nubweig
     I   IRR-1SG-go Lae tomorrow
     'I will go to Lae tomorrow.'

This distinction is a useful one if one keeps in mind that they are not absolute. The discussion on Muyuw shows that neither the Realis nor the Irrealis morpheme is obligatory; they can be omitted without impacting the modal status of the sentence. It is also not possible to classify a language as either joint or non-joint since both can occur in one and the same language, as Palmer himself notes (2001: 146).

Given the foregoing, it might be useful to ask again if the Latin Subjunctive is a marker of the category irrealis. It has already been mentioned that there is a correspondence between the two categories, but no absolute one-to-one match. There are cases in which there is a mismatch between realis-irrealis and Indicative-Subjunctive in Latin. The Indicative is used for Future events, for instance, while the Subjunctive does not even have a Future paradigm (Hale and Buck 1903: 304):

(22) ded-emus   ergo Hannibal-em?
     give.up-1PL.INDIC.FUT then Hannibal-ACC
     'Shall we then give up, Hannibal?'

Although the future can be considered to be an irrealis category, as it refers to events that have not (yet) taken place, it is expressed with the Indicative mood in Latin. The same is true for sentences which contain a negation. As argued below, negation is also an irrealis category, yet it is very much compatible with the Indicative in Latin. There is then a problem in mapping the term *irrealis* onto the Latin Subjunctive. While it is appropriate in certain circumstances, it fails to apply in others.

Should we then give up on the term *irrealis*, as advocated by Bybee (1998)? While it may be tempting to do so, it must also be acknowledged that it fulfills a useful role in linking linguistic categories to the cognitive domain. There is no doubt that irrealis tends to be used as a vague term for anything that is even remotely modal. But it is widely used in grammatical descriptions. In the literature on pidgins and creoles, it is the standard way of referring to modal distinctions (cf. Bickerton 1975; Holm 1988: 164–6).

It may be that the difficulties sketched in this section are insurmountable and that we will have to give up realis and irrealis as linguistic categories. It may also be possible to retain the terms, and to account for variation within these categories. One way of doing so might be with the use of semantic maps, to which we now turn.

5. Semantic map of modality

One of the most powerful tools to analyze the complex interactions of modal meanings in the world's languages is a representation that is the sum total of the semantic possibilities of the category under investigation, what Anderson (1982, 1986) calls *the mental space*. An exponent of this category can then be mapped onto this representation and thus be compared to similar means of expression in other languages.[10]

Semantic maps also can be used for both synchronic and diachronic purposes, i.e., they can be used to chart possible changes in meaning. The latter is put to good use by van der Auwera and Plungian (1998), who apply semantic maps to chart meanings and changes in meaning in modal elements. Their investigation starts with the grammaticization paths of Bybee et al. (1994), which can be considered to be diachronic semantic maps. One such path, the path of development from 'ability,' is shown in (23 = Fig. 6.3. in Bybee et al. 1994: 240):

(23)   Semantic map of path of 'ability'

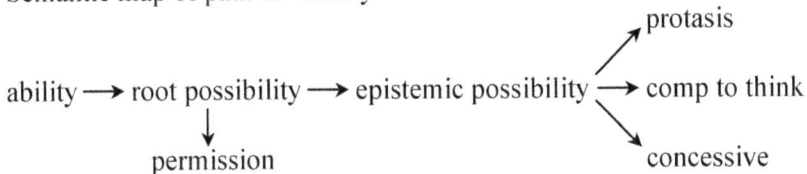

```
                                                        protasis
                                                      ↗
ability ⟶ root possibility ⟶ epistemic possibility ⟶ comp to think
          ↓                                           ↘
       permission                                      concessive
```

This path shows the development of a morpheme meaning 'ability' (in Bybee et al.'s terms, this is an ability *gram*). First, it develops into a marker of root possibility and then into a gram meaning 'permission' or 'epistemic possibility' (or both, as in English *may*). After this, the morpheme may take on additional meanings. This path is taken to be universal and *unidirectional*: a morpheme with an ability meaning will follow the path in (23), and does not skip a step (i.e., an ability morpheme does not change directly into an epistemic possibility gram). This does not mean, of course, that an ability gram necessarily will take on these additional meanings. Language is not deterministic and an ability gram can quite happily remain an ability gram. But if it is going to take on additional meanings, the first one will be that of root possibility.

Bybee et al. provide other grammaticalization paths for mood and modality. Their conclusion (1994: 241) is that the overall developmental path is from agent-oriented modality to the other kinds of modality, with subordinate modality at the end of the path. This corresponds to a development from less to more grammaticalization. The agent-oriented modal grams are typically least likely to be bound, while subordinate modal grams are most likely to be bound. Still, there are problems with this analysis, as the authors freely admit. For instance, it should be predicted that imperative, a speaker-oriented modality, is less frequently bound than subjunctive, a subordinate modality. However, the opposite is the case (1994: 242). Nevertheless, there is a general correlation between the various modal categories and their boundedness.

Van der Auwera and Plungian (1998) take these grammaticalization paths and develop them into a full-blown semantic map. (24 = Fig. 5 in Van der Auwera and Plungian 1998: 91) shows their representation of Bybee et al.'s ability path, otherwise in (23), above:

(24) Semantic map of 'possibility'

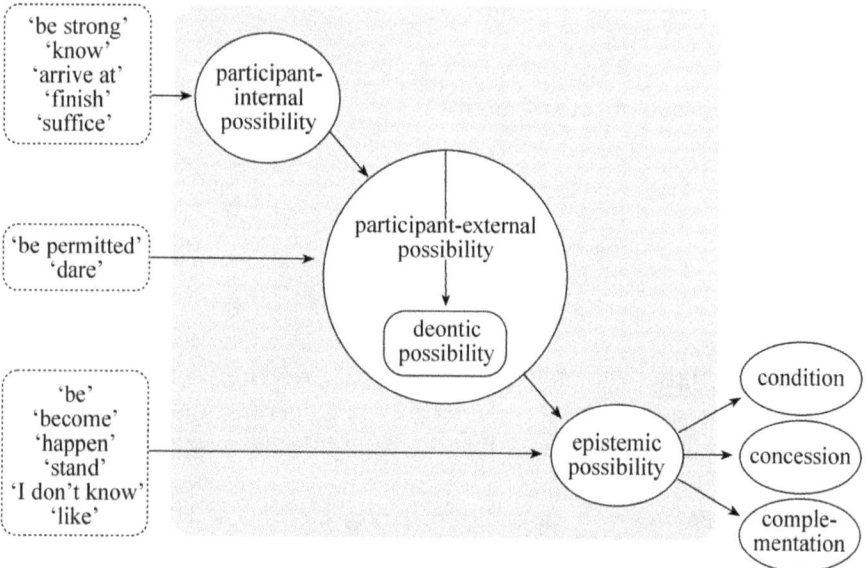

The semantic map is divided in three parts. The main part is the large en-
closed rectangle, which shows the modal domain. To the left side of the
rectangle is the premodal domain, graphically represented by dotted blocks.
This contains the lexical sources for the modal domain. To the right, the
postmodal domain contains further grammaticalization paths for modal
grams, which van der Auwera and Plungian do not consider part of the modal
domain.

Within the modal domain, individual meanings are represented by ovals,
and arrows mark the pathways from one meaning to another. In this representation, meanings can be part of other meanings. As mentioned above,
deontic possibility is part of participant-external possibility in this model.
The arrow wholly within the oval for participant-external possibility shows
the pathway to deontic possibility.

By unifying Bybee et al.'s grammaticization paths, plus adding their
own material, van der Auwera and Plungian end up with the following map
for modality (25=Fig. 19 in van der Auwera and Plungian 1998: 111):

(25) Semantic map of modality

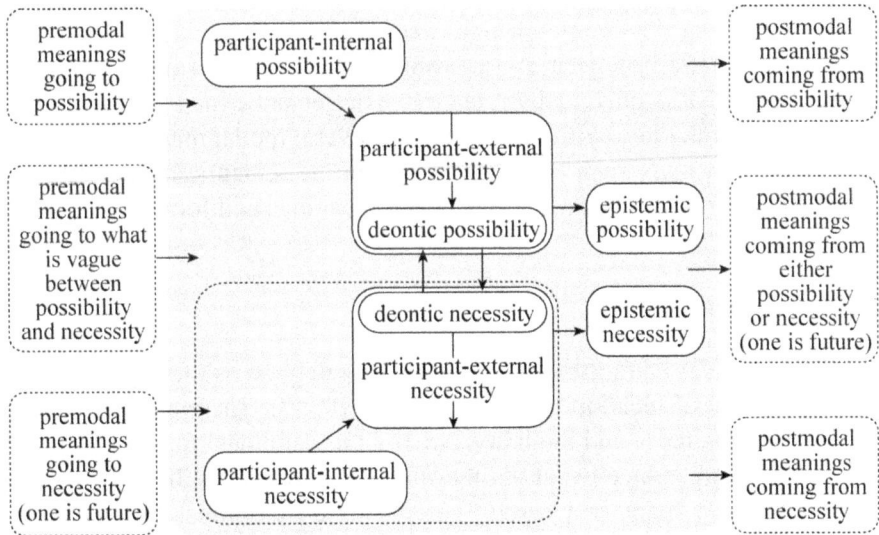

The basic representation is similar to the one shown in (24). Represented
are, from left to right, the premodal, modal, and postmodal domains. The
premodal and postmodal domains are represented abstractly. As before,
grammaticalization paths are denoted by arrows, with the arrows leading

from premodal to modal and those from modal to postmodal being abstract representations.

As is readily visible, some meanings are contained in larger enclosures. For instance, the notions of participant-external possibility and participant-external necessity are grouped together into a larger meaning block. This represents the fact that in some languages, these individual meanings are expressed by one and the same morpheme. An example of this is Swedish *få* 'get,' which is vague between both types of participant-external modality (van der Auwera and Plungian 1998: 103, citing Wagner 1976: 56):

(26)   Lasse får   köra bil
       Lasse gets drive car
       'Lasse gets to drive the car.' 'Lasse may/must drive the car.'

Similarly, there are languages in which all types of participant modality can be expressed with one vague construction. Van der Auwera and Plungian cite the German modal infinitive (sometimes called the *modal passive*, which is similar to English constructions like *We are to meet there at seven*). It is said to be vague between all types of non-epistemic modality.

By combining diachronic changes and synchronic states, one can get a good representation of what is a possible interpretation of a given modal element and what is universally ruled out. The semantic map shown in (24) is certainly not the last word on the matter: several modal meanings are not included in this map, such as imperatives. But the semantic map does go a long way toward a unified picture of modal meanings and forms. [11]

6. Modality and tense

In the typological literature tense is commonly defined as the grammatical-ized expression of location in time (Comrie 1985: 9). There are clear inter-actions between tense and modality. An obvious candidate for such interac-tion is the future. Since events in the future have not (yet) happened, it is easy to see that there is a certain amount of uncertainty surrounding it. Hence there is a connection between future and epistemic modality. The future is sometimes classified as a realis category, and sometimes as an irrealis category.

There is a similar connection between modality and the past tense. This seems at first to be somewhat counterintuitive since the events happened in the past and one can be certain (or, at least, modally neutral) about past events. Nevertheless, the past tense is routinely used to express notions of modality.

6.1. Modality and future tense

The fact that future events can be described both temporally and modally is an observation which goes back a long time. Discussions on the relation between the two areas can be found in Comrie (1985: 43–46), Dahl (1985: 103, 2000b), Bybee (1988), Bybee et al. (1991, 1994) and Palmer (1986, 2001), among others. These studies currently represent the state of the art in the typological thinking on the future.[12]

Future is quite often a part of so-called irrealis morphemes, as discussed above. Nevertheless, as argued previously, there is no one-to-one correlation between the two categories since there are many languages in which the future is a realis category (Maung, Caddo, Latin). Ontologically, future events have not come to pass, and, epistemologically, the speaker cannot know for certain that the event will occur. Despite these logical uncertainties, there are languages in which these considerations either do not play a role or in which there is a choice between various future tense forms to denote various shades of certainty. A language in which the future has been analyzed as a pure tense (that is, it refers to events occurring subsequent to the moment of speech without conveying a modal meaning as well) is the Tibeto-Burman language Manipuri (Bhat 1999: 18–19). In Manipuri, there is a basic future/non-future distinction. That is, there is one morpheme to denote future and one to denote present and past tense. In (27), the morpheme -*ŋi* is used for Non-future (a,b), and -*kə.ni* is used for Future (c).

(27) a. ŋəsi   noŋ məŋ-ŋi
          today rain cloudy-NFUT
          'It is cloudy today.'

      b. ŋəraŋ   noŋ məŋ-ŋi
          yesterday rain cloudy-NFUT
          'It was cloudy yesterday.'

      c. nuŋdaŋwayrəmdə noŋ məŋ-gəni
          evening.LOC   rain cloudy-FUT
          'It will be cloudy in the evening.'

There are languages in which a speaker has a choice between different future morphemes to denote various shades of certainty. In Bybee et al. (1994: 247–248) several languages are listed in which there are two or more future morphemes with various levels of confidence. An example is Southern Agaw, a Cushitic language (Bybee et al. 1994: 248, data cited from Hetzron 1969). The Future certainty morpheme -*áGá* is used when the speaker is certain that the action will occur, while -*e* is the Future possibility morpheme.[13]

(28) a. táq-áGá
          know-2SG-FUT.CERT
          'You will [certainly] know [it].'

      b. dəngéta ča   des-é
          perhaps tomorrow study-FUT.POSS
          'Perhaps tomorrow I shall study.'

Another connection between modality and future is the fact that quite often future morphemes develop from modal (deontic) forms. This has happened in English, of course, where the modal auxiliaries *will* and *shall* were originally modal verbs (see Traugott this volume). The connection between obligation/volition and future is clear: one can oblige someone to do something only in the future. Thus, a sentence such as *you must go to school* means that the action of going to school is necessarily subsequent to the moment at which the obligation was uttered. This is a widespread development, accounting for the vast majority of cases in Bybee et al. (1994). Similarly, Fleischman (1982) discusses the French verb *devoir* 'must, ought to,' which functions in many respects like a marker of future tense rather than obligation (1982: 146):

(29) Je dois dîner avec Joseph la   semaine prochaine
      I   must dine with Joseph ART week   next
      'I must/will have dinner with Joseph next week.'
      'I am to have dinner with Joseph next week.'

Fleischman comments that the modal verb can be replaced by other future forms (the go-future or the synthetic future) without much change in meaning.

6.2. Modality and past tense

While the past tense is usually taken as a pure temporal category, because it refers to events that are immutable and known, there is nevertheless a connection between the past tense and modality. This can be demonstrated even with English. The past tense morpheme -*ed* is usually a pure tense morpheme, yet in certain environments it can mark various modal meanings, as in the following examples, from Comrie (1985:19):

(30) a. If you did this, I would be very happy.
     b. If John was /were here.
     c. I just wanted to ask you if you could lend me a pound.

Sentences (30a) and (30b) are counterfactuals and hypotheticals, which are usually considered to be modal in nature (they are typical irrealis categories). Sentence (30c) is a polite request and refers to a non-actual event as well; a request is a type of wish. Is this an isolated fact of English (in which case examples (30a) and (30b) could be explained away as an instance of homophony: the irrealis forms in (30a) and (30b) are homophonous with the regular past tense forms), or is this a cross-linguistic feature (in which case we can look for a principled account of the phenomenon)?

Steele (1975) discusses the relation between past tense and modality through a reconstruction of part of the tense-aspect-modality system of Proto-Uto-Aztecan. She reconstructs two morphemes: **ta-* as a general Irrealis morpheme, and **ta-* as a Past tense morpheme. She then goes on to state that both are actually the same morpheme and that there is one abstract feature that underlies both categories. This feature is called *dissociative*, as past tense is dissociated from the present, and irrealis is dissociated from reality. Steele suggests that this observation is valid cross-linguistically. This view of past tense as a remoteness device has been echoed in other works, such as James (1982) and Fleischman (1989). Palmer (1986: 211; 2001: 210) considers this line of reasoning circular but does not provide any real alternative. Bybee (1995: 513–516), which is a paper concerned with the development of the past tense forms of the modals *should* and *would*, rejects the notion that it is the past tense alone that is responsible for the modal interpretation. In her view, it is the combination of past tense plus some other element, such as a modal verb, the subjunctive or (per Fleischman 1995) the imperfective aspect.

7. Modality and negation

By itself, negation has been considered by some scholars to be part of modality. The reason for this is that by talking about nonexistent events or
states, we are talking about events or states that are not real. Hence, negation
can be considered an instance of an irrealis category and it is so classified
in some languages as was discussed above. Example (31), from the Native
American language Caddo, is illustrative (Chafe 1995: 355):

(31)   kúyt'áybah / kúy-t'a-yi=bahw
       NEG-1.AG.IRR-see
       'I don't see him.'

When the negative prefix *kúy-* is present, the Irrealis form of the pronominal
prefixes must be used.

   However, in other languages, the presence of a negation has no influence
on the choice of realis/irrealis. Latin has already been mentioned in this
regard, and we can add Central Pomo (Mithun 1995: 380–382) and Amele
(Roberts 1990) to this list. This distinction between negation and irrealis
can occur in very closely related languages. Mithun (1995: 383–384) makes
mention of two dialects of the Yuman language Diegueño, Mesa Grande
and Jamul, where the former has an obligatory irrealis morpheme whenever
a negation is present, but in the latter, negation plays no role in the choice
of irrealis or realis.

   This divergence of irrealis and negation is not to deny additional close
relations between modality and other semantic factors associated with negation. Scope relations, for example, between modality and negation have
been known for at least 2500 years. Ever since Aristotle, philosophers and
logicians have been concerned with this issue. It has attracted the attention
of linguists as well, but only comparatively recently.

7.1. Modals, logic and typology

While modal linguistic issues are different from the issues in modal logic,
the representation system and some of the logical analyses shed light on the
natural language problems (Karttunen 1972). (32) shows the basic symbols
mapped on sample sentences from English (see also Kaufmann, Condoravdi, and Harizanov this volume):

(32) a. John must be a bachelor   □p
    b. John may be a bachelor   ◊p
    c. John must not be a bachelor   □¬p
    d. John need not be a bachelor   ¬□p
    e. John may not be a bachelor   ◊¬p (or ¬◊p)

Two questions concerning the logical structure of modality have been addressed in the recent typological literature:

 – How are modal meanings mapped onto the logical possibilities?
 – How do languages disambiguate possible scope ambiguities?

7.2. Mapping of modals onto logical structures

What types of modals are there and can there be? We know there are modals that express the notions □ and ◊, but are there modals that specifically
and uniquely express the notion □¬ or ¬◊?

In two important papers van der Auwera has studied the connection between modality and negation. Van der Auwera (1996) investigates the inad-
equacy of the well-known *square of oppositions* for dealing with modality
in natural language (see, e.g., Horn 1989 on this issue). Van der Auwera
(2001) is an investigation into which combinations of modality and negation receive a specialized modal element.

In van der Auwera (1996), a distinction is made between two logical
types of possibility. One, known from logic dating back to antiquity, is the
familiar ◊, used in such formulae as (33):

(33) a. ◊p = ¬□¬p   ('it is possible that p = it is not necessary that not-p')
    b. □p → ◊p   ('it is necessary that p' entails 'it is possible that p')

The logical operator ◊ is not always directly translatable into real language
use because it fails to differentiate the uses of the modal *may* in (34a). This
sentence suggests the equivalency shown in (34b), which is absurd from a
logical point of view:

(34) a. John may be there and he may not be there.
    b. ◊p = ◊¬p

Example (34a) illustrates what is called the *contingent* use of the modal *may* and not the *possibility use*. This was first argued by Hintikka (1960) and also noted by Horn (1989) among others. Hence a new symbol is necessary to distinguish between the two uses. Van der Auwera suggests a new operator ♦, which is used for cases like (34a) – the relation between ◊ and ♦ is one of implicature: when something is possible, it is taken for granted that it is also contingent:

(35) p conversationally implicates ♦p

There appear to be no languages in which a lexical distinction is made between weak modals that express possibility and contingency.

Are there specialized modals for every possible logical combination of modality and negation? This question is addressed in van der Auwera (2001) and, to an extent, in de Haan (1997). Van der Auwera surveys a number of languages, mostly European ones, and provides the following cases (Kashmiri added):

(36)
modality	language	element
¬□p	English	*need*
	Dutch	*hoeven*
	Kashmiri	*lagun*
□¬p	Bengali	*nei*
¬◊p	Russian	*nel'zja*
◊¬p	English	*mightn't*

That is, every possible combination is attested in at least one language, with the possible exception of ◊¬p. The combination form *mightn't* is very rare and not accepted by many speakers (its equivalent form *mayn't* is even rarer and even less accepted). The reason for the rarity of specialized ◊¬p forms is possibly the peripheral status of ◊¬p itself.

A further issue is the status of double modals. It is well-known that strong modality can be expressed by means of double negation and a weak modal, to form the logical equivalency of □p = ¬◊¬p. This can be seen in English constructions like (37):

(37) John can't not go to school = John must go to school.

There are languages in which strong modality is expressed only by means of a weak modal and a double negation. That is, there is no separate strong modal in the language, and ¬◊¬p is the only way to express □p:

(38) a. Malagasy

      tsy   main-tsy
      NEG able-NEG
      'Can't not.' (Horn 1989: 220)

   b. Classical Tibetan

      mI-V   mthu   mI-V
      NEG-V ability NEG-V
      'Can't not.' (Beyer 1992: 247–8)

   c. Japanese

      Rekishi no   hon   o   yoma-na-kereba nari-masen
      History GEN book ACC read-NEG-PROV   work.out-NEG
      'I have to read history books.' (Han 1983: 341)

There is also a logical equivalence between ¬□¬p and ◊, but there seem to be no languages that have a weak modal that is made up of a strong modal and a double negation.

7.3. Resolving scope ambiguities

How do languages differentiate between, say, □¬p and ¬□p and resolve scope ambiguity in modality and negation? The basic problem can be illustrated by considering the sentences in (39). In (39a) the negation is in the scope of the modal, while the modal is in the scope of the negation in (39b). The first instance is a case of *narrow scope of negation* and the second one of *wide scope of negation*:

(39) a. John must not go to school.   □¬p
      b. John need not go to school.   ¬□p

As is clear from the example, English uses two different modal verbs to show the difference in scope. The modal verb *must* is used for narrow scope, and *need* is used for wide scope. De Haan (1997) calls this the *Modal Suppletion Strategy* for disambiguation.

Another strategy can be exemplified by a language like Russian, as shown in (40). The modal verb *moč* 'may/can' interacts with the negation *ne* in the following way:

(40) a. Ivan ne   možet   rabotat' $\neg \Diamond p$
          Ivan NEG can.3SG work.INF
          'Ivan is not allowed/able to work.'

      b. Ivan možet ne   rabotat' $\Diamond \neg p$
          Ivan can.3SG NEG work.INF
          'Ivan is allowed/able not to work.'

In Russian, the modal verb stays the same but the place of the negation changes. This strategy is referred to in de Haan (1997) as the *Negation Placement Strategy*. It iconically shows the scope relation: if the negation precedes the modal, it has wide scope, but if it immediately precedes the main verb, it has narrow scope.

English uses primarily the first strategy, but there are some verbs that do not have suppletion. As seen in (32e) above, the verb *may* is ambiguous when a negation is present (and also the verb *can*), although there are prosodic differences depending on scope. Another complication is the fact that languages that use the Negation Placement strategy also tend to have the phenomenon of NEG-raising, which muddies the iconic relation.[14] Since Russian is one of these languages, sentence (41) can be interpreted with a narrow scope reading:

(41) Maša   ne   dolžna   rabotat' $\neg \Box p / \Box \neg p$
      Masha NEG must.FEM work.INF
      'Masha mustn't/needn't work.'

8. Evidentiality

The category of evidentiality deals with the source of evidence a speaker has for his or her statement.[15] Evidential morphemes mark whether a speaker has been a direct witness to the action he/she is describing or whether s/he has received the information about the action or event from another source. Thus evidentiality can be divided into two subcategories, *direct* evidentiality, which marks that the speaker was a witness to the action, and *indirect* evidentiality, which marks that the speaker was not a witness but obtained knowledge about the action from another person (hearsay or quotative evidentiality) or through inference (inferential evidentiality). This is exemplified in (42), from Evenki (Tungusic; Nedjalkov 1996: 239), where the suffix *-re* in (42a) is used for direct evidence, and *-che* in (42b) for indirect evidence. The Turkish data in (43), from Slobin and Aksu (1982) and DeLancey (1997: 37), show the evidential use of the two past tenses, *-di* to show direct evidence, *-miş* indirect evidence (see also (46) below for other uses of *-miş*):

(42) a. eni   eme-re-n
      mother come-NFUT-3SG
      'Mother came (direct evidence).'

    b. eni   eme-che-n
      mother come-PST-3SG
      'Mother came (no direct evidence).'

(43) a. Kemal gel-di
      Kemal come-PAST
      'Kemal came (direct).'

    b. Kemal gel-miş
      Kemal come-PAST
      'Kemal came (indirect).'

Evidentiality has long been considered an exotic category, associated with Native American languages primarily. However, it is a category that manifests itself in languages on every continent, including in some well-studied languages of Europe, such as German. English lacks a grammatical category of evidentiality, but it can be expressed with lexical means like *evidently*, *ostensibly*, and with verbs like *seem*.

The reasoning for treating evidentiality as a modal category in the typological literature. Palmer (1986: 51) distinguishes four kinds of epistemic modality; one is the degree of confidence in the truth discussed above and the other three types are evidential categories. In Palmer (2001) evidentiality and epistemic modality are themselves categories of the hypercategory of *propositional* modality. This point of view is found in other typological studies of modality or evidentiality, such as Bybee (1985), Bybee et al. (1994), Willett (1988), and Frawley (1992).

The reasoning for treating evidentiality as a modal category is the belief that one is inherently less certain about actions one has not witnessed than about those one has witnessed. This belief is anchored in the fact that when one sees something with one's own eyes, one tends to accept that sight as a true representation of the world while a secondhand report is viewed with more suspicion. Hence, indirect evidentiality presents the action as less certain than does direct evidentiality.

While this is an appealing belief, there are some problems with it. First, it is risky to compare grammatical categories across languages, as the typological literature has amply shown. This is especially true for notional categories which are strongly rooted in a subjective environment, like evidentiality and epistemic modality. It is hard to compare modal verbs in related languages, and comparing English to, say, Evenki, might be extremely hard. To illustrate this, example (44) shows a typical Dutch sentence with the modal verb *moeten,* which is cognate with English *must,* and yet a straightforward comparison is not always possible:

(44)   Het moet een goede film   zijn
       It   must a   good movie be
       'It is bound to be a good movie (epistemic).'
       'It is required to be a good movie (deontic).'
       'It seems to be a good movie (evidential).'

Sentence (44) has three possible interpretations (as always, out of context), only two of which have *must* as a possible English translation, (44a) and (44b). In its evidential reading, *must* is not appropriate. Thus, even in two closely related languages there is not always a one-to-one correspondence. Consequently, how can one assess the status of a sentence like (45), from Tuyuca, an Eastern Tucanoan language from the Vaupés River region of Western Amazon (Barnes 1984: 257)?

(45)   diíga apé-yi
       soccer play-INFER
       'He played soccer (I have seen evidence that he played, but I have not seen him play).'

A typical analysis is to equate the Inferential in Tuyuca with the English category of probability (possibly by translating the above sentence as *he must have played soccer*), and lump the two together and claim that the two are synonymous. But this way, the epistemic modality has been introduced through the back door. Still, at no stage of the game has it been shown that the Inferential in Tuyuca is a modal category. Indeed, there is good reason to assume that it is not. Not only does Barnes never use the term (*epistemic*) *modal* in her description, but there are also true epistemic modals in the language. By translating an evidential with the modal *must*, the analysis is prejudiced at best, wrong at worst.

A recent proposal is to analyze evidentiality not as a modal, but as a deictic category (de Haan 2001, 2005a). Frawley (1992) already made an attempt in this direction but called it *modal deixis*, so still a modal category. De Haan (2005a) notes the connection between spatial deictic elements such as demonstratives, temporal deictic elements such as tense, and evidential elements. In all cases, the morphemes in question denote the distance between the speaker and an object (spatial), time (temporal), or the entire proposition (evidential). Hence de Haan (2005a) proposes the term *propositional deixis* for evidentiality.

9. Mirativity

An offshoot from the research into evidentiality is *mirativity*, which refers to the fact that the speaker has received his information from an unexpected source (DeLancey 1997). The connection with evidentiality is that the two categories are usually expressed by the same morphemes in those languages that have both categories. An example is (46), from Turkish (DeLancey 1997: 37, citing Slobin and Aksu 1982, but my translations). It has already been mentioned above that there are two past tenses in Turkish, one for direct information, one for indirect. The Indirect Past tense -*miş* can also be used to mark unexpected information. The context for (46) is that Turkish Prime Minister Ecevit resigned unexpectedly, whereas President Nixon's resignation was widely expected. This warrants the use of the -*miş* Past in (46a) and the -*di* Past in (46b). Note that this parallels the use of the so-called Hot News Perfect in English (McCawley 1971):

(46) a. Ecevit istifa   et-miş
      Ecevit resignation make-PAST.MIR
      'Ecevit has resigned!'

    b. Nixon istifa   et-ti
      Nixon resignation make-PAST.DIR
      'Nixon resigned.'

DeLancey notes (1997) that there is a widespread correspondence between mirative and (indirect) evidential morphemes. He cites examples from Hare,

Slave, several Tibeto-Burman and Dardic languages, and mentions several more, from all parts of the world.

Although a thorough analysis of the connection between evidentiality and mirativity is still to be done, as indeed an analysis of evidentiality and its proper place in grammar, it is clear that this particular area is currently one of the more exciting ones in all of linguistics. There is every reason to think that a convincing analysis of evidentiality and related areas will prove important for all areas of linguistics.

Abbreviations

ABL	ablative	MIR	mirative
ACC	accusative	MP	modal particle
AG	agent	M.PROP	modal proprietive
ALL	allative	NEG	negation
AOR	aorist	NFUT	non-future
ART	article	NOM	nominative
CERT	certainty	OBLIG	obligation
COMP	complementizer	OPT	optative
DAT	dative	PAST	past tense
DS	different subject	PERF	perfect
DIR	direct evidential	PERM	permissive
FEM	feminine	PL	plural
FOC	focus	POSS	possibility
FUT	future	POT	potential
GEN	genitive	PRES	present tense
IMP	imperative	PROB	probability
IND	indicative mood	PRT	particle
INF	infinitive	REAL	realis
INFER	inferential evidential	SG	singular
INSTR	instrumental	SIM	simultaneous
IRR	irrealis	SS	same subject
MASC	masculine	SUBJ	subjunctive mood

Notes

1. This paper has benefited from advice by Johan van der Auwera and Sheila Dooley. Neither of them is responsible for the final product.
2. An excellent recent book on typology is Croft (2003).
3. Many languages make a distinction between physical and mental ability. For instance, German uses the verb *kennen* for mental ability and *können* for physical ability.
4. In recent years, the field of *corpus linguistics* has produced several important studies that deal with modal verbs, ranging from studies that deal with a single modal verb to those that deal with the entire modal system. English is the language best represented here, as should come as no surprise. An early study is Ehrman (1966), which probably has the honor of being the first corpus linguistic study overall. Other significant studies are Palmer ([1979], 1990) and Coates (1983), which are still cited. More recent studies are Westney (1995) and Krug (2000), the latter of which deals mostly with semi-modals. A study of modality as a whole is Perkins (1983). Other languages are lagging behind but are catching up. For German, there is Diewald (1999).
5. In this paper I will follow the typological tradition of making a typographical distinction between language-specific categories (capitalized) and typological categories (not capitalized). An example is: the English Past Tense morpheme does not always indicate past tense.
6. The best typological study on the imperative and related areas is Xrakovskij and Volodin (1986), in Russian.
7. Modality can be marked on the verb as well.
8. Although marking modality on nouns is typologically rare, it does seem to occur elsewhere. Guy (1974: 35–36) describes the case of the Oceanic language Sakao, where (some) nouns may be marked with an irrealis prefix. Verbs are marked for modality as well.
9. Maung has several verb classes, each with its own allomorphs. The above table is therefore not typical for all verbs.
10. For a full discussion on the usefulness of semantic maps in typology see Croft (2003: 133). An easy introduction is Haspelmath (2003). This technique has been applied to various categories. A small sample of (non-modal) studies is: the perfect (Anderson 1982), evidentiality (Anderson 1986), voice (Kemmer 1993), case (Croft 1991), coming and going (Lichtenberk 1991), and indefinite pronouns (Haspelmath 1997). In addition, semantic maps play a prominent role in Radical Construction Grammar (Croft 2001).
11. Hansen (2001) takes the findings of van der Auwera and Plungian (1998) and applies them quite successfully to modality in the Slavic language family.
12. There are several important studies on the use and development of the future in individual languages and language families. Palmer (1990) and Coates (1983)

include sections on the modal verbs with future reference and Fleischman (1982) is an in-depth study on the future in Romance.

13. Hetzron calls these two morphemes the Imperfect Definite and Imperfect Indefinite, respectively. The morpheme *-áGá* has only the one function exemplified in (28a) but *-é* has other meanings besides future possibility.

14. NEG-Raising refers to the process in which the negation associated with an embedded verb is moved ("raised") to a verb higher in the sentence. An example from English is the sentence *I don't think that he will come* in which the negation has been raised from the original *I think that he will not come*. See Horn (1989) for details of this process.

15. Evidentiality currently enjoys an upsurge in popularity, with several important studies being released. An early study (in German) is Haarmann (1970). The classic in the field is Chafe and Nichols (1986), which is a collection of articles on evidentiality in all parts of the world. More recent books are Johanson and Utas (2000) and Aikhenvald and Dixon (2003), which are both collections of articles in the vein of Chafe and Nichols (1986). There is a special issue of the *Journal of Pragmatics* devoted to evidentiality (Dendale and Tasmowski 2001). An early typological study is Givón (1982). Willett (1988) is in need of updating but still useful. A recent book-length treatment is Aikhenvald (2004). Other important articles are de Haan (1999, 2005a), which explore the limits of evidentiality and epistemic modality. De Haan (2005b, c) are studies for the *World Atlas of Language Structures* (Haspelmath et al., 2005) on the existence of evidential morphemes in over 400 languages. Barnes (1984) is an article on the evidential system of the Tucanoan language Tuyuca, which continues to feature prominently in the field. In addition, there are many individual studies on "evidentiality in language X" in the literature, which do not always deal with evidentiality proper.

References

Abraham, Werner
    1991   The grammaticalization of the German modal particles. In *Approaches to Grammaticalization,* F. Traugott and B. Heine (eds.), 331–380. Amsterdam: Benjamins.

Adéwolé, Fémi
    1990   Gbódò 'must': Analysis of a Yoruba modal verb. *Journal of West African Languages* 20: 73–82.

Aikhenvald, A. Y.
    2004   *Evidentiality.* Oxford: Oxford University Press.

Aikhenvald, A. and R. M. W. Dixon
    2003   *Studies in Evidentiality.* Amsterdam: Benjamins.

Anderson, Lloyd B.
1982   The 'perfect' as a universal and as a language-particular category. In
        Tense-aspect: Between Semantics and Pragmatics, P. Harper (ed.),
        227–264. Amsterdam: Benjamins.
1986   Evidentials, paths of change, and mental maps: Typologically regular
        asymmetries. In *Evidentiality*, W. Chafe and J. Nichols (eds.), 273–
        312. Norwood: Ablex.
Asher, N.
1979   *Tamil*. Amsterdam: North Holland.
Barnes, Janet
1984   Evidentials in the Tuyuca verb. *International Journal of American
        Linguistics* 50: 255–271.
Beyer, Stephan V.
1992   *The Classical Tibetan Language*. Albany: SUNY Press.
Bhat, D. N. S.
1991   *Grammatical Relations: The Evidence against their Necessity and
        Universality*. London: Routledge.
1999   *The Prominence of Tense, Aspect, and Mood*. Amsterdam: John
        Benjamins.
Bickerton, Derek
1975   *Dynamics of a Creole System*. Cambridge: Cambridge University
        Press.
Buck, Carl D.
1933   *Comparative Grammar of Greek and Latin*. Chicago: University of
        Chicago Press.
Bugenhagen, Robert D.
1994   The semantics of irrealis in the Austronesian languages of Papua
        New Guinea. In *Topics in Descriptive Austronesian Linguistics*, Ger
        P. Reesink (ed.) 1–39. Leiden: Rijksuniversiteit Leiden.
Bybee, Joan L.
1985   *Morphology: A Study of the Relation between Meaning and Form*.
        Amsterdam: Benjamins.
1988   The diachronic dimension in explanations. In *Explaining Language
        Universals*, John A. Hawkins (ed.). 350–379. Oxford: Blackwell.
1998   'Irrealis' as a grammatical category. *Anthropological Linguistics* 40:
        257–271.
Bybee, Joan, William Pagliuca and Revere Perkins
1991   Back to the future. In *Approaches to Grammaticalization*, E. Traugott
        and B. Heine (eds.), 17–58. Amsterdam: John Benjamins.
Bybee, Joan, Revere Perkins, and William Pagliuca
1994   *The Evolution of Grammar: Tense, Aspect, and Modality in the Lan-
        guages of the World*. Chicago: University of Chicago Press.

Capell, A. and H. E. Hinch
  1970   *Maung Grammar: Texts and Vocabulary.* The Hague: Mouton.
Chafe, Wallace
  1995   The Realis – Irrealis Distinction in Caddo, the Northern Iroquoian
          languages, and English. In *Modality in Grammar and Discourse,* J.
          Bybee and S. Fleischman (eds.), 349–366. Amsterdam: John Benja-
          mins.
Chafe, Wallace and Johanna Nichols (eds.)
  1986   *Evidentiality: The Linguistic Coding of Epistemology.* Norwood, NJ:
          Ablex.
Chung, Sandra and Alan Timberlake
  1985   Tense, aspect and mood. In *Language Typology and Syntactic De-
          scription, vol. III.* Tim Shopen (ed.), 202–258. Cambridge: Cam-
          bridge University Press.
Coates, Jennifer
  1983   *The Semantics of the Modal Auxiliaries.* London: Croom Helm.
Comrie, Bernard
  1985   *Tense.* Cambridge: Cambridge University Press.
Croft, William
  1991   *Syntactic Categories and Grammatical Relations.* Chicago: Univer-
          sity of Chicago Press.
  2001   *Radical Construction Grammar: Syntactic Theory in Typological
          Perspective.* Oxford: Oxford University Press.
  2003   *Typology and Universals* (2nd edition). Cambridge: Cambridge
          University Press.
Dahl, Östen
  1985   *Tense and Aspect Systems.* Oxford: Blackwell.
  2000   The grammar of future time reference in European languages. In
          Tense and Aspect in the Languages of Europe, O. Dahl (ed.), 309–
          328. Berlin/New York: Mouton de Gruyter.
Dahl, Östen (ed.)
  2000   *Tense and Aspect in the Languages of Europe.* Berlin/New York:
          Mouton de Gruyter.
de Haan, Ferdinand
  1997   *The Interaction of Modality and Negation: A Typological Study.*
          New York: Garland.
  1999   Evidentiality and epistemic modality: Setting boundaries. *Southwest
          Journal of Linguistics* 18: 83–101.
  2001   The place of inference within the evidential system. *International
          Journal of American Linguistics* 67: 193–219.
  2005a   Encoding speaker perspective: Evidentials. In *Linguistic Diversity
          and Language Theories,* Z. Frajzyngier, D. Rood and A. Hodges
          (eds.), 379–397. Amsterdam: John Benjamins.

2005b   Semantic distinctions of evidentiality. In *World Atlas of Language Structures*, M. Haspelmath et al, (eds.), 314–317. Oxford: Oxford University Press.

2005c   Coding of evidentiality. In *World Atlas of Language Structures*, M. Haspelmath et al, (eds.), 318–321. Oxford: Oxford University Press.

DeLancey, Scott
1997   Mirativity: The grammatical marking of unexpected information. *Linguistic Typology* 1: 33–52.

Dench, Alan and Nicholas Evans
1988   Multiple case-marking in Australian languages. *Australian Journal of Linguistics* 8: 1–47.

Dendale, P. and L. Tasmowski (eds.)
2001   *Evidentiality*. Special issue of *Journal of Pragmatics* 33 (4).

Diewald, Gabriele
1999   *Die Modalverben im Deutschen: Grammatikalisierung und Polyfunktionalität*. Tübingen: Niemeyer.

Dik, Simon C.
1997   *The Theory of Functional Grammar* (2 volumes). Berlin / New York: Mouton de Gruyter.

Ehrman, Madeleine
1966   *The Meaning of the Modals in Present-Day English*. The Hague: Mouton.

Elliott, Jennifer R.
2000   Realis and Irrealis: Forms and Concepts of the grammaticalization of reality. *Linguistic Typology* 4: 55–90.

Evans, Nicholas D.
1995   *A Grammar of Kayardild, with Historical-Comparative Notes on Tangkic*. Berlin/New York: Mouton de Gruyter.

2003   Typologies of Agreement: Some problems from Kayardild. *Transactions of the Philological Society* 101: 203–34.

Fleischman, Suzanne
1982   *The Future in Thought and Language*. Cambridge: Cambridge University Press.

1989   Temporal distance: A basic linguistic metaphor. *Studies in Language* 13: 1–51.

1995   Imperfective and Irrealis. In *Modality in Grammar and Discourse*, J. Bybee and S. Fleischman (eds.), 519–551. Amsterdam: John Benjamins.

Foley, William A. and Robert D. Van Valin
1984   *Functional Syntax and Universal Grammar*. Cambridge: Cambridge University Press.

Frawley, William
1992   *Linguistic Semantics*. Hillsdale, NJ: Lawrence Erlbaum.

Geerts. C. et al.
    1984   *Algemene Nederlandse Spraakkunst.* Groningen: Wolters Noordhoff.
Givón, Talmy
    1982   Evidentiality and epistemic space. *Studies in Language* 6: 23–49.
    1984   *Syntax, vol. 1.* Amsterdam: John Benjamins.
Guy, J. B. M.
    1974   *A Grammar of the Northern Dialect of Sakao.* Pacific Linguistics
            Series B-33. Canberra: Australian National University.
Haarmann, Harald
    1970   *Die indirekte Erlebnisform als grammatische Kategorie.* Wiesbaden:
            Harrassowitz.
Hale, William G. and Carl D. Buck
    1903   *A Latin Grammar.* Boston/London: Ginn & Co.
Han, Mieko S.
    1983   *Modern Japanese* (2nd edition). Los Angeles: Institute for Inter-
            cultural Studies Press.
Hansen, Björn
    2001   *Das slavische Modalauxiliar. Semantik und Grammatikalisierung im
            Russischen, Polnischen, Serbischen/Kroatischen und Altkirchen-
            slavischen.* München: Verlag Otto Sagner.
Haspelmath, Martin
    1997   *Indefinite Pronouns.* Oxford: Oxford University Press.
    2003   The geometry of grammatical meaning: semantic maps and cross-
            linguistic comparison. In *The New Psychology of Language: Cogni-
            tive and Functional Approaches to Language Structure, vol. 2*, M.
            Tomasello (ed.), 211–242. Mahwah, NJ: Lawrence Erlbaum.
Haspelmath, Martin, Matthew Dryer, David Gil and Bernard Comrie (eds.)
    2005   *World Atlas of Language Structures.* Oxford: Oxford University
            Press.
Hengeveld, K.
    2004   Mood and modality. In *Morphology: A Handbook on Inflection and
            Word-Formation*, G. Booij, C. Lehmann and J. Mugdan (eds.).
            1190–1202. Berlin/New York: Mouton de Gruyter.
Hetzron, Robert
    1969   *The Verbal System of Southern Agaw.* Berkeley: University of Cali-
            fornia Press.
Hintikka, J.
    1960   Modality and quantification. *Theoria* 27: 119–128.
Holm, John
    1988   *Pidgins and Creole, vol. I: Theory and Structure.* Cambridge: Cam-
            bridge University Press.
Horn, Laurence R.
    1989   *A Natural History of Negation.* Chicago: University of Chicago Press.

James, Deborah
    1982   Past tense and the hypothetical: a cross-linguistic study. *Studies in Language* 6: 375–403.

Johanson, Lars and Bo Utas (eds.)
    2000   *Evidentials*. Berlin/New York: Mouton de Gruyter.

Karttunen, Lauri
    1972   Possible and must. In *Syntax and Semantics, vol. 1*, John P. Kimball (ed.), 1–20. New York: Academic Press.

Keesing, Roger
    1988   *Melanesian Pidgin and the Oceanic Substrate*. Stanford: Stanford University Press.

Kemmer, Suzanne
    1993   *The Middle Voice*. Amsterdam: John Benjamins.

Kimball, Geoffrey D.
    1991   *Koasati Grammar*. Lincoln: University of Nebraska Press.

Krug, Manfred G.
    2000   *Emerging English Modals: A Corpus-Based Study of Grammaticalization*. Berlin/New York: Mouton de Gruyter.

Lewis, G. L.
    1967   *Turkish Grammar*. Oxford: Oxford University Press.

Lichtenberk, F.
    1991   Semantic change and heterosemy in grammaticalization. *Language* 67: 475–509.

Lyons, John
    1977   *Semantics*. Cambridge: Cambridge University Press.

Matthews, Steven and Virginia Yip
    1994   *Cantonese: A Comprehensive Grammar*. London: Routledge.

McCawley, James D.
    1971   Tense and time reference in English. In *Studies in Linguistic Semantics*, Charles Fillmore and D. Terence Langendoen (eds.), 96–113. New York: Holt, Rinehart and Winston.

Mithun, Marianne
    1995   On the relativity of irreality. In *Modality in Grammar and Discourse*, J. Bybee and S. Fleischman (eds.), 367–88. Amsterdam: John Benjamins.

Nedjalkov, Igor
    1996   *Evenki*. London: Routledge.

Nuyts, Jan
    2001   *Epistemic Modality, Language, and Conceptualization: A Cognitive-Pragmatic Perspective*. Amsterdam: John Benjamins.

Palmer, Frank R.
    1990   [1979] *Modality and the English Modals* (2nd edition). London: Longmans.

Palmer, Frank R.
  1986   *Mood and Modality*. Cambridge: Cambridge University Press.
  1995   Negation and the modals of possibility and necessity. In *Modality in Grammar and Discourse to Grammaticalization*, J. Bybee and S. Fleischman (eds.), 453–72. Amsterdam: John Benjamins.
  2001   *Mood and Modality* (2nd edition). Cambridge: Cambridge University Press.
Perkins, Michael R.
  1983   *Modal Expressions in English*. London: Frances Pinter.
Rice, Keren D.
  1987   *A Grammar of Slave*. Berlin / New York: Mouton de Gruyter.
  2000   *Morpheme Order and Semantic Scope: Word Formation in the Athapaskan Verb*. Cambridge: Cambridge University Press.
Roberts, John R.
  1990   Modality in Amele and other Papuan languages. *Journal of Linguistics:* 26: 363–401.
Slobin, Dan I. and Ayhan Aksu
  1982   Tense, aspect and modality in the use of the Turkish evidential. In *Tense-Aspect: Between Semantics and Pragmatics*, P. Hopper (ed.), 185–200. Amsterdam: John Benjamins.
Steele, Susan
  1975   Past and irrealis: Just what does it all mean? *International Journal of American Linguistics* 41: 200–217.
Sweetser, Eve E.
  1990   *From Etymology to Pragmatics: Metaphorical and Cultural Aspects of Semantic Structure*. Cambridge: Cambridge University Press.

Thompson, Sandra A. and Anthony Mulac
  1991   A quantitative perspective on the grammaticization of epistemic parentheticals in English. In *Approaches to Grammaticalization*, E. Traugott and B. Heine (eds.), 313–329. Amsterdam: John Benjamins.
Traugott, Elizabeth Closs and Richard B. Dasher
  2002   *Regularity in Semantic Change*. Cambridge: Cambridge University Press.
van der Auwera, Johan
  1996   Modality: The Three-layered Square. *Journal of Semantics* 13: 181–195.
  2001   On the typology of negative modals. In *Perspectives on Negation and Polarity Items*, J. Hoeksema, H. Rullmann, V. Sánchez-Valencia and T. van der Wouden (eds.), 23–48. Amsterdam: John Benjamins,
van der Auwera, Johan and Vladimir Plungian
  1998   Modality's semantic map. *Linguistic Typology* 2: 79–124.

van der Auwera, Nina Dobrushina and Valentin Goussev
　　2005　　Imperative-Hortative Systems. In *World Atlas of Language Structures*, M. Haspelmath et al. (eds.), 294–297. Oxford: Oxford University Press.
von Wright, E. H.
　　1951　　*An Essay in Modal Logic.* Amsterdam: North Holland.
Wagner, Johannes
　　1976　　Eine kontrastive Analyse von Modalverben des Deutschen und Schwedischen. *International Review of Applied Linguistics in Language Teaching* 14: 49–66.
Westney, Paul
　　1995　　*Modals and Periphrastics in English: An Investigation into Semantic Correspondence between Certain English Modal Verbs and their Periphrastic Equivalents.* Tübingen: Niemeyer.
Willett, Thomas L.
　　1988　　A cross-linguistic survey of the grammaticization of evidentiality. *Studies in Language* 12: 51–97.
Xrakovskij, V. S. and A. P. Volodin.
　　1986　　*Semantika i tipologija imperativa.* Leningrad: Nauka.
Young, Robert and William Morgan
　　1987　　*The Navajo Language: Grammar and Dictionary.* Albuquerque: University of New Mexico Press.

Formal approaches to modality

Stefan Kaufmann, Cleo Condoravdi
and Valentina Harizanov

1. Modal logic

Modal notions are pervasive in the meaning of a wide range of expressions from grammatical categories, such as tenses, to the lexical semantics of particular words, such as modal adverbials (*probably*, *necessarily*) and modal auxiliaries (*must*, *may*, *can*). The best known modalities are the alethic[1] modalities *necessary* and *possible*. Other modalities include temporal, deontic, epistemic, and doxastic ones, and modalities pertaining to disposition, ability, provability, mood, aspect, and so on. Temporal modalities deal with time. Deontic[2] modalities deal with obligation and permission. Epistemic[3] modalities deal with knowledge, and doxastic[4] modalities deal with belief. Although modals have been thoroughly studied since Aristotle, the formal theory of modality was revolutionized in the 1960's with the introduction of the possible world semantics by Hintikka and Kripke.

In our formal approach to the semantic analysis of modal expressions, we will employ the model-theoretic apparatus of modal logic. In modal logic, modals correspond to sentential operators, whose semantic role is to qualify the truth of the sentences in their scope. For example, the sentence *He is possibly right* is represented by a formula that is roughly equivalent to *It is possibly true that he is right*. Likewise, the sentence *Nature must obey necessity* is represented as *It is necessarily true that nature obeys necessity*. Given a sentential symbol p, we use the square notation $\Box p$ for the statement p *is necessarily true*, and the diamond notation $\Diamond p$ for the statement p *is possibly true*. Thus, *necessarily* and *possibly* are formalized as modal operators that act on sentences. Most modal expressions, though by no means all, are treated similarly.

The modal operators $\Box$ and $\Diamond$ are interdefinable. Even Aristotle in his *De Interpretatione* established that the negation of *It is necessary that p* is *It is not possible that not-p*. Similarly, *It is possible that p* is equivalent to *It is not necessary that not-p. It is contingent that p* is equivalent to *It is possible that p, but not necessary that p.*

We will formalize this as follows. Let the symbol ¬ be used for sentential negation. That is, ¬*p* stands for *It is not the case that p.* The *Law of Double Negation* implies that the negation of this sentence is equivalent to *p*. Formally:

(1) $\neg\neg\varphi \Leftrightarrow \varphi$,

where ⇔ is the symbol for equivalence and φ is a variable over arbitrary sentences. While □ and ◊ are unary sentential operators (combining with single sentences to produce new sentences), ⇔ is a binary relational symbol that is not part of the standard language of modal logic, but rather part of the metalanguage – i.e., used to make statements *about* the sentences of the formal language. If we have $\varphi \Leftrightarrow \psi$, then we also have $\neg\varphi \Leftrightarrow \neg\psi$. The statement *It is not necessary that p* is equivalent to *It is possible that not-p.* Thus:

(2) $\neg\Box p \Leftrightarrow \Diamond\neg p$, and so

(3) $\neg\neg\Box p \Leftrightarrow \neg\Diamond\neg p$

Therefore, by the Law of Double Negation, we could define □ in terms of ◊ by:

(4) $\Box p \Leftrightarrow \neg\Diamond\neg p$

Similarly, we could define ◊ in terms of □ and ¬ :

(5) $\Diamond p \Leftrightarrow \neg\Box\neg p$

The above are general properties that modal operators have under all interpretations. Within particular modalities (deontic, epistemic, etc.) the same operators take on different flavors and support additional inference patterns, which are quite distinct from case to case. In deontic logic, □*p* usually stands for *It must be the case/is required that p.* The sentence ◊*p* is equivalent to ¬□¬*p*, which means *It is not required that not-p*, or equivalently, *It may be the case/is permissible that p.* The sentences *It is required that p* and *It is required that not-p* cannot both be true – they are *contraries* in the square of negation (cf. Horn 2001). On the other hand, *It is permissible that p* and *It is permissible that not-p* cannot both be false – they are *subcontraries*. There is also general agreement that in deontic logic, we have that $\Box p \Rightarrow \Diamond p$ (if *p* is required, it is allowed), but not $\Box p \Rightarrow p$ (just because *p* is required, it does not follow that it is true).

In epistemic logic, $\Box p$ stands for *It is known that p*, where *known* here has to mean 'known to someone.' Let us assume that the possessor of the knowledge is the speaker. This is one common interpretation, although others are certainly possible. Thus $\Box p$ is interpreted as *The speaker knows that p*. Accordingly, the dual sentence $\Diamond p$ is equivalent to *It is not true that the speaker knows that not-p*, which is equivalent to *It is possible, for all the speaker knows, that p*. Similarly, in doxastic logic, $\Box p$ stands for *The speaker believes that p*. Thus the dual $\Diamond p$ is equivalent to *The speaker does not believe that not-p*, which is again equivalent to *It is compatible with the speaker's beliefs that p*. Both in epistemic and doxastic logic, the interpretation of $\Box p$ relative to some particular individual *i* is sometimes indicated explicitly by an index on the operator. Thus, for instance, $\Box_i p$ stands for *i knows that p* or *i believes that p*.

1.1. Propositional modal logic: syntactic approach

For now, we will limit our discussion to sentences, ignoring the words and phrases they are composed of. Formally, we will use a language $\mathcal{L}_\mathcal{A}$ based on a set $\mathcal{A}$ of atomic propositional letters *p, q, r,* ... , the sentential connectives $\wedge, \vee, \rightarrow$ and $\neg$ for conjunction (*and*), disjunction (*or*), material conditional (*if-then*), and negation (*it is not the case that*), respectively, parentheses (shown only where needed to avoid ambiguity), and modal operators $\Box$ and $\Diamond$. Using Greek letters, such as φ and ψ, as variables over strings built from these symbols, we define the language $\mathcal{L}_\mathcal{A}$ as follows:

(6)   a.   All atomic propositional letters are sentences in $\mathcal{L}_\mathcal{A}$:
            $\mathcal{A} \subseteq \mathcal{L}_\mathcal{A}$

        b. $\mathcal{L}_\mathcal{A}$ is closed under the truth-functional connectives:
            If $\varphi, \psi \in \mathcal{L}_\mathcal{A}$, then $\varphi \wedge \psi, \varphi \vee \psi, \varphi \rightarrow \psi, \neg\varphi \in \mathcal{L}_\mathcal{A}$

        c. $\mathcal{L}_\mathcal{A}$ is closed under the unary modal operators:
            If $\varphi \in \mathcal{L}_\mathcal{A}$, then $\Box\varphi, \Diamond\varphi \in \mathcal{L}_\mathcal{A}$

        d.   Nothing else is in $\mathcal{L}_\mathcal{A}$.

The standard language of (non-modal) propositional logic is obtained by omitting clause (6c).

Classical propositional logic can be axiomatized by several axiom schemata[5] and one rule of inference, *Modus Ponens:*

$$(\text{MP}) \quad \frac{\varphi, \; \varphi \rightarrow \psi}{\psi}$$

This rule asserts that from φ and $\varphi \rightarrow \psi$ as hypotheses, we can derive ψ as a conclusion. Equivalently, if φ and $\varphi \rightarrow \psi$ are provable, then ψ is provable as well. The following set of axioms is one way to characterize classical logic, jointly with the rule of Modus Ponens.

(7)   a. $\varphi \rightarrow (\theta \rightarrow \varphi)$
        (truth follows from anything: if φ is true, then so is $(\theta \rightarrow \varphi)$ for any θ).

      b. $(\varphi \rightarrow (\theta \rightarrow \psi)) \rightarrow ((\varphi \rightarrow \theta) \rightarrow (\varphi \rightarrow \psi))$
        (distributivity of implication: if $\theta \rightarrow \psi$ follows from φ, then $\varphi \rightarrow \psi$ follows from $\varphi \rightarrow \theta$).

      c. $(\neg\psi \rightarrow \neg\varphi) \rightarrow ((\neg\psi \rightarrow \varphi) \rightarrow \psi)$
        (proof by contradiction: if the falsehood of φ follows from the falsehood of ψ, then showing that the truth of φ follows from the falsehood of ψ establishes the truth of ψ).

We now define the following notions, which are at the center of the syntactic approach to modal logic, as well as other axiomatic systems. The key notion is that of a *derivation*: a finite sequence of sentences, each of which is either an axiom or obtained from axioms and sentences already in the sequence by applying an inference rule of the system (Modus Ponens in our case). In addition, a derivation from *hypotheses* allows the use of hypotheses in the derivation sequence. Although the set of hypotheses can be infinite, every derivation must be finite. A *derived rule* is a rule whose conclusion has a derivation from its hypotheses. A *proof* for a sentence φ is a derivation sequence whose last member is φ. A *theorem* is a sentence that has a proof. Hence axioms are (trivially) theorems.

In addition to the above axioms, all propositional modal systems have the following axiom schema:

(K) $\Box\,(\varphi \rightarrow \psi) \rightarrow (\Box\varphi \rightarrow \Box\psi)$

(distributivity of $\Box$ over $\rightarrow$: if ψ necessarily follows from φ, then the necessity of ψ follows from the necessity of φ).

Furthermore, all propositional modal systems have the additional inference rule, the *Necessitation* rule (introduced by Gödel):

(N) $\dfrac{\varphi}{\Box\varphi}$

This rule says that if φ is provable, then φ is necessarily true. It does *not* say that φ implies $\Box\varphi$. The sentence $\varphi \rightarrow \Box\varphi$ is not a theorem in all systems of modal logic.

The most basic propositional modal system is called K (named after Kripke). It contains, in addition to the axioms of classical propositional logic, only the axiom (K) and, in addition to Modus Ponens, the Necessitation rule.

So, for example, in system K, we can derive $\Box p \rightarrow \Box q$ from $p \rightarrow q$. Here is a derivation sequence beginning with the hypothesis and ending with the conclusion:

(i)	$p \rightarrow q$	(hypothesis)
(ii)	$\Box\,(p \rightarrow q) \rightarrow (\Box p \rightarrow \Box q)$	(axiom (K))
(iii)	$\Box\,(p \rightarrow q)$	(from (i) by Necessitation)
(iv)	$\Box p \rightarrow \Box q$	(from (ii) and (iii) by Modus Ponens)

Based upon the central notion of derivation, we define the following notions, which are at the heart of all logical systems:

(8)   A set Φ of sentences is syntactically *consistent* if and only if there is no derivation of a sentence of the form $\varphi \wedge \neg\varphi$ (a contradiction) from Φ.

Furthermore, we say that a sentence φ is syntactically consistent with a set Φ of sentences iff $\Phi \cup \{\varphi\}$ is consistent (i.e., φ can be added to Φ consistently). A consistent set Φ is *maximally consistent* if no sentence outside Φ can be added to Φ consistently. Every consistent set of sentences can be extended to a maximally consistent one.

(9)   A sentence φ is a syntactic *consequence* of a set Φ of sentences if and only if there is a derivation of φ from Φ.

1.2. Propositional modal logic: semantic approach

The central notion in the semantic interpretation of modal logic is that of *possible worlds*. The history of this concept can be traced back to Leibniz, who believed that we live in a world which is one of infinitely many possible worlds created by God (and, fortunately for us, the best one among them!). In philosophical logic, the notion was introduced only in the 1960's, independently by Hintikka (1961) and Kripke (1963). Its ontological status continues to be controversial among philosophers. These debates will not concern us here, however. The utility of possible worlds as a methodological tool in semantic analysis has been amply demonstrated in recent decades and does not depend on any particular stance on metaphysical questions, such as whether worlds other than ours "exist" in any real sense. For our purposes, they are nothing but abstract entities which help us in modeling certain semantic relations among linguistic expressions.

Towards this end, we only need to assume that possible worlds fix the denotations of the relevant expressions – truth values for sentences, properties for verb phrases, and so on. For now we will limit the discussion to sentences, and we will continue to use the formal language we introduced.

Possible worlds play a central role in defining the denotations of sentences. The meaning of a sentence is analyzed in terms of its role in distinguishing between possible worlds. Assuming that every sentence is guaranteed to be either true or false (the *Law of Excluded Middle*),[6] but not both true and false (the *Law of Non-Contradiction*), each possible world determines the truth values of all atomic sentences, as well as, via the interpretation of the logical connectives, those of their Boolean combinations.

To be more precise, we define a *model* as a pair $M = \langle W, V \rangle$, consisting of a nonempty set W (the set of possible worlds) and a function V which, for each world w in W, assigns truth values to the atomic sentences in the language. We write 1 and 0 for the values 'true' and 'false,' respectively. The truth values of complex sentences are defined recursively by the following clauses.[7]

(10) For atomic p, $V_w(p)$ is either 1 or 0.

$$V_w(\neg\varphi) = \begin{cases} 1 & \text{if } V_w(\varphi) = 0 \\ 0 & \text{otherwise} \end{cases}$$

$$V_w(\varphi \wedge \psi) = \begin{cases} 1 & \text{if } V_w(\varphi) = 1 \text{ and } V_w(\psi) = 1 \\ 0 & \text{otherwise} \end{cases}$$

$$V_w(\varphi \vee \psi) = \begin{cases} 1 & \text{if } V_w(\varphi) = 1 \text{ or } V_w(\psi) = 1 \\ 0 & \text{otherwise} \end{cases}$$

$$V_w(\varphi \rightarrow \psi) = \begin{cases} 1 & \text{if } V_w(\varphi) = 0 \text{ or } V_w(\psi) = 1 \\ 0 & \text{otherwise} \end{cases}$$

Given the assignment function, each sentence in the language distinguishes between those worlds in which it is true and those in which it is false. We may, therefore, associate each sentence φ with the set of those worlds in which it is true. Thus we introduce a function $[\![\cdot]\!]^M$ for our model M, mapping sentences to sets of worlds:

(11) $[\![\varphi]\!]^M =_{\text{def}} \{w \in W \mid V_w(\varphi) = 1\}$

We call $[\![\varphi]\!]^M$ the *denotation* of sentence φ in M. We will omit the superscript M when the choice of model makes no difference. The term *proposition*, in its technical use in this context, is reserved for sets of worlds. Hence the denotation of the sentence *It is raining* is the proposition 'that it is raining,' the set of just those worlds in which it is raining.

We can now characterize standard logical properties of sentences set-theoretically in terms of the propositions they denote:

(12) A sentence φ is:
    a. *tautologous* iff $W \subseteq [\![\varphi]\!]$
    b. *contradictory* iff $[\![\varphi]\!] \subseteq \varnothing$
    c. *contingent* otherwise (i.e., iff $\varnothing \subset [\![\varphi]\!] \subset W$)

Likewise, semantic relationships between sentences can be defined in terms of the propositions they denote. For instance, the interpretation of the logical connectives gives rise to the following relations between the denotations of complex sentences and the parts they are composed of ($\cap$, $\cup$, and \ stand for intersection, union, and relative complement or set subtraction, respectively):

(13) $[\![\neg\varphi]\!] = W \setminus [\![\varphi]\!]$

$\qquad [\![\varphi \wedge \psi]\!] = [\![\varphi]\!] \cap [\![\psi]\!]$

$\qquad [\![\varphi \vee \psi]\!] = [\![\varphi]\!] \cup [\![\psi]\!]$

$\qquad [\![\varphi \rightarrow \psi]\!] = W \setminus ([\![\varphi]\!] \setminus [\![\psi]\!]) = (W \setminus [\![\varphi]\!]) \cup [\![\psi]\!]$

The clause for conjunction states that the denotation of *It is raining and it is cold* is the intersection of the denotations of *It is raining* and *It is cold*, i.e., the set of worlds in which both of these sentences are true. This idea can be generalized to arbitrary sets Φ of propositions, writing $[\![\Phi]\!]$ for the set of worlds in which all sentences in Φ are true – i.e., the intersection of their respective denotations:[8]

(14) $[\![\Phi]\!]^M =_{\text{def}} \cap \{[\![\varphi]\!]^M \mid \varphi \in \Phi\}$

Using this notation, we can now define the central notions of modal logic semantically.

(15) Consistency

    a. A set Φ of sentences is semantically *consistent* iff there is some world in which all sentences in Φ are true; i.e., iff $[\![\Phi]\!] \neq \varnothing$.

    b. A sentence φ is semantically consistent with a set Φ of sentences iff $\Phi \cup \{\varphi\}$ is consistent (φ can be added to Φ consistently); i.e., iff $[\![\Phi \cup \{\varphi\}]\!] \neq \varnothing$.

(16) Consequence

    A sentence φ is a semantic *consequence* of a set Φ of sentences if and only if φ is true in all possible worlds in which all sentences in Φ are true; i.e., iff $[\![\Phi]\!] \subseteq [\![\varphi]\!]$.

We often use these terms relative to Φ consisting of just a single sentence. In a slight abuse of terminology, we will speak of a sentence being consistent with, or a consequence of, such a single proposition, rather than the singleton set containing it. This is a safe move to make since $[\![\{\psi\}]\!] = [\![\psi]\!]$.

    Much of the work in modal logic explores the relationship between axiomatic systems and the semantic relationships they give rise to. For instance, it is easy to check that all the axioms in (7) above are tautologies, and that Modus Ponens preserves the property of being a tautology. Hence all theorems in this system are tautologies. This property of a formal system is called *soundness*. What is remarkable is that the converse also holds. Every tautology can de derived as a theorem in this system, i.e., the classical propositional logic is *complete* with respect to this axiomatic system (for a proof by Kalmár see Mendelson 1987). The completeness theorem establishes that being provable in a sound formal system is equivalent to being true in every model. As a corollary, it follows that any given set Φ of sentences is syntactically consistent if and only if Φ has a model (i.e., is semantically consistent).

By adding more axioms, we obtain systems which may be sound and complete with respect to some restricted class of models, rather than all models. We will see a few illustrations of this in later sections. In general, the task of identifying the class of models relative to which a given axiomatic system is sound and complete can be difficult. We will not discuss it in more detail in this chapter.

2. Modal bases

Above, we defined the notions of consistency and consequence relative to the proposition $[\![\Phi]\!]$, the set of those worlds at which all sentences in Φ are true. Following Kratzer (1977, 1981, 1991) we call this set of worlds the *modal base*. Kratzer calls the set of propositions whose intersection forms the modal base *conversational background*. In this section we give a more direct definition of modal bases, sidestepping conversational backgrounds.

Modal bases constitute a central parameter in all formal treatments of modality. They serve to distinguish between the different readings of modals (epistemic, deontic, etc.) we identified earlier. Thus it is customary to speak of epistemic, deontic, and other types of modal bases. The intuition is that on each occasion of use the modal base is the set of just those worlds that are compatible with all of the speaker's beliefs or desires, the applicable laws, and so on. The contents of speakers' beliefs, of laws, etc. are of course themselves contingent and, therefore, may vary from world to world. Thus the contents of, say, an epistemic modal base do not remain constant across different worlds. Just like the truth values of the sentences in our language, the modal base depends on the world of evaluation.

Formally, a modal base is given by a function from possible worlds to propositions. We will reserve the letter R as a general symbol for such functions, using superscripts to distinguish between them, such as R^{epist} and R^{deont} for epistemic and deontic modal bases, respectively. Given a world w

of evaluation, we will write R_w^{epist} for the (speaker's) epistemic modal base at w, i.e., the set of exactly those worlds that are compatible with the speaker's beliefs in w. We will use the Greek letter ρ as a variable over modal bases.

The second major parameter in the interpretation of modality is the *modal force*. Unlike the modal base, which is usually left implicit and contextually given, the modal force is an integral part of the lexical meaning of all modals. For instance, both (17b) and (17c) below can be used as assertions about either the speaker's beliefs (*given what I know...*) or John's options and obligations (*given the rules and John's age...*), but the logical relations invoked in the two sentences are unambiguously possibility and necessity, respectively. With respect to the intended modal base, this difference between (17b) and (17c) corresponds to consistency and consequence.

(17)   a.   John is at the party.
       b.   John may be at the party.
       c.   John must be at the party.

We can now give the first version of the truth conditions for modalized sentences such as (17b,c). We assume that in both cases the modal auxiliary functions as a sentential operator which takes (17a) as its argument. For simplicity, we assume that the intended modal base ρ is given, and extend the valuation function V as follows:

$$(18)\quad V_w(\Diamond_\rho \varphi) = \begin{cases} 1 & \text{if } V_{w'}(\varphi)=1 \ \text{ for some } w' \in \rho_w \\ 0 & \text{otherwise} \end{cases}$$

$$(19)\quad V_w(\Box_\rho \varphi) = \begin{cases} 1 & \text{if } V_{w'}(\varphi)=1 \ \text{ for all } w' \in \rho_w \\ 0 & \text{otherwise} \end{cases}$$

Modal operators are thus quantifiers over possible worlds, with the modal base providing the domain of quantification. Relative to modal base ρ, $\Diamond_\rho$ and $\Box_\rho$ are duals.

We can now identify the meaning of necessity modals with the interpretation of $\Box$, and that of possibility modals with the interpretation of $\Diamond$. The truth-conditional content of a modal is given relative to a context of use that fixes the modal base, that is, the appropriate index ρ for the operators $\Box$ and $\Diamond$. For instance, supposing the modal base of an utterance of (17b) is determined to be epistemic, (17b) is true in a world w iff there exists $w' \in R_w^{epist}$

such that *John is at the party* is true in w'. If instead the modal base of an utterance of (17b) is determined to be deontic, the only thing that would change in determining whether (17b) is true in w is the domain of quantification. In general, R^{epist} and R^{deont} are distinct so an utterance of (17b) expresses a different proposition, depending on whether the modal is construed with an epistemic or a deontic modal base.

As we mentioned earlier, our definition of modal bases is a shortcut compared to Kratzer's treatment. There the modal base is defined indirectly via a conversational background, the latter being a function from worlds to sets of propositions. Our more direct definition is not meant to deny the utility of the notion of conversational background (the examples to which we apply it here do not illustrate its specific advantages), nor is it merely for the sake of simplicity. Rather, it takes us to the area of contact between the Kratzer-style theory and another, equally influential approach in terms of *accessibility relations* between possible worlds. For any function ρ from worlds to sets of worlds, there is a relation R_ρ which pairs up each world w with all and only the worlds in ρ_w:

(20) $R_\rho =_{def} \{\langle w, w' \rangle \mid w' \in \rho_w\}$

Many authors, especially in the area of philosophical logic, take such relations between possible worlds as basic, rather than define them in terms of modal bases. In technical discussions of modal logic, they are given as part of the model. Assuming for simplicity that we are only interested in one accessibility relation R, we can define a model to be a triple $\langle W, R, V \rangle$, where W and V are as before. The pair $\langle W, R \rangle$, the set of worlds and the accessibility relation, is called a *frame*. For a fixed frame, certain axioms may be guaranteed to hold solely in virtue of the properties of the accessibility relation, regardless of what truth values V assigns to the sentences of the language at individual worlds. We will discuss some of them, and the structural properties they correspond to, in the following subsection. In the course of the discussion, it will be useful to switch back and forth between modal bases as functions from worlds to propositions and as accessibility relations. In light of the close formal affinity between these two perspectives, we will use the same symbol R for both.

2.1.   Properties of modal bases

The modal base is not only a useful parameter to capture the variability and context dependence of modal expressions. It is also the right place to state generalizations about the properties of particular readings of modals. The investigation of such general properties and their logical consequences is the topic of modal logic; the reader is referred to introductions to this field, such as Hughes and Cresswell (1996), for discussions going far beyond what we can cover here. We will only mention a few such conditions which have turned out to be important in linguistic analysis. For concreteness, unless otherwise stated, we will restrict the discussion in this subsection to the special case of a *doxastic* modal base – i.e., one that represents the speaker's beliefs. We will write R instead of R^{dox} for simplicity.

2.1.1. Consistency

The first general condition one can impose on modal bases is that they be *consistent*. Formally, this corresponds to the requirement that for all worlds w, the set R_w be nonempty. Alternatively, in relational terms, the requirement is that R be *serial*: for every world w of evaluation, there is at least one world w' that is accessible from w via R.

In linguistic theory, consistency is generally taken to be a requirement for all modal bases. An inconsistent modal base may result in the interpretation of sentences by quantification over an empty set of worlds, leading to presupposition failure.

2.1.2. Realism

Next, one may impose the condition that a modal base be *realistic,* in the sense that none of the sentences supported by the modal base for a world w (i.e., true at all worlds in R_w) is false at w. Formally, this condition means that each world w must itself be a member of R_w. In relational terms, the analog of this condition is that R is reflexive – i.e., each world w is related to itself by R.

Realism is a sensible condition for some modalities, but not for others. For doxastic modality, the condition means that all of the speaker's beliefs are true. This property is often taken to distinguish *knowledge* from *belief* or, equivalently, *epistemic* from *doxastic* accessibility relations. Deontic modality is generally not realistic. Assuming otherwise would amount to the claim that all obligations are fulfilled.[9]

2.1.3. Introspection

Under a doxastic interpretation, R_w is the set of those worlds that are *compatible with what the speaker believes at w*. These worlds will differ from each other with respect to the truth values of non-modal sentences, such as *It is raining*. In addition, they may also differ with respect to the speaker's beliefs. Each world w' in R_w is one in which the speaker has certain beliefs, represented in the set $R_{w'}$. What this means for w is that the modal base does not only encode the speaker's beliefs about the facts, but also her beliefs about her own beliefs.

Little reflection is required to see that some conditions ought to be imposed on these beliefs about one's own beliefs. Suppose the speaker believes in w that it is raining (i.e., all worlds in R_w are such that it is raining), and suppose further that there are two worlds w', w'' in R_w, such that in w' the speaker believes that it is raining, and in w'' she believes that it is not. While there is nothing wrong with this scenario from a formal point of view, it is very peculiar indeed as a representation of a speaker's beliefs. It amounts to the claim that the speaker has a very definite opinion on the question of whether it is raining, but does not know what that opinion is.

Such outcomes are avoided by imposing constraints governing the relationship between speakers' actual beliefs and the beliefs they have at the worlds compatible with their beliefs, i.e., the worlds in the corresponding modal bases. The two most commonly encountered conditions of this kind are those of positive and negative introspection.

Positive introspection is the requirement that at every world compatible with what the speaker believes (i.e., each world in R_w), she has all the beliefs that she actually has at w (and possibly more). Formally, this means that for each such belief-world w', the speaker's doxastic modal base $R_{w'}$ is a subset of the actual modal base R_w. The corresponding condition on the accessibility relation is that it be *transitive*. The following two statements are equivalent, and each imposes the requirement of positive introspection, provided it is true at every world w:

(21) a. For all $w' \in R_w$, we have $R_{w'} \subseteq R_w$
     b. If wRw' and $w'Rw''$, then wRw''

It is helpful to visualize this formal constraint by illustrating the kind of case it rules out. Such a case is shown in Figure 1. The modal bases R_w and $R_{w'}$ are indicated as partial spheres (whether the worlds are in their respective modal bases, and whether there is any overlap between R_w and $R_{w'}$ is not relevant here). Positive introspection fails because $R_{w'}$ is not fully contained in R_w: there is at least one world, w'', which is in $R_{w'}$, but not in R_w. Equivalently, in terms of the accessibility relation, there is a path leading from w to w'', but w'' is not directly accessible from w. Now, suppose some sen-

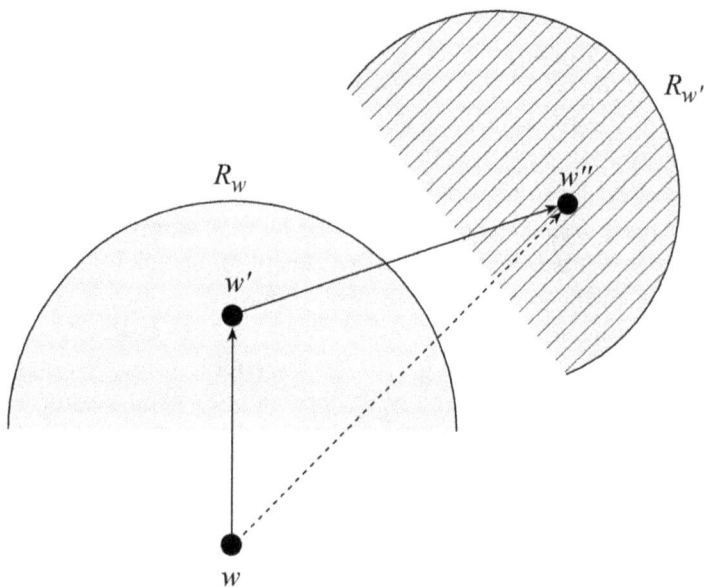

Figure 1. A violation of transitivity. No direct accessibility link leads from w to w''; $R_{w'}$ is not a subset of R_w.

tence φ is true at all worlds in R_w, but false at w''. Thus there is a sentence, φ, which the speaker believes at w but not at w'. Since w' is compatible with what the speaker believes at w, the picture shows a speaker who at w thinks she may not believe that φ, even though she actually believes φ at w. To rule out such cases, positive introspection is usually imposed as a condition on epistemic and doxastic modal bases.

Negative introspection is the corresponding requirement that there be no world compatible with what the speaker believes at which she holds any beliefs that she does not actually hold. In relational terms, this requires R to be *euclidean.* Formally:

(22) a. For all $w' \in R_w$, we have $R_w \subseteq R_{w'}$

   b. If wRw' and wRw'', then $w'Rw''$

As before, we can illustrate the effect of this condition by giving an example in which it is violated, as illustrated in Figure 2:

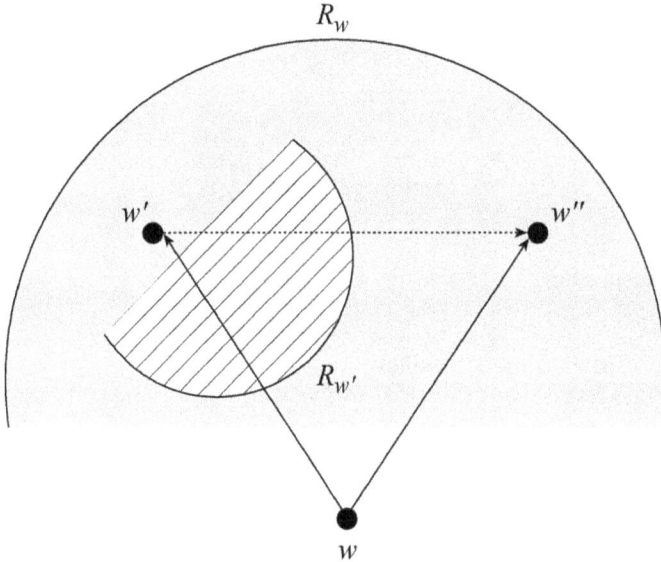

Figure 2. A violation of euclidity. No direct accessibility leads from w' to w'' (or *vice versa*); R_w is not a subset of $R_{w'}$.

The accessibility relation in Figure 2 is not euclidean, and the modal base R_w lacks the property of negative introspection. Even though w' and w'' are both accessible from w, the world w'' is not directly accessible from w'. Suppose φ is true at w'' and false at worlds in $R_{w'}$. Then the situation depicted is one in which the speaker does not believe that φ is false at w, but does believe that it is false at w'. In other words, the speaker thinks she may believe that φ is false, but is not sure if she does. To rule out such counterintuitive models, negative introspection (i.e., euclidity) is usually required of epistemic and doxastic modal bases.

Table 1 summarizes these properties of modal bases and the corresponding properties of accessibility relations, along with the axioms of modal logic that are guaranteed to hold for any modal base with the respective properties.

Table 1. Correspondences between some properties of modal bases and accessibility relations, and their characteristic axioms. (Free variables w, w', w'' are universally quantified over.)

Modal Base	Accessibility Relation	Axiom	
consistency $R_w \neq \varnothing$	seriality $(\exists w')\, wRw'$	$\Box_R \varphi \to \Diamond_R \varphi$	(D)
realism $w \in R_w$	reflexivity wRw	$\Box_R \varphi \to \varphi$	(T)
total realism $R_w = \{w\}$	identity $wRw' \Leftrightarrow w = w'$	$\Box_R \varphi \leftrightarrow \varphi$	
positive introspection $w' \in R_w \Rightarrow R_{w'} \subseteq R_w$	transitivity $wRw' \wedge w'Rw'' \Rightarrow wRw''$	$\Box_R \varphi \to \Box_R \Box_R \varphi$	(4)
negative introspection $w' \in R_w \Rightarrow R_w \subseteq R_{w'}$	euclidity $wRw' \wedge wRw'' \Rightarrow w'Rw''$	$\Diamond_R \varphi \to \Box_R \Diamond_R \varphi$	(5)

In most applications, it is some combination of these conditions that in its totality determines the properties of a particular modal base and distinguishes it from others. For instance, *doxastic* modal bases are generally taken to be consistent and fully introspective, whereas *epistemic* ones (modeling knowledge, rather than mere belief) are, in addition to these properties, realistic. Positive or negative introspection is rarely imposed on modal bases other than epistemic or doxastic ones.

2.2. Ordering sources

Our discussion so far has shown how the great variability in the readings of modal expressions can be reduced to the specification of their modal force in their lexical meaning and the contextual determination of a modal base on a particular occasion of use. Natural language, though, abounds in modal expressions that exhibit a wider variety of modal forces than plain necessity and possibility, appropriately relativized to a modal base. Expressions of graded modality, such as *may well*, *barely possible*, and *more likely than*, for instance, show that our semantics had better incorporate a gradable notion of possibility, built around the absolute notion of consistency.

As argued by Kratzer, the interpretation of modal expressions requires an additional parameter, which she terms *ordering source*. This parameter enables us to specify a wider range of modal forces, such as weaker necessity than in (19) and stronger possibility than in (18), as well as to cover expressions of gradable modality. In this subsection we motivate ordering sources by discussing first the need for weaker necessity in the epistemic domain and then the use of ordering sources in avoiding potential inconsistencies.

Consider the necessity modals *should* and *must* in (23b) and (24b) below, supposing they are construed with an epistemic (hence realistic) modal base. If they quantified universally over R_w^{epist}, for any w, then (23b) and (24b) would entail (23a) and (24a), respectively, but no such entailment is in fact present:

(23) a. John has reached Athens by now.
    b. John should have reached Athens by now.

(24) a. It rained overnight.
    b. It must have rained overnight.

Rather, (23b) and (24b) carry an implication of uncertainty that (23a) and (24a) do not. A speaker who chooses to assert (23b) or (24b), over (23a) or (24a), indicates that she does not have direct knowledge about John's whereabouts, or the reason for the wet ground, but can only infer where John is, or what explains the wet ground, based on other facts she knows and certain reasonable assumptions. Conversely, a speaker who has direct knowledge of John's whereabouts or witnessed the rain directly would choose (23a) and (24a), over (23b) or (24b).

The conclusion to be drawn is that the universal quantification of epistemic necessity modals needs to be further relativized. The sentences (23b) and (24b) claim that (23a) and (24a) are true *provided* some additional assumptions are brought to bear. In the case of (23b), such an implicit assumption can be that John's trip is following the planned itinerary; in the case of (24b), that rain is the most plausible explanation for the overt evidence at hand, the wet ground.

The meaning of epistemic necessity modals thus makes reference to a set of contextually determined assumptions, construed as a set of propositions. This set of propositions, which for epistemic modals must be nonempty, is the ordering source parameter. By using an epistemic necessity modal, a speaker is signaling uncertainty as to whether these implicit assumptions are true, that is, whether the actual world is one conforming to the planned course of events, or whether the actual world is one to which the most plausible explanation for the evidence at hand applies.

Next we consider potential inconsistencies arising when facts of the matter are not appropriately distinguished from rules, laws, aims, desires, etc. Suppose the sentences in (25) below are uttered in a situation in which John was caught speeding and the law both prohibits speeding and requires that anyone caught speeding pay a fine. In such a situation, with the modals construed deontically, (25a) is true and (25b) false:

(25) a. John must pay a fine for speeding.
      b. John need not pay any fine for speeding.

So far, we have identified deontic modals as those whose modal base is deontic, a mapping from any world w to the set of those worlds in which the dictates of the law in w are adhered to. This leads to two interrelated problems arising from the fact that the proposition that John was speeding has to be true in all worlds in the modal base. This has to be the case if (25a) is to come out true. The first problem is an unavoidable inconsistency. Given the prohibition against speeding and John's speeding, the modal base ends up being inconsistent and, in that case, both (25a) and (25b) are verified. The second problem is an unwanted entailment of (25a), namely (26).[10]

(26) John was required to be speeding.

In order for these two problems to be avoided, the propositions corresponding to the relevant actual facts and the propositions corresponding to the content of the law must constitute distinct parameters. The modal base of deontic modals is not itself deontic, but determined by the relevant actual facts, for instance, that John was speeding. The deontic parameter in the interpretation of deontic modals is the ordering source, determined by the contents of the law in every world. Different mappings from a world w to a set of propositions determine a moral ideal, a normal course of events, a likely scenario, etc., for w. Moreover, each such mapping can be used to rank the worlds in ρ_w. For instance, the relevant ranking for the interpretation of (25a) is one where worlds in which what is prohibited in w is never committed are ranked higher than worlds in which violations occur; worlds in which violations occur but are punished are in turn ranked higher than worlds with violations but no punishment.

More formally, we say that, for any world w, a set of propositions P induces a *preorder*[11] $\leq_w$ on a set of worlds as follows: $w'' \leq_w w'$ if and only if any proposition in P that is true at w' is also true at w''. We can also define ordering sources more directly, just as we did for modal bases, as functions from worlds to preorders between worlds. We will follow this more direct method here and use o as a variable over ordering sources. For any function o from worlds to preorders, there is a ternary relation relating each world w with the members of all and only the pairs in o_w:

(27) $\leq_o =_{\text{def}} \{\langle w, w', w'' \rangle \mid \langle w', w'' \rangle \in o_w\}$

We can now give the semantics of a doubly modal necessity operator, making reference to both modal bases and ordering sources:[12]

(28) $V_w(\Box_{\rho,o}\, \varphi) = \begin{cases} 1 & \text{if for all } w' \in \rho_w \text{ there is some } w'' \in \rho_w \\ & \text{such that } \langle w'', w' \rangle \in o_w \text{ and} \\ & \text{for all } u \in \rho_w,\ V_u(\varphi) = 1 \text{ if } \langle u, w'' \rangle \in o_w \\ \\ 0 & \text{otherwise} \end{cases}$

The reader is referred to Kratzer (1981, 1991) for definitions of other doubly relative modal notions, such as 'good possibility,' 'slight possibility,' or 'better possibility.' Formally, the order induced by the ordering source is similar to the relation of comparative similarity between possible worlds, which is central to the Stalnaker/Lewis theory of counterfactuals (see Lewis 1981 for a comparison).

2.3. Interim summary

So far we outlined some of the basic apparatus in which formal accounts of modal expressions are usually framed. We saw that modals are treated as quantifiers over possible worlds, whose domains of quantification at any given world of evaluation are determined by accessibility relations with certain properties. These basic ingredients were introduced more than twenty years ago and have formed the mainstay of the formal semantics of modality ever since.

3.   Modality and time

In this section, we turn to modal aspects of expressions of tense and temporal reference. The semantic interactions between the temporal domain and modality are so pervasive that no analysis of one can be complete without an account of the other. We will be focusing on ways in which temporal reference determines and constrains modal interpretations. As part of this discussion, we will further develop and refine the formal tools we have so far introduced.[13]

3.1. The English present tense

The present tense in English can be used with both present and future reference times. Thus, as far as temporal reference is concerned, the Present complements the Past. Consider the following examples:

(29) a. Megan was in her office yesterday.
      b. Megan is in her office (now).
      c. Megan is in her office tomorrow.

Based on (29), it would appear that there are two tenses in English, Past and Non-Past, illustrated by (29a) on the one hand, and (29b,c), on the other. However, the formal semantic literature on tense in English presents a different picture. While there is general agreement that (29a,b) differ only in tense and temporal reference, most authors maintain that the futurate Present in (29c) differs rather dramatically from both. Specifically, for the truth of (29c) it is not sufficient that a certain state holds in the future, but this occurrence has to be *predetermined*, in some sense, at speech time. No such connotation is observed in either (29a) or (29b).

Notice that the sentences in (29) are *stative*. A slightly different pattern is observed with non-stative predicates:

(30) a. Megan came to her office yesterday.
      b. Megan comes to her office (now).
      c. Megan comes to her office tomorrow.

Here, both (30b) and (30c) call for a *scheduling* reading. The contrast between (29b) and (30b) is accompanied by a difference in temporal reference: (29b) asserts that a state holds at speech time, whereas the event in (30b) is asserted to occur in the (near) future. A full analysis of these differences would lead us far beyond the scope of this section and into the area of aspectual classes. We merely note that the reference time follows the speech time in all and only the sentences in (29c) and (30b,c). Our goal in this subsection is to show that, with the right model-theoretic setup, the presence or absence of the scheduling reading falls out from this fact about temporal reference alone, with a simple and uniform analysis of the tenses and no further stipulations. This is a modest goal, but first we must further develop the technical apparatus.

3.1.1. Some background

Like many interesting phenomena at the intersection of modality and temporality, the connection between temporal reference and the scheduling reading can be traced to a fundamental and, it appears, virtually universally shared background assumption speakers make about the nature of time: that there is an important difference between a *fixed* past and an *open* future. The past up to and including the present time has (now) no chance of being different from what it actually has been. Consequently, sentences whose truth or falsehood depends solely on times no later than the speech time are either unequivocally true or unequivocally false, regardless of whether their truth values are known or not.

The situation is different with respect to the future. To use a well-known example from Aristotle (*De Interpretatione* 9), consider the claim that there will be a sea battle tomorrow. It is intuitively clear that the truth or falsehood of this claim will, in time, be fully determined by the course of events. There either will or will not be a sea battle, and there can be no two ways about it. However, most speakers share with Aristotle the intuition that, regardless of which way history eventually settles the question, at present it is still possible for things to turn out otherwise. It is precisely with regard to this intrinsic non-determinacy that the future differs from past and present.

The rigorous treatment of this old idea in present-day formal logic starts with the work of Prior (1967). In our brief discussion of this topic, we will focus on two issues: the notion of truth in time, and temporal constraints on the interaction between two kinds of uncertainty – objective (metaphysical) and subjective (epistemic/doxastic).

3.1.2. Two notions of truth

In Aristotle's example, the statement that there will be a sea battle tomorrow and its negation, the statement that there will not be a sea battle, have a similar semantic status at the present time. Both have a certain chance of being true, and neither is verified or falsified by the facts accumulated through history up until now. Aristotle was concerned with the implications of this judgment for the validity of the logical principles of Excluded Middle and Non-Contradiction. When applied to the sea battle example, these two general principles entail that one of the sentences is true and the other is false, contrary to intuition.

In formal two-valued logic, there are two ways of reconciling the intuition with the logical principles, depending on which of two notions of truth one considers appropriate for statements about the future. The first, known as the *Ockhamist* notion of truth, upholds Excluded Middle and Non-Contradiction for such statements and asserts that they are indeed *already* either true or false, even though it may be impossible, even in principle, to *know* their truth values ahead of time. This was Aristotle's own answer to the problem.

The second notion of truth, sometimes called *Peircean*, maintains, in contrast, that neither of the statements about tomorrow's sea battle is true until the facts actually settle the question. Until such time, both are false. Does this mean that Excluded Middle is not applicable to future statements under this view? Not necessarily, if the notion of truth for such statements is properly construed. The idea is to treat them as *modal* statements, involving the modal force of necessity. It is a straightforward consequence of the interpretation of the modal operators that relative to any given modal base ρ, two statements $\Box_\rho \varphi$ and $\Box_\rho \neg\varphi$ may both be false (or, for that matter, vacuously true) without any violation of logical principles.[14]

3.2. The temporal dimension

Let us consider in some detail a formal implementation in which these distinctions can be clarified. To integrate time into our model-theoretic apparatus, we add a temporal dimension to the possible worlds, which in the previous sections had no internal structure at all. Technically, we can achieve this by introducing an ordered set $(T, <)$ of times, where $<$ is the *earlier-than* relation. We assume that $<$ has the following properties for all $t, t', t'' \in T$:

(31) a. irreflexivity: not $(t < t)$
      b. transitivity: if $t < t'$ and $t' < t''$, then $t < t''$
      c. linearity: $t < t'$ or $t' < t$ or $t = t'$

The inverse $<^{-1}$ of the earlier-than relation is the *later-than* relation, defined as:

(32) $t' <^{-1} t$ iff $t < t'$

The properties of $<$ ensure that its inverse is also irreflexive, transitive and linear (these properties are 'preserved under inverse'). We will refer to both relations below, writing $<$ for *earlier-than* and $>$ for *later-than*.

Each single world $w \in W$ is now associated with a set of pairs $\langle w, t \rangle$ for $t \in T$; temporal precedence is extended to these pairs as expected:

(33) $\langle w, t \rangle < \langle w', t' \rangle$ iff $w = w'$ and $t < t'$

The same holds for $>$.[15]

Notice that these temporal relations are themselves modal accessibility relations – though 'modal' only in the technical sense of modal logic; we have not yet employed them in the interpretation of linguistic expressions of modality. However, we can now use the same formal tools as before to evaluate statements at individual world-time pairs in this structure, analogously to our definitions in (18)–(19) for single worlds. For instance, $>_{\langle w, t \rangle}$ is the set of all world-time pairs $\langle w, t \rangle$ such that $t > t'$ – i.e., all world-time pairs that precede $\langle w, t \rangle$ in time. Similarly, we define the set $<_{\langle w, t \rangle}$. We also have the set $\leq_{\langle w, t \rangle}$, which differs from $<_{\langle w, t \rangle}$ only in that it includes $\langle w, t \rangle$. The sets $>_{\langle w, t \rangle}$ and $<_{\langle w, t \rangle}$, illustrated in Figure 3, are the analogs of modal bases in the temporal dimension (although the term *temporal base* has never been proposed for them):

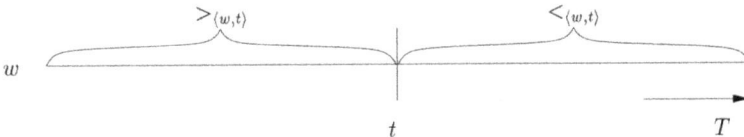

Figure 3. Temporal *accessibility*. The sets of world-time pairs preceding and following $\langle w, t \rangle$ are labeled '$>_{\langle w, t \rangle}$' and '$<_{\langle w, t \rangle}$,' respectively.

Thus:

$$(34) \quad V_{\langle w,\, t\rangle}(\lozenge_{>}\varphi) = \begin{cases} 1 & \text{if } V_{\langle w,\, t'\rangle}(\varphi) = 1 \text{ for some } \langle w,\, t'\rangle \in >_{\langle w,\, t\rangle} \\ 0 & \text{otherwise} \end{cases}$$

Under this definition, the expression $\lozenge_{>}\varphi$ states that φ happened at some time in the past. Prior (1957, 1967) used the special symbol P for $\lozenge_{>}$, and H for its dual $\square_{>}$, the latter meaning roughly *it has always been the case that*.... Notice that the truth conditions for these operators make no reference to worlds other than the world w of evaluation.

There are various ways in which this basic idea can be extended to include present and future reference. For our purposes, the best way to proceed is to ignore for the moment the modal implications of future statements; we will account for them shortly. Regarding temporal reference on its own, we will say that statements about the future are evaluated just like those about the past, but with respect to the relation $<$. The by-now familiar truth definition for modal operators gives us the counterpart to (34) with non-past reference:

$$(35) \quad V_{\langle w,t\rangle}(\lozenge_{<}\varphi) = \begin{cases} 1 & \text{if } V_{\langle w,\, t'\rangle}(\varphi) = 1 \text{ for some } \langle w,\, t'\rangle \in <_{\langle w,\, t\rangle} \\ 0 & \text{otherwise} \end{cases}$$

Prior used the symbols F and G for $\lozenge_{<}$ and $\square_{<}$, respectively.

In defining the truth conditions in (35), we have followed the Ockhamist tradition. Recall that, in this approach, the truth value of a statement such as $\lozenge_{<}\varphi$ is determined at all times, depending solely on the truth values of φ at various times in the world of evaluation. Accordingly, our definition treats past and non-past symmetrically and leaves no room for uncertainty about the future.

We did *not* claim that expressions of the form $\lozenge_{<}\varphi$ are suitable logical translations of well-formed English sentences such as *It rains tomorrow* or *It will rain tomorrow*. Before we turn to the interpretation of natural language expressions, let us continue our discussion of the formal apparatus and incorporate the asymmetry between past and future. For this purpose, we will add a modal dimension to our temporal model.

3.2.1. *Modal/temporal two-dimensional semantics*

Modal notions are introduced in our system as before, by postulating a multitude of possible worlds (or world-lines, as illustrated in Figure 3). We will assume here that all of these worlds are aligned with the same temporal dimension, given by $(T, <)$.[16] One can picture these alternative worlds as lines running in parallel, illustrated in Figure 4:

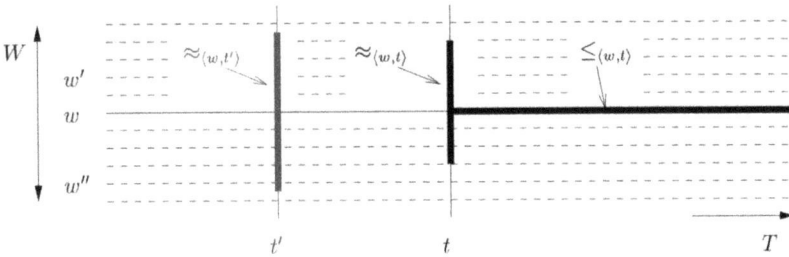

Figure 4. Two-dimensional modal logic. The thick lines represent the sets of indices accessible from $\langle w, t \rangle$ by the modal relation $\approx$ (vertical) and the temporal relation $\leq$ (horizontal). For example, the worlds accessible via $\approx$ from w at t are also accessible at t', but not necessarily vice versa.

Modal bases are given by accessibility relations, as before. However, we are now interested in the way they change over time. Our current *tomorrow* is part of the *open* future from today's perspective, but will be part of the *fixed* past from next week's.

Thus modal accessibility relations, such as the temporal ones introduced before, will be time-sensitive, defined between world-time pairs, rather than just worlds. Expressions such as $\langle w, t \rangle \rho \langle w', t' \rangle$ or, alternatively, $\langle w', t' \rangle \in \rho_{\langle w, t \rangle}$ state that $\langle w', t' \rangle$ is accessible from $\langle w, t \rangle$. We will say that *modal* accessibility relations are those which link only world-time pairs whose time coordinate is constant (i.e., if $\langle w, t \rangle \rho \langle w', t' \rangle$, then $t = t'$). *Temporal* relations, on the other hand, link only world-time pairs whose world coordinate is constant (i.e., if $\langle w, t \rangle \rho \langle w', t' \rangle$, then $w = w'$). In Figure 4, modal and temporal relations operate "vertically" and "horizontally," respectively. Notice that aside from this difference in direction, modal and temporal accessibility relations are the same kind of semantic object. Technically, there is no reason to restrict ourselves to just modal and temporal relations, but we will do so in this chapter for simplicity.[17]

With the formal tools developed so far, we are now ready to give a precise formal account of the intuitive difference between a fixed past and an open future. To this end, we employ a special modal accessibility relation $\approx$, whose intended role is to identify *historical alternatives*. The intention is that the historical alternatives of a world w at time t are worlds that are just like w at all times up to and including t, but may differ from w at times later than t.

We impose certain conditions on the relation $\approx$ to ensure its suitability. Recall that $\langle w, t \rangle \approx \langle w', t \rangle$ is to be read as the statement 'w' is just like w up to time t.' Little reflection is needed to see that this relation of 'being-just-like (up to t)' should have the following properties (some of which we have already encountered before):

(36) a. reflexivity: $\langle w, t \rangle \approx \langle w, t \rangle$
     b. symmetry: if $\langle w, t \rangle \approx \langle w', t \rangle$, then $\langle w', t \rangle \approx \langle w, t \rangle$
     c. transitivity: if $\langle w, t \rangle \approx \langle w', t \rangle$ and $\langle w', t \rangle \approx \langle w'', t \rangle$,
                    then $\langle w, t \rangle \approx \langle w'', t \rangle$

Together, these properties ensure that $\approx$ is an *equivalence relation*, which is our first condition. Next, we want to ensure that two worlds which are each other's historical alternatives at some time t, *have been* historical alternatives at all times up to t. This, of course, is simply part of what it means to share the same past up to t, but we need to make the condition explicit. Formally, it means that the worlds that are accessible from w at a given time must also be accessible at all earlier times. In Figure 4, with $\approx$ for ρ, this condition is respected by the modal bases at t and the earlier t'.

Finally, our last condition concerns the idea that being 'just like w' at a given time implies being indistinguishable from w by all atomic sentences of the language that are evaluated at that time (and thus also all truth-functional compounds which do not include temporal operators). This is stated as a condition that the truth assignment function V must respect. To summarize, we impose the following conditions on the relation $\approx$ of 'being a historical alternative to':

(37) a. $\approx$ is modal
     b. $\approx$ is an equivalence relation
     c. If $\langle w, t \rangle \approx \langle w', t \rangle$ and $t' < t$, then $\langle w, t' \rangle \approx \langle w', t' \rangle$
     d. If $\langle w, t \rangle \approx \langle w', t \rangle$, then for all atomic sentences p,
         $V_{\langle w, t \rangle}(p) = V_{\langle w', t \rangle}(p)$

Within this formal setup, we can easily capture the asymmetry between a fixed past and an open future, as well as shed some light on the two notions of truth introduced above.

3.2.2. *Truth and settledness*

Recall the informal characterization of the two notions of truth: truth at individual worlds (Ockhamist) as opposed to truth at all possible continuations of history (Peircean). In terms of the technical distinctions we introduced, this amounts to *truth simpliciter* on the one hand, and truth at all historical alternatives, i.e., necessity with respect to the accessibility relation ≈, on the other.[18] This kind of necessity is commonly referred to as *historical necessity* or *settledness.* Notice that it can easily be defined in terms of truth, but not *vice versa.* Peircean truth is Ockhamist settledness, but Ockhamist truth has no analog in the Peircean approach.

Now, in a model in which the accessibility relation ≈ and the truth value assignment respect all the conditions we introduced above, these two notions are not independent: they *coincide* for all sentences whose truth value does not depend on times later than time of evaluation. This is guaranteed to be the case for all formulas not containing the operators $\Diamond_<$ or $\square_<$. Historical alternatives at time t are indistinguishable at all times up to and including t, and, therefore, for any given world, sentences whose truth values depend only on the states of affairs at such times are either true at all of its historical alternatives or at none of them. It is only with respect to future reference that historical alternatives may disagree.

3.3. Present tense revisited

With these formal preliminaries in mind, we can now return to the data we cited at the beginning of this section in (29) and (30). As we noted earlier, data such as these have been at the center of much controversy in the literature on English tenses and temporal reference. With the tools now at our disposal, we can give a very simple explanation for the fact that the settledness reading arises with (29c) and (30b,c), and not with (29a,b) or (30a). First, we assume that two tenses are involved in the above sentences, Past and Present, whose temporal interpretation is 'past' and 'non-past,' respectively. Accordingly, their formal representation will involve the accessibility relations > for the Past and ≤ for the Present.

How, then, do we account for the settledness reading arising in (29c) and (30b,c)? Recall the generalization that this reading arises just in case the reference time of the sentence follows the speech time of evaluation. This is the case in (29c) and (30c) due to the adverbial *tomorrow*, and in

(30b) because of the aspectual properties of the predicate. Now it is evident that this is precisely the pattern we predict if we assume, against the background of a model as introduced above, that *all* of the six sentences assert that it is not merely true, but *settled* that Megan is in her office at the time in question.

Thus, assuming that our language contains an untensed atomic sentence *Megan be in her office*, we can say that the following sentences in (38a,b) are equivalent to the respective formulas:

(38) a. Megan was in her office.
$\Box_\approx \Diamond_>$ (Megan be in her office)

   b. Megan is in her office.
$\Box_\approx \Diamond_\le$ (Megan be in her office)

The role of the adverbials *now* and *tomorrow* in (29b,c) is to restrict the domain of the operators $\Diamond_>$ and $\Diamond_\le$. The sentences in (30b,c) are treated similarly.

We have shown in this section how the techniques of modal logic are applied in both the modal and the temporal domain, and how due consideration for the interaction between these dimensions can lead to very simple linguistic analyses, here illustrated with the example of the English Present tense. Key to the explanation of the settledness reading was the claim that the interpretation of sentences such as those in (29) and (30) involves the settledness operator $\Box_\approx$.

We stated above that the interpretation of sentences such as (29a,b) is equivalent to the respective formulas with the settledness operator, but we have so far avoided a commitment as to the status of this universal force. Is it part of the truth-conditional meaning of these sentences, or does it enter the interpretation as a pragmatic effect of some kind? On this question, too, there is little agreement. Dowty (1979), for instance, treated it as part of the truth-conditional meaning of sentences of the form *tomorrow* φ (though not of sentences with past and present reference – in this respect, our analysis is more uniform), whereas other authors, notably Steedman (2000), sought a pragmatic explanation. Kaufmann (2002) also argued for a pragmatic explanation, but Kaufmann (2005) took the opposite position in the face of evidence from *if*-clauses and argued that settledness is part of the truth conditions.

While the data behind this distinction are somewhat intricate and beyond the scope of this chapter, it is illuminating to discuss in some detail the theoretical assumptions that made the pragmatic argument compelling in the first place. We will do so in the next subsections. Again, in the course of the discussion we will have occasion to extend and refine our formal framework in ways that will enable us to account for a range of other data as well.

3.4. Objective and subjective uncertainty

Historical necessity, the topic of the last subsection, is a means of dealing formally with the asymmetry between a fixed past and an open future. We saw that settledness is represented as necessity with respect to the set of historical alternatives to the world and time of evaluation. Of central importance was the condition imposed by the relation $\approx$ on admissible truth value assignments in the model: all historical alternatives of a world w at time t are indistinguishable from w at all times up to t. Worlds may part ways only at times later than t.

The kind of uncertainty that this model is designed to capture is *objective* or *metaphysical* uncertainty. The assumption is that the future course of events is literally not determined at present. Accordingly, our uncertainty about the future is not solely due to ignorance of the relevant facts. Rather, it is impossible, even in principle, to know how things will turn out in the future. Even if we could resolve all of our uncertainty about past and present facts, some residual uncertainty about the future would necessarily remain.[19]

In contrast to the future, the model mandates that there can be no uncertainty about past or present facts. Now, clearly, this constraint would be too strong if imposed on speakers' beliefs. Ordinary speakers do not know much more about the past than they do about the future. The doxastic accessibility relations encoding speakers' belief states, therefore, must have somewhat different properties from $\approx$. In particular, they must allow for uncertainty about the past: It should be possible for doxastically accessible worlds at time t to differ from each other with regard to facts at times earlier than t.

However, two assumptions about the interaction between doxastic and metaphysical accessibility are intuitively plausible, and it is these assumptions that will ultimately facilitate our account of certain linguistic data. First, it is reasonable to assume that doxastic states themselves are subject to historical necessity; that is, the relation modeling a speaker's beliefs at a

given world-time pair $\langle w, t \rangle$ should be constant across all historical alterna-
tives $\langle w', t \rangle$ such that $\langle w, t \rangle \approx \langle w', t \rangle$. This is because intuitively the contents
of a speaker's belief state are facts, just like the *ordinary* facts about the
world, and not subject to objective uncertainty at later times.

   The second assumption concerns limits on what speakers can rationally
believe at a given world and time. Specifically, speakers cannot have full
confidence about the truth values of sentences whose truth they also believe
is not yet objectively settled. Having such beliefs would imply that the
speaker (believes that she) can "look ahead" in history, an attitude which
we will assume (perhaps somewhat optimistically) is not attested.

   We will use the symbol $\sim$ to stand for doxastic accessibility relations.[20]
We assume that $\sim$, like the metaphysical accessibility relation $\approx$, is modal
(i.e., holds only between indices, or world-time pairs, which share the same
temporal coordinate), and that it is serial, transitive and euclidean (i.e., that
the corresponding modal base is consistent and fully introspective). The
two modal bases are illustrated in Figure 5:

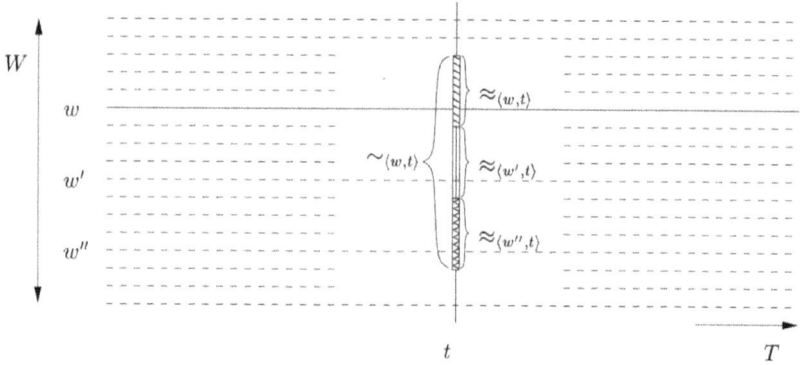

Figure 5. Objective and subjective modal bases, represented by $\approx$ and $\sim$, respectively. At any given index $\langle w, t \rangle$, the doxastic modal base $\sim_{\langle w, t \rangle}$ must
contain $\approx_{\langle w', t \rangle}$ for all $\langle w', t \rangle \in \sim_{\langle w, t \rangle}$.

Now, the two properties discussed can be formalized as the following constraints on the interaction between the two relations:

(39) a. historicity
        If $\langle w, t \rangle \sim \langle w', t \rangle$ and $\langle w, t \rangle \approx \langle w'', t \rangle$, then $\langle w'', t \rangle \sim \langle w', t \rangle$
     b. lack of foreknowledge
        If $\langle w, t \rangle \sim \langle w', t \rangle$ and $\langle w', t \rangle \approx \langle w'', t \rangle$, then $\langle w, t \rangle \sim \langle w'', t \rangle$

Condition (39a) states that two indices cannot be historical alternatives unless they agree on the set of indices that are doxastically accessible. Condition (39b) ensures that if an index $\langle w', t \rangle$ is doxastically accessible, then so are all its historical alternatives. Together, these two constraints guarantee that the two relations interact in the way we discussed above; in particular, in virtue of (39b), objective uncertainty invariably gives rise to subjective uncertainty (though not *vice versa*): Only what is settled can already be known.

3.5. Settledness and scheduling

Using a model that conforms to the conditions introduced above, it is now quite straightforward to account for the modal connotations of the English Present tense. The generalization was that whenever the reference time lies in the future from the perspective of the evaluation time, the Present is only felicitous on a scheduling reading. Earlier we suggested that scheduling in this context corresponds to settledness, or historical necessity. The sentence is not merely asserted to be true in the world of evaluation, but true in all of its historical alternatives. We also argued that *all* sentences with bare tenses carry this strong reading, not just those in the bare Present.

This assumption is in line with the fact that only future reference gives rise to a settledness condition that is felt as an additional semantic element over and above the mere condition that the sentence be true. Recall now that settledness and truth coincide for all sentences whose truth depends solely on past and present facts. Indeed, by attributing settledness to all such sentences, we can immediately account for the fact that the Present sometimes does and sometimes does not carry the settledness reading. It does so if the reference time lies in the future (as it must with non-statives), but not if the evaluation is co-temporal with the evaluation time (as it can be with statives).

However, why should it be that sentences carry this strong modal force? While the pragmatic account stops short of including the modal element into the truth conditions, it nevertheless gives a simple and compelling answer to this question: because they are *asserted*.

Two assumptions about the assertion of sentences are sufficient to derive this explanation:

(40) a. In asserting a sentence, the speaker signals that she believes that it is true.

b. If the linguistic transaction is successful, the listener will end up believing that the sentence is true.

While these statements gloss over a number of important fine details about the way communication comes to succeed, they are widely accepted and part of the standard pragmatic account of what goes on in standard communicative situations.[21]

Now, relative to a doxastic accessibility relation $\sim$, a sentence p is believed to be true at world w and time t if and only if it is true at all world-time pairs $\langle w', t \rangle$ such that $\langle w, t \rangle \sim \langle w', t \rangle$. Furthermore, given the conditions imposed on the interaction between the relations $\sim$ and $\approx$, p is believed to be true if and only if it is believed to be settled – recall that for any world-time pair $\langle w', t \rangle$ accessible via $\sim$, the historical alternatives of $\langle w', t \rangle$ are also accessible via $\sim$. Thus the speaker, in asserting p, signals that she believes that p is not only true, but settled.

Consider, on the other hand, the update to the listener's belief state that results from her accepting the speaker's assertion. It is standardly assumed that this update proceeds by elimination of all those world-time pairs in which the sentence is false. Given the constraints we introduced, this update may lead to an inadmissible belief state in the case of future reference – i.e., a doxastic relation which accesses some world-time pairs, but fails to access all of their historical alternatives. Of course, the listener also knows, from the very fact that the speaker asserted the sentence, that she believes it to be settled. In reaction to this evidence, and to ensure that the conversation proceeds smoothly, she may also eliminate from her belief state those indices in which the truth or falsehood of the sentence is not yet determined. This amounts to an *accommodation* of the information that the truth value of p is objectively settled.

4. Conclusion

In this chapter, we covered fundamental concepts and approaches to the formal treatment of modality in semantic theory. The introduction of formal modal logic into linguistic theory was a significant step forward. Among its main early achievements was the ability to bring order to the class of modal auxiliaries and adverbials, and to analyze what had been a bewildering polysemy, in terms of a few basic modal parameters. We described some of the standard formal modal logic tools that are widely employed in semantic theory, and illustrated their use with examples from expressions that are traditionally considered *modal*. At the same time, the appeal to modality alone is not sufficient for the proper analysis of even the most prototypical modal expressions. Invariably, other notions interact with modality in intricate ways. Hence we also discussed and analyzed some more subtle examples showing the interaction between modality and other grammatical categories. These interactions have been at the center of much recent theoretical work (see, for example, Condoravdi 2002, Ippolito 2003, Kaufmann 2005). The area of modality continues to be exciting and rife with new ideas and further questions.

Acknowledgement

The authors would like to thank William Frawley for continuous support and encouragement, as well as assistance with the manuscript.

Notes

1. From Greek *aletheia* 'truth.'
2. From Greek *deon* 'obligation.'
3. From Greek *episteme* 'knowledge.'
4. From Greek *doxa* 'belief.'
5. An axiom is a sentence whose provability is guaranteed by assumption. An axiom schema is a sentence of a certain form, for example $\varphi \to (\theta \to \varphi)$, where φ and θ stand for arbitrary propositional sentences.
6. This is a simplification. Sentences carrying semantic presuppositions are commonly assumed to be neither true nor false at worlds at which their presuppositions are not satisfied.
7. To be sure, none of the logical connectives adequately captures the semantic richness of the English words that are customarily associated with it. However, as our primary goal in this chapter is a discussion of modals, we will adopt the connectives without further discussion.
8. One could think of $[\![\Phi]\!]^M$ as the denotation of the conjunction of all members of Φ, but this analogy breaks down if Φ has infinitely many members. In this case, $[\![\Phi]\!]^M$ is still defined, but our language does not include the corresponding infinite conjunction.
9. Notice that the absence of the condition does not mean that w cannot be a member of R_w – it merely does not have to be.

10. This kind of problem is known as the *Samaritan paradox*.
11. A binary relation on a set is a preorder if it is reflexive and transitive.
12. The semantics in (28) could be simplified if it were guaranteed that there were minimal elements in the preorder.
13. The formal apparatus introduced in this section is partly based on Thomason (1984).
14. Another compelling possibility, which we will not discuss here, is to consider multi-valued logic, or to say that sentences whose truth value is not yet determined are not false, but truth-valueless (e.g., see Thomason 1970 for discussion).
15. World-time pairs of this sort are also behind Montague's (1973) treatment of intensionality. It is fair to say, though, that the analysis of modality is not among the areas in which Montague himself made very substantive contributions.
16. This assumption has nontrivial logical consequences, which are immaterial for our purpose.
17. Kaufmann (2005) argues that hybrid modal-temporal relations that operate "diagonally" are required for the analysis of certain conditionals.
18. *Truth simpliciter* is equivalent to necessity with respect to the identity relation.
19. It is immaterial in this connection whether physicists tell us that the world is in fact deterministic or non-deterministic. What matters for our purpose is that we talk *as if* certain things could not be known in advance.
20. Belief states are subjective, tied to individual agents. We assume here that we are speaking about the beliefs of a particular speaker, but, for simplicity, we do not indicate this formally.
21. See Stalnaker (1978) for an early exposition.

References

Condoravdi, Cleo
    2002   Temporal interpretation of modals: Modals for the Present and for the Past. In *The Construction of Meaning*, D. I. Beaver, L. D. Casillas Martínez, B. Z. Clark and S. Kaufmann (eds.), 59–87. Stanford: CSLI Publications.
Dowty, David R.
    1979   *Word Meaning and Montague Grammar*. Berlin: Springer.
Hintikka, Jaako
    1961   Modality and quantification. *Theoria* 27: 119–128.
Horn, Laurence R.
    2001   *A Natural History of Negation*. Stanford: CSLI Publications (originally Chicago: University of Chicago Press).

Hughes, George E. and Maxwell J. Cresswell
  1996   *A New Introduction to Modal Logic.* London: Routledge.
Ippolito, Michela
  2003   Quantification over times in subjunctive conditionals. In *Proceedings of Semantics and Linguistic Theory* XIII, R. B. Young and Y. Zhou (eds.), 145–186. Cornell University: CLC Publications.
Kaufmann, Stefan
  2002   The presumption of settledness. *Chicago Linguistic Society* 38: 313–328.
  2005   Conditional truth and future reference. *Journal of Semantics* 22: 231–280.
Kratzer, Angelika
  1977   What 'must' and 'can' must and can mean. *Linguistics and Philosophy* 1: 337–355.
  1981   The notional category of modality. In *Words, Worlds, and Contexts: New Approaches in Word Semantics*, H. J. Eikmeyer and H. Rieser (eds.), 38–74. Berlin/New York: Mouton de Gruyter.
  1991   Modality. In *Semantik: Ein Internationales Handbuch der Zeitgenössischen Forschung*, A. von Stechow and D. Wunderlich (eds.), 639–650. Berlin/New York: Mouton de Gruyter.
Kripke, Saul
  1963   Semantical analysis of modal logic, I. Normal modal propositional calculi. *Zeitschrift für Mathematische Logik und Grundlagen der Mathematik* 9: 67–96.
Lewis, David
  1981   Ordering semantics and premise semantics for counterfactuals. *Journal of Philosophical Logic* 10: 217–234.
Mendelson, Elliot
  1987   *Introduction to Mathematical Logic.* Pacific Grove, CA: Wadsworth.
Montague, Richard
  1973   The proper treatment of quantification in ordinary English. In *Approaches to Natural Language*, J. Hintikka, J. M. E. Moravcsik and P. Suppes (eds.), 221–242. Dordrecht: Reidel.
Prior, Arthur N.
  1957   *Time and Modality.* Oxford: Clarendon Press.
  1967   *Past, Present and Future.* Oxford: Clarendon Press.
Stalnaker, Robert
  1975   Indicative conditionals. *Philosophia* 5: 269–286.
  1978   Assertion. In *Syntax and Semantics, vol. 9*, P. Cole (ed.), 315–332. New York: Academic Press.
Steedman, Mark
  2000   *The Syntactic Process.* Cambridge, Mass.: MIT Press.

Thomason, Richmond H.
    1970   Indeterminist time and truth-value gaps. *Theoria* 36: 264–281.
    1984   Combinations of tense and modality. In *Handbook of Philosophical Logic: Extensions of Classical Logic, vol. II*, D. M. Gabbay and F. Guenthner (eds.), 135–165. Dordrecht, Reidel.

Historical aspects of modality

Elizabeth Closs Traugott

1. Introduction[1]

In this chapter some of the most widely-discussed changes that have been observed in the course of the development of expressions of modality will be outlined. In languages for which we have long historical records (most European languages, Chinese, and Japanese) it appears that expressions of modality are ultimately derived from non-modal expressions. Morphosyntactically the following findings have been made:

- In the verbal domain modal auxiliaries and affixes, including markers of future tense, usually derive from main verbs.
- In the domain of "tags"or "epistemic parentheticals," sources are likely to be found in main clauses with first-person subjects and verbs of cognition (e.g., *I think*).
- In the adverbial and modal particle domains, there are more varied sources, e.g., manner adverbials, measure adverbials, and epistemic parentheticals.[2]

Semantically, the following paths have been the focus of many studies:

- Possession/intention > deontic > epistemic conclusion
  (e.g., the type *You have to go > You have to be kidding*), but not vice versa.
- Ability > root possibility > epistemic possibility
  (e.g., the type *I can swim > wherever I can be found*) or

  ability > root possibility > permission
  (e.g., the type *I can swim, I have had a lot of lessons > I can swim, Mom doesn't mind*), but not vice versa.

In the next section, I outline some of the most important theoretical issues and debates in historical linguistics that underpin work on the history of modality, including grammaticalization and processes of semantic change.

Historical cross-linguistic typological work on modality is discussed thereafter. Subsequently, I turn to findings based in historical corpora of English, particularly those that take frequency into account; the section ends with comments on some recent changes in the history of English modal expressions.

2.   Some basic issues in historical work

2.1. Functional and formal approaches

Like almost all theoretically-based historical studies in the last forty years, those on modality have been pursued from the perspective of both functional and formal theories of linguistics. The history of English core auxiliaries in general and of core modals in particular had pride of place in studies from the nineteen-sixties in large part because of the prominent role they played Chomsky's *Syntactic Structures* (1957), and in part because of the publication between 1963 and 1973 of Visser's major multivolume study of the history of English syntax, which focuses on the verb, and devotes much of both parts of the third volume to core modals.

Given the grounding in different perspectives, it is inevitable that some studies have paid more attention than others to semantics, even when the overall topic is syntactic change. Functionally-oriented views of the history of (morpho)syntactic aspects of English modality include work by Plank (1984), Denison (1993), Bybee, Perkins, and Pagliuca (1994), Hopper and Traugott (2003 [1993]) (see also Fleischman 1982 on developments in Romance; Sun 1996 and Peyraube 1999 on Chinese). In these works, the study of modal development has been embedded in the study of grammaticalization. Among more formal approaches are those by Lightfoot (1979, 1991), Kemenade (1992), Warner (1993), and Roberts and Roussou (2002, 2003) (see also Roberts 1993 on the development of the future in Romance and Benincà and Poletto 1997 on several modals of necessity in Italian).

One fundamental point of disagreement has been over what a theory of change is about. From the functionalist perspective, it is use (Croft 2000); from the formalist, it is competence or differences in individual grammars (Lightfoot 1991). For proponents of change in use, innovation in individual grammars alone does not constitute change; instead, there must be interspeaker transfer (see Weinreich, Herzog, and Labov 1968). For proponents of change in grammars, innovation is regarded as change, while transfer to others is regarded as spread (Lightfoot 1991; Harris and Campbell 1995). Another point of disagreement has been whether the search for universals of language is a search for strong tendencies, which allow for exceptions (the functionalist view), or absolute universals, which do not (a formalist view expressed most clearly in Newmeyer 1998).

Differences at this level are so fundamental that researchers on each side may be in danger of serious misunderstanding. However, over the last decade the possibility of reaching some common ground has seemed more feasible, because of increased interest among formalists in variation and the availability of corpora (and hence of empirical evidence against which to test hypotheses). For example, while adopting a parametric view of syntactic change, and assuming a universal hierarchy of functional heads, Roberts and Roussou allow for the "language device" (individual learners' acquisition) to be subject to preferences, even though UG (universal grammar) is not (2003: 232). Still, the debates continue, not only at this abstract level but also at the level of more particular problems in morphosyntactic change (see, e.g., Rohdenburg and Mondorf 2003).

Some of the major questions in the debate are as follows:

− *Does semantic change trigger syntactic change or vice versa?* On the whole functionalists assign semantics (including pragmatics) a major role in triggering the change, whereas formalists assign it less or none, arguing that semantic change is an outcome of syntactic change. However, Bybee (e.g., 1988) takes a different position saying that in many cases it is frequency of use that triggers meaning change.[3]

− *What is the role of frequency not only in determining whether a change as opposed to an innovation has occurred, but also in triggering change?*

− *Should significant changes be regarded as local, gradual, micro-changes* (e.g. Denison 1993), *or global, discrete, and "catastrophic"* (e.g., Lightfoot 1979)? As more has come to be known about the development of auxiliaries in English, and as theories have been refined over time, it has come to be generally agreed that change must be understood as local, even if the changes leading to the syntactic properties of core modals do appear to have crystallized around the early part of the sixteenth century.

− *How robust is the hypothesis of unidirectionality?* Largely associated with work on grammaticalization, it has its origins at least in part in the observation that in language after language auxiliaries are derived from other sources, such as main verbs.

Virtually all work in the domain of semantic change has been pursued from a functional perspective and with the assumption that polysemy is a viable theoretical construct.[4] Two basic questions in the work are as follows:

- *To what extent is semantic change systematic (replicated and unidirectional) rather than random?* Unidirectional hypotheses have been put forward in considerable part based on discoveries about modals in the context of work on grammaticalization. Particularly important has been the hypothesis that if a modal expression has deontic and epistemic polysemies, the latter is derived from the former.
- *How should a theory of semantic change be modeled?* Should we use a primarily cognitive theory of metaphor or a communicative as well as cognitive theory of pragmatic inferencing?

2.2. Grammaticalization

Grammaticalization has been defined as "the change whereby lexical items and constructions come in certain linguistic contexts to serve grammatical functions, and once grammaticalized, continue to develop new grammatical functions" (Hopper and Traugott 2003 [1993]: 18). For modality the basic idea is that certain main verbs (lexical items) may over time become modal auxiliaries and these auxiliaries may in turn become affixes (mood and tense markers). This broad characterization needs constraining, of course. Only main verbs with particular content meanings such as *want, desire, obtain, go* are subject to such changes, and only in particular syntactic contexts, most notably when they take a complement verb. At least initially, new uses coexist with earlier ones, i.e., there is a split in uses, a fact unfortunately obscured by notations typical of historical linguistics, such as Main Verb > Auxiliary > Affix.

Changes such as those represented in the previous schema are often referred to as unidirectional "paths," "clines," or "chains," of change. These terms have often been misunderstood, and it is worth pausing to note that "path" is not meant to denote a hard-wired neurological path that makes trajectories of change cognitively inevitable (cf. Newmeyer 1998). Rather, along with "cline" and "chain," it is a metaphor for a macro-schema summarizing overarching types of change that may take place over several hundred years or even millennia (Andersen 2001). At the same time the term is meant to invoke micro-steps by which such changes occur; they are conceptualized in terms of a continuum with focal ("cluster") points (the named categories, like morphosyntactic *Auxiliary, Affix*, or semantic *Deontic, Epistemic*).[5] The micro-steps are said to be examples of gradual change; gradualness is the historical counterpart of gradience in synchronic linguistics (see, e.g., Denison 2001). Like physical paths, grammatical paths need not be gone down. Paths are schemas characterizing possible, but not necessary, changes. Change never has to happen.

One can, of course, always turn around on a physical path, but the hypothesis basic to most work on grammaticalization is that the predominant tendency is for change to be unidirectional. Once a main verb has become an auxiliary, it will not normally become a main verb again; once an auxiliary has become an affix it will not normally become an auxiliary again (Bybee, Perkins, and Pagliuca 1994: 13). Some possible counterexamples to unidirectionality from the domain of modality are discussed below. Unidirectionality is variously interpreted as originating in strategic interaction between speakers, "in the need to be more specific, in the tendency to infer as much as possible from the input, and in the necessity of interpreting items in context" (Bybee, Perkins, and Pagliuca 1994: 300; also Hopper and Traugott 2003 [1993]), in cognitive constraints on metaphor (Sweetser 1990; Gamon 1993), in problem-solving (Heine, Claudi, and Hünnemeyer 1991), and in preferences exercised by the "learning device" (Roberts and Roussou 2003: 232). Assuming a minimalist syntax, Roberts and Roussou associate unidirectionality with reanalysis of lexical material to functional heads, and of structural change "upward" along the hierarchy of functional heads to more abstract members of the hierarchy (2003: 202).[6] Citing Joseph (1983) they give the example of Gk. *thelo* 'want' > auxiliary > future marker, i.e., "from V (lexical) to v (dynamic/root), to T (epistemic)" (2003: 202).

One type of unidirectionality is known as *bleaching*, the loss of concrete, referential, and content meaning. While bleaching might suggest that grammaticalized forms become devoid of meaning, "semantic bleaching is not just the random loss of content. It is rather the loss of non-logical content such as argument structure and the retention – in the case of modals – of modal content. We consider this to be an instance of the retention of logical meaning (here having to do with quantification over possible worlds)" (Roberts and Roussou 2003: 221). Furthermore, former non-referential implicatures typically become enriched or strengthened (Sweetser 1988; Hopper and Traugott 2003 [1993]: 94–98); an example is the strengthening of future meaning associated with *shall* (< OE *scul-* 'owe'), and *will* (< OE *will-* 'intend').

If bleaching is understood to be related to the development of auxiliaries as functional heads, it is not surprising that one of the unidirectionalities closely connected with modality is scope increase, both syntactic and semantic. Syntactic scope increases include shifts of epistemic modals and moods to the outer positions in phrasal or morphological sequences. Bybee (1985: 33–35, 196–200) shows that in a sample of fifty languages, all but one show the order mood-tense-aspect (or aspect-tense-mood), as in *might have been leaving*, where *might* expresses modality/mood, *have* expresses tense, and *be + ing* expresses aspect. Nagle (1994: 206) suggests that the order of double modals in American English shows the same constraint: *may/might/must* expressing epistemic possibility or probability precede *can/could/should/will/would*, which express "ability, futurity, or deontic readings of permission or necessity"; he goes on to argue that American *can* is more grammaticalized than Scots, which allowed only *will can*, *may can* (1994: 208). Semantic scope increase is identified as a major factor in the development of both deontic and epistemic modality in German (Gamon 1993) and English (Nordlinger and Traugott 1997).

Despite notations of the type in A>B>C, such changes not only overlap in time, but also never occur out of context. For example, Gk. *thelo* became an auxiliary only in the context of the infinitive complements introduced by *(h)ina* 'to.' As work on contexts for change has been refined, it has become increasingly clear that changes in modality expressed by verbs are enabled or constrained by synchronic contexts, such as the subject (first, second, or third person, animate or inanimate), the meaning of the complement verb, the tense and the aspect of the complement verb, and by adverbs (especially negation markers, modal adverbs). All these factors need to be investigated as possible constraints in studying the development of modality. Romaine (1995: 420) further advises that some overlap should always be expected across tense, aspect and modality.

Most importantly, it has come to be recognized that certain areas of modality are synchronically indeterminate or vague in certain contexts. Van der Auwera and Plungian (1998: 101), for example, point out that modal passives may be "not only vague between possibility and necessity, but also between participant-internal and participant-external modality." One of the claims of recent work on grammaticalization and semantic change is that at periods of change, indeterminacy (rather than ambiguity, which presupposes discrete alternatives) is to be expected (e.g., Denison 2001; Enfield 2003) and can last a long time (centuries, even millennia). It is striking that when epistemic meanings of ME *mot-/most-* were emerging, many examples are not only indeterminate between deontic and epistemic meanings, but include the adverb *nede(s)* 'necessarily,' which was itself indeterminate between deontic and epistemic necessity (Goossens 1999; Traugott and Dasher 2002), as in (1):

(1) Ah heo *most nede*   beien, þe mon þe ibunden bið
     But he must necessarily submit, the man that bound   is
     'But he who is bound ought necessarily to submit/necessarily submits.'
                  (c.1225 (?1200) *Layamon's Brut*, 1051 [MED *moten* 2c])

Note (1) is also generic, another contributor to the indeterminacy, since present as well as future temporality is implied. Bybee suggests that past tense modals in English came to mark hypotheticality because "past modals offer two areas of vagueness: (i) whether or not the predicate event was completed; and (ii) whether or not the modality remains in effect"(Bybee 1995: 506). Enfield refers to indeterminate and ambiguous utterances at an intermediate stage of change as "bridging contexts" (2003: 28).

2.3. Invited inferencing and subjectification

Important in studies of both grammaticalization and semantic change has been the question of whether to conceptualize it as resulting primarily from the activity of metaphorizing (mapping concrete domains on abstract ones, see, e.g., Bybee and Pagliuca 1985; Sweetser 1990; Heine, Claudi, and Hünnemeyer 1991), or primarily from that of inferencing, which is a kind of cognitive metonymizing (cf. Bybee, Perkins, and Pagliuca 1994; Traugott and Dasher 2002; Hopper and Traugott 2003 [1993]; Enfield 2003). While neither mechanism precludes the other, and indeed can be shown ideally to work together, since many metaphors are based in metonymy (see Barcelona 2000) and also contribute to the context in which metonymic inferencing becomes salient, it appears that metonymic inferencing plays a leading role as speakers and hearers negotiate meaning and adopt innovations; the outcome of many changes, however, functions metaphorically from a synchronic perspective.

    In the domain of modality, Sweetser (1990) proposed that one way to conceptualize the synchronic polysemic relationship between root/obligation and epistemic modality is in terms of metaphorical mapping of image-schemata. Building on aspects of Talmy's (1988) theory of force dynamics, she hypothesized that the *may* of permission (*Kim may leave, I allow it*) expresses "an absent potential barrier in the sociophysical world," and epistemic *may* (*Kim may be there*) "is the force-dynamically parallel case in the world of reasoning"(Sweetser 1990: 59). Root *must* (*You must go*) indicates a real-world force that compels the subject to act, while epistemic *must* (*You must be tired*) indicates that "an epistemic force applied by some body of premises"compels the speaker to "reach the conclusion embodied in the sentence"(1990: 64). She argued that meaning change in the modals is a unidirectional metaphorical mapping from content > reasoning meanings, not vice versa, because "viewing X as Y is not the same as, and does not imply, viewing Y as X" and metaphorical mapping is "inherently unidirectional" (1990: 19).

However, Traugott and Dasher (2002) argue that this same development is best understood, when looking at the textual data rather than at citation forms out of context, in terms of the Invited Inferencing Theory of Semantic Change.[7] This theory builds on Levinson's (2000) revival of Grice's distinction between (a) utterance token implicatures that are by hypothesis universal and arise on the fly in the context of strategic interaction between speakers and hearers (and writers and readers), (b) utterance type implicatures that are conventionalized in particular communities and languages, and (c) coded meanings that are conventions of a language at a given time. According to this model, utterance token implicatures may become salient and normative types in a community; at this point meanings may be indeterminate or ambiguous (Enfield's "bridging contexts"). Change occurs when utterance type implicatures are semanticized, that is, when the earlier meaning of an item would not make sense in a particular utterance (the earlier type implicature has been reanalyzed as a distinct meaning of a form-meaning pair *f*, whether lexical or grammatical). The inference may, of course, not always be semanticized. Furthermore, it may persist for centuries, even millennia (cf. *after*, the causal implicature of which has not been semanticized).

Enfield characterizes this as follows: "an interpretation of *f* as merely implicating 'q' (on the basis of 'p') or as actually *meaning* 'q' (as distinct from 'p') become [sic] functionally equivalent"(Enfield 2003: 29; italics original). Since contexts are typically redundant, it does not really matter at the moment of interaction whether the speaker intends or is even aware of implicating q, or, if the speaker intends to implicate q, whether the hearer understands it as a conversational implicature, a generalized one, or a semanticized meaning. It is only when an implicated q is used in a new context that is neither indeterminate nor redundant that the first step toward change occurs.

The term *invited inferencing* is used to highlight the fact that change occurs in strategic interaction: speakers/writers invite hearers/readers to infer meanings beyond what is said. It is a process of pragmatic enrichment. Roberts and Roussou's approach to bleaching, cited above, conceptualizes bleaching as loss of content meaning and retention of logical meaning. This may be sufficient to account for shifts from non-modal to modal meaning, but is inadequate to account for further shifts typically found in grammaticalization, e.g., future *be going to* > inferential *be going to* as in (2):

(2)   Petaluma *is going to* be sixty miles north of here.

(2) may be said in acknowledgement of the likelihood that the hearer may not know where Petaluma is (equivalent, in other words, to *That would be sixty miles north of here*). Here future is bleached, and the present tense is enriched to express speaker's certainty and expectation of hearer's future information state.

Invited inferencing is an associative process in the syntagmatic flow of speech. Metonymically based association of what is said with the speaker's attitudes and speech act purposes, by which speakers and writers recruit meanings to express and to regulate beliefs, attitudes, etc., leads to changes known as *subjectification* (Traugott 1989; 2003)[8]. Subjectification encompasses shifts from adverbs with concrete descriptive meanings to modal adverbs (*probably* 'in a provable manner' > 'presumably'; see Hanson 1987).[9] Since modality is by definition somewhat subjective, subjectification in historical modality involves shifts from less to more subjectively construed obligation, epistemic attitude, etc. Note that while subjectification encompasses some developments to modal speaker-orientedness, in the sense of Bybee, Perkins, and Pagliuca (1994), it is orthogonal to it, and covers a far larger group of modalities, including inferences based in the speaker (see Goossens 2000 on the development of subjective meanings of *must*).

Subjectification, construed as emerging metonymically from inferences that arise in the act of communication between speaker and hearer, not surprisingly also includes intersubjectification, or paying attention to the hearer (Traugott 2003). Examples include the development of inferential *be going to* cited in (2), and many modal discourse markers that project speaker attitude not only to what is said but also toward the hearer in the immediate communication context, e.g., present-day uses of *actually* as the "hedge" 'I am telling you this in confidence' as in *I was determined to get married actually* (Aijmer 1986: 126).

3.   Cross-linguistic typological studies

3.1. The work of Bybee and her associates

The foundational work on cross-linguistic modality is Bybee, Perkins, and Pagliuca (1994). Part of a study from the perspective of grammaticalization (they call it *grammaticization*) of tense, aspect and modality in the languages of the world, it is based on materials from a sample of seventy-six languages selected to represent different language families, most from phyla with more than twenty-two members.[10] The authors start from a distinction between open class verbs that are relatively free and closed class items "whose class membership is determined by some unique grammatical behavior, such as position of occurrence, co-occurrence restrictions"(1994: 2). They are concerned with determining what commonalities there are across languages in the meanings expressed by closed-class grammatical morphemes such as affixes, stem changes, reduplication, auxiliaries, particles (they call these grammatical morphemes *grams*). Following Dahl (1985), universal categories such as future, past, and imperfective are taken to be the atoms of their theory and are referred to as *cross-linguistic gram-types* (Bybee, Perkins, and Pagliuca 1994: 3). While tense and aspect are in their view relatively easily defined grammatically, modality and mood are not. Taking mood, which is usually expressed as an inflectional affix, as the ultimate target of change,[11] they concur with Bybee (1985: 193) that it covers a large, rather heterogeneous set of categories – imperatives, subjunctives, epistemics and conditionals – and is hardly a conceptual category, and that mood is best understood in terms of its historical development. They therefore seek "to establish the major paths of development for mood and modality notions, and to try to determine how and why particular grammatical meanings arise in this domain" (Bybee, Perkins, and Pagliuca 1994: 176).

Since most sources are reference grammars, little discourse data is provided. Therefore the contexts for change must often be inferred. Furthermore, the histories of many of the languages represented are unknown or have been known for only a short time because of the absence of written records (e.g., American Indian languages like Cheyenne, or Australian aboriginal languages like Alawa). Therefore the results of the study are hypotheses about development. The methods and assumptions for establishing historical paths include the following:

- The hypothesis of morphosyntactic and semantic unidirectionality.
- Evidence from languages groups such as Germanic, Romance and Slavic, the histories of which are accessible through long text-based traditions.
- The hypothesis of "semantic retention": "the meaning of the source construction determines the subsequent grammatical meaning" (Bybee, Perkins, and Pagliuca 1994: 15–16). An example is the contrast in English represented below (Bybee, Perkins, and Pagliuca 1994: 16):

(3)   a.   Shall I call you a cab?
      b.   Will I call you a cab?
      c.   Will you/he call me a cab?

Although *shall* is largely obsolescent in English, it is "appropriate in first person questions because its obligation sense implies external imposition of duties" (Bybee, Perkins, and Pagliuca 1994: 16). *Will* as in (3b) is not appropriate because the older sense 'desire' suggests that the speaker is asking about his or her own willingness. On the other hand, use of *will* in second and third person questions such as (3c) is appropriate since one can question other people's willingness.

- The hypothesis that "semantic change is predictable" (1994: 18): as grammatical forms emerge, they become semantically more general and abstract (*bleached*). Therefore multiple uses of a single gram can be arranged on a grammaticalization path (1994: 17).
- Parallel reduction of semantic and phonological structures: over time grams lose content meaning and phonetic substance, i.e., they become shorter (grammatical items are typically monosyllabic). This means that when there are several exponents of a gram-type (e.g., future), the longer, more contentful, form can be hypothesized to be newer (see especially Bybee, Pagliuca, and Perkins 1991). Despite strong hypotheses about the "coevolution of meaning and form" (Bybee, Perkins, and Pagliuca 1994: 20), in some languages like English, modals have in fact shown considerable resistance to phonetic reduction, e.g., *may, could, should, must, ought, need*; in contrast, some, e.g., *will, would,* have been subject to reduction (to *'ll, 'd* respectively) since the sixteenth century (McElhinney 1992).
- Grams have higher frequency than lexical items because they are more generalized in meaning, often obligatory or "default"categories, specifi-

cally "the more generalized a gram is, the higher its incidence of use" (Bybee, Perkins, and Pagliuca 1994: 20). Bybee (1985, 2003) has made the important distinction between token and type frequency. Token frequency concerns the number of instances of a form, e.g., how often *want* or *will* is used. By contrast, type frequency concerns the number of categories or constructions with which an item co-occurs, e.g., how many main verbs co-occur with epistemic as opposed to deontic *must.*[12]

As described in fuller detail by de Haan (this volume), Bybee, Perkins, and Pagliuca construe modality as involving four conceptual categories:

- Agent-oriented (the agent is influenced in some way); this includes obligation, necessity, desire, ability, and root possibility.
- Speaker-oriented (the speaker enables the situation); this includes directives and imperatives.
- Epistemic (possibility, probability, inferred certainty).
- Subordinating (essentially mood), what van der Auwera and Plungian (1998) usefully call *post-modal.*

Schemas are posited for paths of development of modal expressions, and finally, in subordinate clauses, into mood (Bybee, Perkins, and Pagliuca 1994: 240). There are three sets of paths (ignoring post-modal developments):

- From ability (the schema for this path is cited in de Haan, this volume): this path has two routes – via root possibility to epistemic possibility and via root possibility to permission. Lexical sources include *finish, know (how to), get, obtain, arrive* (1994: 188).
- From obligation: this has three routes – via intention to future, via imperative, and via probability. Lexical sources include, among others, *need, good, be, sit, stand, owe, mete, measure, be fitting* (1994: 182–185). At least in English, the emergence of impersonal or raising constructions seems to be essential for the development of probability (epistemic) meanings (see Denison 1990; Warner 1990).
- From desire (e.g., *want*) and movement toward (e.g., *go*): both may lead via intention to future.

3.2. Other cross-linguistic studies

A major work on cross-linguistic grammaticalization as evidenced by African languages is Heine, Claudi, and Hünnemeyer (1991). Absent historical data for African languages, various hypotheses were developed using Bybee and her associates' criteria, as well as drawing on work on metaphorical mapping (e.g., Sweetser 1990). While Bybee's and Sweetser's work on modality is cited, only passing attention is paid to modal developments, except as illustrated by the development of the future, in which goal-oriented activity is seen as a major channel for future markers (Heine, Claudi, and Hünnemeyer 1991: 174). However, in the *World Lexicon of Grammaticalization*, which draws on the languages of the world, Heine and Kuteva (2002) list a number of studies of different modal developments under entries for concepts such as WANT, and, most usefully a Source-Target List (2002: 317–326) and a Target-Source List (2002: 327–336).[13] For example, in the Source-Target List we find not only sources with modally-related meanings like ABILITY > (1) PERMISSIVE, (2) POSSIBILITY, but also ARRIVE > ABILITY (317), and in the Target-Source List ABILITY < (1) ARRIVE, (2) GET, (3) KNOW, (4) SUITABLE (327).

While Heine and his associates for the most part adopted Bybee and her associates' typology of modality, including the category agent-oriented modality, van der Auwera and Plungian (1998), in developing their semantic map of modality, modified Bybee, Perkins, and Pagliuca's typology to contrast internal vs. external degree of force and degree of certainty. They present a unidirectional map from pre-modal to post-modal meanings with a streamlined set of modal meanings; the truly intermediate stages are, in their view, first either participant-internal or participant-external possibility, then participant-external possibility or participant-external necessity, including deontic possibility and necessity, and finally either epistemic possibility or epistemic necessity (van der Auwera and Plungian 1998: 111; see de Haan, this volume, for their figure summarizing these developments).

All the typological studies mentioned so far have taken some version of the agent-oriented/deontic > epistemic hypothesis as key to historical modality. But like all testable hypotheses, it has raised many questions. For one, it is largely based on the well-known histories of languages which happen to have clear examples that can be interpreted this way, where a verb meaning 'owe' or 'have' has been assigned a meaning of strong obligation, and has subsequently been assigned an epistemic conclusion meaning, for example,

Lat. *debe*re 'owe'; Eng. *ought to* 'owe,' *have to.* However, even in these languages, some difficulties with the hypothesis have been noted. For example *be supposed to* developed obligation meanings somewhat late. However, the latter change has recently been treated as an instance of contextually-determined meaning and therefore not a real counterexample (Visconti 2004; see also Ziegeler, 2004, who focuses on the genericity of contexts for the development of deontic implicatures). More importantly, investigators into languages that do not have expressions for strong obligation, such as Japanese, have found the change agent-oriented/deontic > epistemic to be largely irrelevant. Akatsuka (1992) argues that the concessive conditional construction *S1 temo, S2* is equivalent to the *may* of permission, and that the double negative conditional construction *S1 tewa, S2* or *S1 ba, S2* is equivalent to deontic *must.*

The domain of ability has proved particularly problematic. As noted earlier, Bybee, Perkins, and Pagliuca (1994) posit separate schemas for ability and obligation. Nevertheless one of the paths in the ability schema is from root possibility to permission, often construed as an agent-oriented/ root/deontic meaning, perhaps partly because their examples are from English *may* and *can*. *May* is sometimes cited on the scale of obligation (*might-may-must*, see Horn 1972). Furthermore, in English and German *mot-* (later Eng. *must*, Gm. *müssen*) 'be mete, be able' came to express strong obligation (deontic). This type of interaction between the ability and the obligation schemas is unusual (and possibly not really attested) in Asian languages, where ability appears to be the dominant schema for modality, and where "permission" is often more appropriately interpreted as 'nothing prevents' rather than as 'I/he/she permit,' (cf. Sun 1996 on Chinese *de* 'obtain' > 'be able, be permitted' > root possibility (and, in a different word order, > epistemic).[14] In discussing the development of polyfunctionality of *daj*[4] 'come to have'/'succeed'/'can' in Lao, Enfield (2003: 125–128) points out that it is one of a set of verbs for ACQUIRE in mainland South East Asia; such verbs typically have inanimate subjects and mean 'come to have' and are therefore quite unlike GET, which has agentive subjects (2003: 367). Narrog (2002) proposes that although the Old Jp. suffix *-beshi* could be said to express both deontic 'should' (usually following a verb of volitional action) and epistemic 'be possible' (usually following a non-volitional one), the analysis is more properly 'be appropriate' in volitional contexts (allowing inducement and intention readings), and root possibility in non-volitional ones (allowing imminent appearance and conclusion readings) (2002: 157). Clearly, the histories of ability modals that do and do not interact with obligation modality need to be better understood (see Narrog 2005, for a model of semantic change in modality that highlights the role of ability).

3.3. Counterexamples to unidirectionality in the domain of modality

As an empirical hypothesis, morphosyntactic unidirectionality (grammaticalization) has rightly been contested (see especially Janda 2001; and for modality and mood in Gk., Tsangalidis 2004). So has the hypothesis of unidirectionality in semantic change. While counterexamples are to date few in number and tend to be idiosyncratic, a number of them can be found in the domain of modality. A few are mentioned here.

Burridge (2002) discusses how in Pennsylvania German the auxiliary *wotte*, the preterite subjunctive of *welle* 'would,' has been converted into a main verb 'wish, desire.' "All the morphosyntactic changes which it underwent during its transition to auxiliaryhood" have been undone (Burridge 2002: 219). This change appears to be motivated by preemption of a form for the ideological purposes of the community. It is a kind of euphemism, adopted by the community of Mennonites as a way of avoiding expressing a wish too bluntly.

Not all examples of "demodalization" to more contentful meaning and/or more regular morphology appear to have such external motivations, however. Van der Auwera and Plungian cite the development of Lat. *posse* 'be able' < *potis esse* 'able be' into what is usually considered a pre-modal (more concrete, less grammatical) meaning 'to have influence, to avail' (1998: 106). There have also been what some researchers have regarded as splits into two verbs, one retaining the defective morphology of modality, the other developing regular morphology and pre-modal meaning, and ousting the defective form, e.g., Swed. *må* 'may,' which in Middle Swed. came to be paired with a homonymous regular verb *må* 'feel' (as in 'feel good') (1998: 105); Beths (1999) has cited Eng. *dare* as a similar example (but see Taeymans 2004 on evidence that modal *dare* is still strongly entrenched in British Eng., though recessive in American Eng.). In Russian there was an imperfective verb 'may' that originally disallowed a perfective derivation. However, in the twentieth century this derivation (*s- moč* came to be allowed, and a new modal meaning 'manage' developed (van der Auwera and Plungian 1998: 105–106). As Ziegeler (2003) points out, the examples cited do not make a unified set. While in some cases (*wotte, moč*) a new lexical verb is created, in others (*må, dare*) the main verb and auxiliary forms have coexisted for a very long time, although used with different frequencies over time. These are not examples of splits but of revival of old forms that have been retained alongside the newer auxiliaries.

Another type of counterexample to the unidirectionalities posited is the formation of adverbs from modals, e.g., *maybe*. Using the term *lexicalization* to refer to the use of grammatical as lexical material,[15] Ramat and Ricca (1994: 297) say "[t]he most widespread lexicalization seems, indeed, to be the 'may/can be' (or 'happen')-type for the modal epistemic adverb 'perhaps', like in Fr. *peut-être*, Engl. *maybe.*" Other forms cited include Du. *misschien* < *mach scien* '(it) may happen,' Polish *može byt'* 'may be' (see also Nuyts 2000: 125, who in addition cites Du. *mogeliijk* 'possible/ possibly,' Gm. *möglich(erweise)* 'possible/possibly,' which both derive from cognates of the English auxiliary *may*).

What is striking about these examples except for *wotte* is that they involve participant-internal possibility in different European languages. Whether this is a feature peculiar to this type of modality or to European languages remains to be determined.

3.4. Constraints on changes in modality

The hypothesis of the unidirectionality of modal paths is part of more far-reaching hypotheses that lexical items will be recruited to do grammatical work (grammaticalization) and that meanings will be recruited to express speaker attitudes and evaluations (subjectification). Some other constraints that are more specific to modality have also been suggested. These have to do with the likelihood that the modality 'not necessary that' will not be expressed (i.e., that there will be gaps in coding of certain modal meanings); or if they are expressed they will in all likelihood be used in a different syntactic structure from 'necessary that not,' be suppletive, or be merged with modals meaning 'necessary that not' (see de Haan, this volume). Building on Aristotelean squares of opposition and the neoGricean maxims, Horn (1989: 259–260) gives an account of this phenomenon (along with even stricter constraints on negation, cf. *all, some, no,* **nall* 'some are not'): since the *may* of possibility entails 'not necessary that' and *some* entails 'some are not,' expressing these negative concepts would be uninformative. Historically, in the case of modals, there is a unidirectional shift from expressions of 'not necessary that' (if they occur) to expressions of 'necessary that not.' Syntactic distinctions in word order between the two also tend to be lost (Horn 1989: 261–262; van der Auwera 2001).

4. Corpora and frequency studies of English

Until the 1990's, the major repositories of information on the historical development of English modals were the *Oxford English Dictionary* and Visser (1963–1973: Vol. III). The advent of electronic corpora revolutionized the study of English and allowed far more through investigations of the exact contexts for change than were feasible before. The corpus that has largely defined historical work on changes in earlier English is the Helsinki Corpus of English Texts, Diachronic Part; this million and a half word corpus covers the periods 850–1710, and is designed to represent varieties of English that led to the development of Standard English in the eighteenth century (see Rissanen, Kytö, and Palander-Collin 1993). The ARCHER corpus (A Representative Corpus of Historical English Registers) is a corpus of about one million seven hundred thousand words, two-thirds British, and one-third American, and covers the periods 1650–1990 (see Biber, Finegan, Atkinson, Beck, Burges, and Burges 1994). These can be supplemented with several corpora of relatively recent English, such as the Brown corpus of American texts from 1961 on (see Francis and Kučera 1989 [1964]) and the BNC (the British National Corpus; see Aston and Burnard 1998). For discussion of these and other databases, see Krug (2000), Leech (2003), and Lindquist and Mair (2004). Nothing so extensive appears to be available for the histories of other languages, which is a major reason why English has continued to be the language most studied with respect to change. Book-length studies of modality based on the Helsinki Corpus include Kytö (1991) on the development of *can/could* vs. *may/might* and of *shall/should* vs. *will/would* in Early American English, compared to British English; Gotti, Dossena, Dury, Facchinetti, and Lima (2002) on the core modals in late ME and EModE; Krug (2000) on the emergence of semi-modals is based on ARCHER and the BNC.

Corpora have allowed researchers to correlate various factors with change, including sex, age, text type, spoken vs. written medium (in recent periods), and variety (e.g., British vs. American). Most particularly they have allowed researchers to study language change in progress. Close inspection of texts such as early twentieth century American dramas and the interaction between characters led Myhill (1995, 1997) to suggest that the decline of strong deontic modals like *must, ought to* and intentional *will* found in the texts reflects the fact that these modals were perceived as too prototypically authoritarian and insistent on group norms; in a democratizing society that disfavors overt markers of group power and favors individuality, *got to, should,* and *be gonna* are favored, as their meanings are modally weaker. Agreeing in principle with Myhill's view that there has been a democratizing trend in language use, Smith (2003: 263) notes that in British English in the second half of the twentieth century, while *(have) got* to is rapidly replacing deontic *must* in spoken data, *need to* rather than *be going to* is the modal most widely used in printed texts for strong obligation (see also Leech 2003: 235).

5.   Major changes in the English modal system

In the next sections I review some major changes in the English modal system over the last hundred years or less that have been the subject of particular attention in studies of modality. Although the central concern of historical studies of modality in English has been the system of auxiliary verbs, the emergence of other kinds of modal expression has not been ignored. I begin with studies of adverbials and epistemic parentheticals, and end with comments on the auxiliary system.

5.1. Modal adverbials

A class of sentential adverbs and adverbials with at least partially modal meaning has existed ever since OE. Swan (1988, 1991) shows that in OE there was a small set of truth intensifiers that emphasize the truth or importance of the statement. Of these, *witodlice* and *soþlice* were the most frequent. They are intersubjective in that they serve to legitimize the speaker's utterance. The number of these adverbs increased in the ME period. Some, like *certes* 'certainly,' *clerly* 'clearly,' were borrowed from French. In EModE adverbs with high, medium and low probability meanings began to appear (often in clause-internal position), notably *probably, presumably, possibly, conceivably.* During the twentieth century, such adverbs came to be used significantly more frequently; low-probability adverbs "occur initially in very high proportions much more so than high-probability modal adverbs – as if modern speakers hedge where Old English speakers emphasise!" (Swan 1991: 418). It is possible that this change is related to the "de-mocratization" of modals that Myhill proposed. It is certainly part of the increasingly significant role of adverbs and adverbials in English, an increase noted already by Western (1906), who said: "No other Teutonic language has developed to the same degree the faculty of expressing so much by a single adverb as English"(cited in Swan 1991: 421).

The increasing repertoire of adverbials includes various phrasal constructions like *indeed* and *in fact* that have been grammaticalized[16] as sentential modal adverbials, a subset of discourse markers (see Traugott and Dasher 2002) and stance adverbs (Biber and Finegan 1988; Biber 2004a). They also include the epistemic parentheticals like *I think,* which has lost its status as matrix clauses and has come to function as "a discourse marker or modal particle which is syntactically a speech-act adverbial"(Aijmer 1997: 1) (for the earlier history of such adverbials see Brinton 1996; Palander-Collin 1997). Other sentence-initial modal markers that have sometimes been considered to be adverbs include the first modal in double-modal constructions (see Nagle 1994).

5.2. The auxiliary system

In recent years two types of changes in the auxiliary system have attracted attention. One is the use of *may* instead of *might* in counterfactual main clauses, and modal perfects like *would have.* Considering the rarity of counterfactual expressions, and modal perfects (some of which are counter-factual), these changes are somewhat on the margins of the system. The other is a broad-sweeping change that has been occurring since the beginning of Modern English -- the spread of modals with *to* (the so-called semi-modals or quasi-modals).

In OE counterfactual expressions had pluperfect in both protasis (subordinate clauses) and apodosis (main clause). This was a symmetric construction, and it continued to be used through the nineteenth century, as in (4):

(4) *Had* I yielded to the first impulse … how different *had* been my present situation.   (1814 Scott, *Waverley* 23 [Molencki 2000: 317])

From the mid-fourteenth century on, the pluperfect in the apodosis could be expressed by a modal (*wolde* or *scholde*) + *have* + past participle. This allowed for an asymmetric construction:

(5)   The former *would have* been ruined if he *had* not saved it by betraying
       his party.   (1674, *History of Charles II*, 1.1.179 [Ibid.)

New symmetrical *would have* … *would have* constructions are also found,
like the following:

(6)   If the world *would have* begunne as I *would have* wished.
              (1513 (1641) *Richard III* 235 [Molencki 2000: 321, citing OED])

Molencki (2000: 325) comments that "the struggle between parallelism and
asymmetry is by no means over."
       Indeed, a new asymmetry, discussed in Denison (1992), developed in
the 1980's and appears to be spreading: the use of *may have* for *might have,*
as in (7):

(7)   Had we known about Mrs Westbrook's illness we would have taken
       this into consideration, and the case *may* not have ended up in court.
                 (Dec. 17th, 1982, *The Guardian* [Denison 1992: 232])

While most speakers may not identify *might* as past tense, they do presumably identify it as remote or hypothetical, whereas *may* is not remote.
Denison (1992) investigates several possible modal uses which might have
served as templates for this new construction, including open possibility as
in *The editor may have served his reader better by...* (1992: 234), but suggests that the most likely reason for the appearance of counterfactual *may* is
the obsolescence of the *may/might* distinction (confirmed in Leech 2003:
28 for the periods 1961–1992) – dying forms tend to be used in haphazard
ways.
       Boyland (1998) discusses a different but semantically related change in
the use of *should have, would have, could have, had have* (she calls them
modal perfects). They appear to have been grammaticalized into a single
unit. Evidence is provided by the fact that they can both precede the subject
in inversion as in (8a). They can also precede *have* as in (8b), or a past
tense as in (8c). This suggests that the *have* cliticized to the modal is no
longer recognized as *have*:

(8)   a. What *would've* you done.
       b. But do you think the QCs *would have* still have linked...
                                                      (COBUILD corpus)
       c. If you *'d'a* ran to the bus stop. (Boyland 1998: 3, 5, 2 respectively)

Boyland notes that (8c) is interpreted as *would have* by US speakers, but as *had have* by UK speakers. She traces it back to the eighteenth century, but says it spread in the nineteenth and gained considerably in the twentieth in spoken data. In (9), from the nineteenth century, note the position of the quantifier *all*:

(9)   But it *would have* all availed me nothing.

(R. H. Dana 1849 [Boyland 1998: 3])

Doubtless the most significant change that English is undergoing with respect to modality is the decline of the core modals. At the same time, semi-modals are on the increase, especially *be going to, (have) got to, want to, need to, want to* (Krug 2000, 2001; Leech 2003). They may even be emerging as a new category, neither core modal nor main verb (Krug 2000, 2001).

Even though semi-modals may in the distant future replace core modals, current data suggest the adjustment is proceeding slowly, and, as has been true for the history of the modals over the last two thousand years, form by form, polysemy by polysemy (Leech 2003). Most importantly, they are not increasing at the same rate as the core modals are declining. Biber notes that "semi-modals have shown noteworthy increases only in drama and personal letters" in the past hundred years (2004b: 210), and mainly in American English. Leech points out that in the written corpora he studied for the period 1961–1992, overall use of core modals had declined about 9% in British English and 12% in American English. Furthermore, there has been a tendency to specialize meanings of individual modals: *may* is used primarily to express epistemic possibility, *should* to express weak obligation. While showing that *be going to, need to* and *want to* increased dramatically in American English over the thirty years studied (51.6%, 123.2%, and 70.9% respectively), in British English only *need to* increased significantly (249.1%), while most other semi-modals declined (Leech 2003: 229). Biber (2004b: 211) hypothesizes that verbal expressions of modality are being replaced by other means of modal expression, such as stance adverbs and complement clauses (see Biber 2004a).

Attempts to explain the rise of semi-modals as in any way the necessary outcome of other changes seem mistaken. For example, in his study of the development of the properties of syntactic Aux (behavior in negation, inter-rogatives, tags, and emphatics) Lightfoot (1979: 112) suggested that their development was the consequence of the development of the core modals as members of Aux. Noting that the semi-modals "are for most purposes semantically identical to the modals *shall/will, must, can*," he analyzes them as "true verbs"and says, "It is as if the re-analysis of *can, may, must,* etc., as modals created a vacuum, which the grammar immediately filled by creating a new set of semantically equivalent verbs"(Lightfoot 1979: 112). Actually Lightfoot himself cites examples of semi-modals from the OED that precede the emergence of syntactic Aux by a hundred years, so they were clearly already available (see Plank 1984, who also shows that several semi-modals already had modal meanings in the OE period). It is unclear what kind of vacuum there could have been since the core modals were still available to express modal meanings, and adverbials were also abundant; furthermore, even in their early stages the semi-modals did not behave syntactically exactly like main verbs (see Visser, 1963–73, Vol. III), and came over time to behave less like them. If the semi-modals had "filled a vacuum," they would surely have proceeded faster and more systematically, and the core modals would have disappeared. Fischer (1994) suggests the loss of past uses of the core modals necessitated the development of semi-modals. However, while most semi-modal constructions, especially *have to*, the subject of Fischer's study, and *be going to, dare to, need to*, clearly do allow past tense expressions, others do not, e.g., *ought to, used to*, and newer semi-modals like *(had) better* and *might as well* (Mitchell 2003) are largely fixed in past tense forms. Fischer has apparently more recently revised her (1994) hypothesis, and considers "the contemporary shape of the grammar and iconic pressure" as the contexts for the auxiliation of *have to*, a change that did not have to take place (Fischer 2003: 464).

It seems best to conclude that because modality is a gradient notion, semantically as well as morphosyntactically, it can be represented in a variety of morphosyntactic ways. Furthermore, because it is an enormously complex system that directly expresses speakers' beliefs and evaluative attitudes, it is not surprising that certain subparts may non-deterministically come to be focal or "gravitational" areas (Krug 2000: 242–247) "verb by verb, submeaning by submeaning, dialect by dialect" (Kemenade 1992: 306).

Notes

1. In this paper, the following abbreviations are used: Du. (Dutch), EModE (Early Modern English c.1500–1750), Eng. (English), Fr. (French), Gm. (German), Jp. (Japanese), Lat. (Latin), ME (Middle English c. 1150–1500), OE (Old English c. 650–1150), Russ. (Russian), Swed. (Swedish). The following symbols are also used: > (becomes, has the later form/meaning), < (derives from), +> (invites the inference).
2. The semantic sources can be very varied: see Abraham (1991) on Gm. modal particles, which originate in such meanings as 'nakedly' (*bloss*), 'equally high' (*eben*), 'much easy' (*vielleicht*).
3. Bybee (1988) is a study of, among other things, the way in which *can* recently came to have permission meaning, and "knocked off" (261) the permission meaning of *may* (*may* is now almost entirely used in the possibility sense). However, the outcome of competition between meanings does not account for why the meanings came to be established in the first place.
4. See, however, Papafragou (2000) for some proposals about how to conceptualize the development of core modals in terms of monosemous Relevance Theory.
5. Goossens (1992) provides a detailed account of overlapping semantic categories with reference to the history of *can* in terms of changes within a radial category (shifts in the saliency of prototype cores or centers).
6. Gelderen (2004) elaborates on Roberts and Roussou (2003), focusing on commonalities between deontic modals and aspect markers.
7. Heine, Claudi and Hünnemeyer (1991: 70) refer to a similar process as *context-induced reinterpretation*.
8. See Benveniste (1971 [1958]) and Lyons (1982) on synchronic subjectivity.
9. Contrast Langacker (e.g., 1990), who restricts subjectification to changes in the interpretation of the syntactic subject characteristic of raising constructions, e.g., the shift from restriction to animate subjects in motion *be going to* constructions to the availability of inanimate or expletive subjects in future/epistemic constructions (*There is going to be an earthquake*).
10. Details of the sample, known as GRAMCATS, can be found in the Appendix to Bybee, Perkins and Pagliuca (1994).
11. Despite the teleological implicature of the word *target*, Bybee, Perkins and Pagliuca soundly reject the notion that change is directed to any intentional goal (1994: 297–298).
12. Increase in type-frequency and hence in range of collocations has been called *host-class expansion* by Himmelmann (2004), who regards this type of expansion as criterial of grammaticalization, along with two additional types of expansion: syntactic (new syntactic possibilities become available, e.g., the use of tags or epistemic parentheticals in various positions in the clause), and semantic-pragmatic expansion (generalization, e.g. of past tense modals such as *could, would* to express hypotheticality).

13. Source > Target is a semasiological perspective, in which source form is treated as (relatively) constant, and meaning change is tracked; Target < Source is an onomasiological perspective, in which target meaning is treated as constant, and shift of forms to this meaning is tracked.
14. However, Sun (1996) uses the deontic terminology for the permission meaning.
15. Although it has until recently been quite widely accepted in the grammaticalization literature, this is actually a rather unusual use of the term *lexicalization*, which is more widely used to refer to the idiomatization and loss of compositionality of a word-formation (Lipka 2002 [1990]); Brinton and Traugott (2005) provide an account of different uses of the term.
16. Aijmer (1997) has proposed that they are "pragmaticalized" on the grounds that they have primarily pragmatic content; however, discourse markers in general, including sentential modal adverbials, belong to the grammar of language and are "pragmaticalized" only in so far as they are highly subjectified and, like other grammatical markers, have lost referential content while gaining non-referential content (have been bleached).

References

Abraham, Werner
  1991   The grammaticalization of the German modal particles. In *Approaches to Grammaticalization vol. 2*, E. Traugott and B. Heine (eds.), 331–380. Amsterdam: John Benjamins.
Aijmer, Karen
  1986   Why is *actually* so popular in spoken English? In *English in Speech and Writing: A Symposium*, G. Tottie and I. Bäcklund (eds.), 119–129. Uppsala: Almqvist and Wiksell.
  1997   *I think* -- an English modal particle. In *Modality in Germanic Languages: Historical and Comparative Perspectives*, T. Swan and O. Westvik, (eds.), 1–47. Berlin/New York: Mouton de Gruyter.
Akatsuka, Noriko
  1992   Japanese modals are conditionals. In *The Joy of Grammar*, D. Brentari, G. Larson, and L. MacLeod (eds.), 1–10. Amsterdam: John Benjamins.
Andersen, Henning
  2001   Actualization and the unidirectionality of change. In *Actualization: Linguistic Change in Progress*, H. Andersen (ed.), 225–248. Amsterdam: John Benjamins.
Aston, Guy and Lou Burnard
  1998   *The BNC Handbook Exploring the British National Corpus with SARA*. Edinburgh: Edinburgh University Press.

Barcelona, Antonio (ed.)
   2000   *Metaphor and Metonymy at the Crossroads: A Cognitive Perspective.*
             Berlin/New York: Mouton de Gruyter.
Benincà, Paola and Cecilia Poletto
   1997   The diachronic development of a modal verb of necessity. In *Para-
             meters of Morphosyntactic Change*, A. van Kemenade and N. Vincent
             (eds.), 94–118. Cambridge: Cambridge University Press.
Benveniste, Emile
   1971   [1958]. Subjectivity in language. In *Problems in General Linguistics,*
             223–230. Trans. by Mary Elizabeth Meek. Coral Gables: FL: Uni-
             versity of Miami Press. (Publ. as De la subjectivité dans le langage.
             Problèmes de Linguistique Générale, 258–266. Paris: Gallimard,
             1966 [1958]).
Beths, Frank
   1999   The history of *dare* and the status of unidirectionality. *Linguistics*
             37: 1069–1110.
Biber, Douglas
   2004a   Historical patterns for the grammatical marking of stance: A cross-
             register comparison. *Journal of Historical Pragmatics* 5: 107–136.
   2004b   Modal use across registers and time. In *Studies in the History of the
             English Language II: Unfolding Conversations*, A. Curzan and K.
             Emmons (eds.), 189–216. Berlin/New York: Mouton de Gruyter.
Biber, Douglas and Edward Finegan
   1988   Adverbial stance types in English. *Discourse Processes* 11: 1–14.
Biber, Douglas, Edward Finegan, Dwight Atkinson, Anne Beck, Dennis Burges
and Jean Burges
   1994   The design and analysis of the ARCHER corpus: A progress report.
             In *Corpora across the Centuries: Proceedings of the First Interna-
             tional Colloquium on English Diachronic Corpora*, M. Kytö, M.
             Rissanen, and S. Wright (eds.), 3–6. Amsterdam: Rodopi.
Boyland, Joyce Tang
   1998   A corpus study of *would* + *have* + past-participle. In *Historical Lin-
             guistics 1995. Selected Papers from the 12th International Confer-
             ence on Historical Linguistics, vol. II. Germanic Linguistics*, R.
             Hogg and L. van Bergen (eds.), 1–17. Amsterdam: John Benjamins.
Brinton, Laurel J.
   1996   *Pragmatic Markers in English: Grammaticalization and Discourse
             Function.* Berlin/New York: Mouton de Gruyter.
Brinton. Laurel J. and Elizabeth Closs Traugott
   2005   *Lexicalization and Language Change.* Cambridge: Cambridge Uni-
             versity Press.

Burridge, Kate
  2002   Changes within Pennsylvania German grammar as enactments of
            Anabaptist world view. In *Ethnosyntax: Explorations in Grammar
            and Culture*, N. J. Enfield (ed.), 207–230. Oxford: Oxford University
            Press.
Bybee, Joan L.
  1985   *Morphology: A Study of the Relation between Meaning and Form.*
            Amsterdam: John Benjamins.
  1988   Semantic substance vs. contrast in the development of grammatical
            meaning. *Berkeley Linguistic Society* 14: 247–264.
  1995   The semantic development of past tense modals in English. In *Mo-
            dality in Grammar and Discourse,* J.L. Bybee and S. Fleischman
            (eds.), 503–517. Amsterdam: John Benjamins.
  2003   Mechanisms of change in grammaticization: The role of frequency.
            In *The Handbook of Historical Linguistics*, B. Joseph and R. Janda
            (eds.), 602–623 Malden: Blackwell.
Bybee, Joan L. and William Pagliuca
  1985   Cross-linguistic comparison and the development of grammatical
            meaning. In *Historical Semantics: Historical Word-Formation*, J.
            Fisiak (ed.), 59–83. Berlin/New York: Mouton de Gruyter.
Biber, Joan L., William Pagliuca and Revere Perkins
  1991   Back to the future. In *Approaches to Grammaticalization, vol. 2*,
            E. Traugott and B. Heine (eds.), 17–58. Amsterdam: John Benjamins.
Bybee, Joan, Revere Perkins and William Pagliuca
  1994   *The Evolution of Grammar: Tense, Aspect, and Modality in the Lan-
            guages of the World.* Chicago: University of Chicago Press.
Chomsky, Noam
  1957   *Syntactic Structures.* The Hague: Mouton.
Croft, William
  2000   *Explaining Language Change: An Evolutionary Approach.* Harlow:
            Pearson Education.
Dahl, Östen
  1985   *Tense and Aspect Systems.* Oxford: Blackwell.
Denison, David
  1990   The Old English impersonals revived. In *Papers from the 5th Inter-
            national Conference on English Historical Linguistics*, S. Adamson,
            V. Law, N. Vincent , and S. Wright (eds.), 111–140. Amsterdam:
            John Benjamins.
  1992   Counterfactual *may have*. In *Internal and External Factors in Syn-
            tactic Change*, M. Gerritsen and D. Stein (eds.), 229–256. Berlin/
            New York: Mouton de Gruyter.
  1993   *English Historical Syntax.* Oxford: Oxford University Press.

2001   Gradience and linguistic change. In *Historical Linguistics 1999. Selected Papers from the 14th International Conference on Historical Linguistics, Vancouver, 9–13 August 1999*, L. J. Brinton (ed.), 119–144. Amsterdam: John Benjamins.

Enfield, N. J.
2003   *Linguistic Epidemiology: Semantics and Grammar of Language Contact in Mainland Southeast Asia.* London: Routledge.

Fischer, Olga C. M.
1994   The development of quasi-auxiliaries in English and changes in word order. *Neophilologus* 78: 137–164.
2003   Principles of grammaticalization and linguistic reality. In *Determinants of Grammatical Variation in English*, G. Rohdenburg and B. Mondorf (eds.), 445–478. Berlin/New York: Mouton de Gruyter.

Fleischman, Suzanne
1982   *The Future in Thought and Language: Diachronic Evidence from Romance.* Cambridge: Cambridge University Press.

Francis, Nelson and Henry Kučera
1989   [1964]. *Manual of Information to Accompany a Standard Corpus of Present-Day Edited American English, for Use with Digital Computers.* Providence: Department of Linguistics, Brown University.

Gamon, David
1993   On the development of epistemicity in the German modal verbs *mögen* and *müssen. Folia Linguistica Historica* 14: 125–176.

Gelderen, Elly van
2004   *Grammaticalization as Economy.* Amsterdam: John Benjamins.

Goossens, Louis
1992   CUNNAN, CONNE(N), CAN: The development of a radial category. In *Diachrony within Synchrony: Language History and Cognition. Papers from the International Symposium at the University of Duisburg*, G. Kellermann and M. D. Morrissey (eds.), 377–384. Frankfurt am Main: Peter Lang.
1999   Metonymic bridges in modal shifts. In *Metonymy in Language and Thought*, K. Panther and G. Radden (eds.), 193–210. Amsterdam: John Benjamins.
2000   Patterns of meaning extension, "parallel chaining," subjectification, and modal shifts. In *Metaphor and Metonymy at the Crossroads: A Cognitive Perspective*, A. Barcelona (ed.). Berlin/New York: Mouton de Gruyter.

Gotti, Maurizio, Marina Dossena, Richard Dury, Roberta Facchinetti and Maria Lima
2002   *Variation in Central Modals: A Repertoire of Forms and Usage in Late Middle English and Early Modern English.* Bern: Peter Lang.

Hanson, Kristin
  1987   On subjectivity and the history of epistemic expressions in English. *Chicago Linguistic Society* 20: 133–147.
Harris, Alice C. and Lyle Campbell
  1995   *Historical Syntax in Cross-linguistic Perspective.* Cambridge: Cambridge University Press.
Heine, Bernd, Ulrike Claudi and Friederike Hünnemeyer
  1991   *Grammaticalization: A Conceptual Framework.* Chicago: University of Chicago Press.
Heine, Bernd and Tania Kuteva
  2002   *World Lexicon of Grammaticalization.* Cambridge: Cambridge University Press.
Himmelmann, Nikolaus P.
  2004   Lexicalization and grammaticalization: Opposite or orthogonal? In *What Makes Grammaticalization – a Look from its Fringes and its Components*, W. Bisang, N. Himmelmann and B. Wiemer (eds.), 19–40. Berlin/New York: Mouton de Gruyter.
Hopper, Paul J. and Elizabeth Closs Traugott
  2003   [1993]. *Grammaticalization* (2nd revised ed.) Cambridge: Cambridge University Press.
Horn, Laurence R.
  1972   On the semantic properties of logical operators in English. Unpublished Ph.D. Dissertation, UCLA.
  1989   *A Natural History of Negation.* Chicago: University of Chicago Press.
Janda, Richard D.
  2001   Beyond "pathways" and "unidirectionality": On the discontinuity of transmission and the counterability of grammaticalization. *Language Sciences* 23: 265–340.
Joseph, Brian
  1983   *The Synchrony and Diachrony of the Balkan Infinitive: A Study in Areal, General, and Historical Linguistics.* Cambridge: Cambridge University Press.
Kemenade, Ans van
  1992   Structural factors in the history of English modals. In *History of English: New Methods and Interpretations in Historical Linguistics*, M. Rissanen, O. Ihalainen, T. Nevalainen, and I. Taavitsainen (eds.), 287–309. Berlin/New York: Mouton de Gruyter.
Krug, Manfred G.
  2000   *Emerging English Modals: A Corpus-Based Study of Grammaticalization.* Berlin/New York: Mouton de Gruyter.
  2001   Frequency, iconicity, categorization: Evidence from emerging modals. In *Frequency and the Emergence of Linguistic Structure*, J. Bybee and P. Hopper (eds.), 209–335. Amsterdam: John Benjamins.

Kytö, Merja
  1991   *Variation and Diachrony, with Early American English in Focus.*
          Frankfurt am Main: Peter Lang.
Langacker, Ronald W.
  1990   Subjectification. *Cognitive Linguistics* 1: 5–38.
Leech, Geoffrey
  2003   Modality on the move: The English modal auxiliaries 1961–1992. In
          Modality in Contemporary English, R. Facchinetti, M. Krug and F.
          Palmer, (eds.), 223–240. Berlin/New York: Mouton de Gruyter.
Levinson, Stephen
  2000   *Presumptive Meaning: The Theory of Generalized Conversational
          Implicature.* Cambridge: MIT Press.
Lightfoot, David
  1979   *Principles of Historical Linguistics.* Cambridge: Cambridge Univer-
          sity Press.
  1991   *How to Set Parameters: Arguments from Language Change.* Cam-
          bridge: MIT Press.
Lindquist, Hans and Christian Mair (eds.)
  2004   *Corpus Approaches to Grammaticalization in English.* Amsterdam
          and Philadelphia: John Benjamins.
Lipka, Leonhard
  2002   [1990]. *English Lexicology: Lexical Structure, Word Semantics, and
          Word-Formation,* 3rd revised ed. of *An Outline of English Lexicology.*
          Tübingen: Max Niemeyer Verlag.
Lyons, John
  1982   Deixis and subjectivity: *Loquor, ergo sum?* In *Speech, Place, and
          Action: Studies in Deixis and Related Topics,* R. J. Jarvella and W.
          Klein (eds.), 101–124. New York: Wiley.
McElhinney, Bonnie
  1992   The interaction of phonology, syntax and semantics in language
          change: The history of modal contraction in English. *Chicago Lin-
          guistic Society* 28: 367–381.
Mitchell, Keith
  2003   *Had better* and *might as well*: On the margins of modality? In *Mo-
          dality in Contemporary English,* R. Facchinetti, M. Krug, and F.
          Palmer (eds.), 129–149. Berlin/New York: Mouton de Gruyter.
Molencki, Rafael
  2000   Parallelism vs. asymmetry: The case of English counterfactual con-
          ditionals. In *Pathways of Change: Grammaticalization in English,* O.
          Fischer, A. Rosenbach and D. Stein (eds.), 311–328. Amsterdam:
          John Benjamins.

Myhill, John
  1995   Change and continuity in the functions of the American English modals. *Linguistics* 33: 157–211.
  1997   *Should* and *ought:* The rise of individually oriented modality in American English. *Journal of English Linguistics* 1: 3–23.
Nagle, Stephen J.
  1994   The English double modal conspiracy. *Diachronica* 11: 199–212.
Narrog, Heiko
  2002   Polysemy and indeterminacy in modal markers – the case of Japanese *beshi. Journal of East Asian Languages* 11: 123–167.
  2005   Modality, mood, and change of modal meanings – a new perspective. *Cognitive Linguistics* 16: 677–731.
Newmeyer, Frederick J.
  1998   *Language Form and Language Function* Cambridge: MIT Press.
Nordlinger, Rachel and Elizabeth Closs Traugott
  1997   Scope and the development of epistemic modality: Evidence from *ought to. English Language and Linguistics* 1: 295–317.
Nuyts, Jan
  2000   Discourse structure and conceptual semantics: The syntax of epistemic modal expressions. *Studies in Language* 24: 103–135.
Palander-Collin, Minna
  1997   A medieval case of grammaticalization, *methinks.* In *Grammaticalization at Work: Studies of Long-Term Developments in English*, M. Rissanen, M. Kytö and K. Heikkonen (eds.), 371–403. Berlin/New York: Mouton de Gruyter.
Papafragou, Anna
  2000   *Modality. Issues in the Semantics-Pragmatics Interface.* Amsterdam: Elsevier.
Peyraube, Alain
  1999   On the modal auxiliaries of possibility in Classical Chinese. In *Selected Papers from the 5th International Conference on Chinese Linguistics*, H.S. Wang, F. Tsao and C. Lien (eds.), 27–52. Taipei: Crane Publishing.
Plank, Frans
  1984   The modals story retold. *Studies in Language* 8: 305–364.
Ramat, Paolo and Davide Ricca
  1994   Prototypical adverbs: On the scalarity/radiality of the notion of ADVERB. *Rivista di Linguistica* 6: 289–326.
Rissanen, Matti, Merja Kytö, and Minna Palander-Collin (eds.)
  1993   *Early English in the Computer Age: Explorations through the Helsinki Corpus.* Berlin/New York: Mouton de Gruyter.

Roberts, Ian
    1993   A formal account of grammaticalisation in the history of Romance futures. *Folia Linguistica Historica* 13: 219–258.
Roberts, Ian and Anna Roussou
    2002   The history of the future. In *Syntactic Effects of Morphological Change*, D. W. Lightfoot (ed.), 23–56. Oxford: Oxford University Press.
    2003   *Syntactic Change: A Minimalist Approach to Grammaticalization*. Cambridge: Cambridge University Press.
Rohdenburg, Günter and Britta Mondorf (eds.)
    2003   *Determinants of Grammatical Variation in English*. Berlin/New York: Mouton de Gruyter.
Romaine, Suzanne
    1995   The grammaticalization of irrealis in Tok Pisin. In *Modality in Grammar and Discourse*, J. L. Bybee and S. Fleischman (eds.), 388–427. Amsterdam: John Benjamins.
Smith, Nicholas
    2003   Changes in the modals and semi-modals of strong obligation and epistemic necessity in recent British English. In *Modality in Contemporary English*, R. Facchinetti, M. Krug and F. Palmer (eds.), 241–266. Berlin/New York: Mouton de Gruyter.
Sun, Chaofen
    1996   *Word Order Changes and Grammaticalization in the History of Chinese*. Stanford: Stanford University Press.
Swan, Toril
    1988   *Sentence Adverbials in English: A Synchronic and Diachronic Investigation*. Oslo: Novus Verlag.
    1991   Adverbial shifts: Evidence from Norwegian and English. In *Historical English Syntax*, D. Kastovsky (ed.), 409–438. Berlin/New York: Mouton de Gruyter.
Sweetser, Eve E.
    1988   Grammaticalization and semantic bleaching. *Berkeley Linguistic Society* 14: 389–405.
    1990   *From Etymology to Pragmatics: Metaphorical and Cultural Aspects of Semantic Structure*. Cambridge: Cambridge University Press.
Talmy, Leonard
    1988   Force dynamics in language and cognition. *Cognitive Science* 22: 49–100.
Taeymans, Martine
    2004   An investigation into the marginal modals DARE and NEED in British present-day English: A corpus-based approach. In *Up and down the Cline – The Nature of Grammaticalization,* O. Fischer, M. Norde, and H. Perridon (eds.), 97–114. Amsterdam: John Benjamins.

Traugott, Elizabeth Closs
    1989   On the rise of epistemic meanings in English: An example of sub-
             jectification in semantic change. *Language* 57: 33–65.
    2003   From subjectification to intersubjectification. In *Motives for Lan-
             guage Change*, R. Hickey (ed.), 124–139. Cambridge: Cambridge
             University Press.
Traugott, Elizabeth Closs and Richard B. Dasher
    2002   *Regularity in Semantic Change.* Cambridge: Cambridge University
             Press.
Tsangalidis, Anastasios
    2004   Unidirectionality in the grammaticalization of modality in Greek. In
             Up and down the Cline – The Nature of Grammaticalization, O.
             Fischer, M. Norde and H. Perridon (eds.), 193–209. Amsterdam:
             John Benjamins.
van der Auwera, Johan
    2001   On the typology of negative modals. In *Perspectives on Negation
             and Polarity Items*, J. Hoeksema, H. Rullmann, V. Sánchez-
             Valencia, and T. van der Wouden (eds.), 23–48. Amsterdam: John
             Benjamins.
van der Auwera, Johan and Vladimir A. Plungian
    1998   Modality's semantic map. *Linguistic Typology* 2: 79–124.
Visconti, Jacqueline
    2004   Conditionals and subjectification: Implications for a theory of se-
             mantic change. In *Up and down the Cline – The Nature of Gram-
             maticalization*, O. Fischer, M. Norde, and H. Perridon (eds.), 169–
             192. Amsterdam: John Benjamins.
Visser, F. Th.
    1963–73 *An Historical Syntax of the English Language, 3* vols. Leiden: Brill.
Warner, Anthony R.
    1990   Reworking the history of the English auxiliaries. In *Papers from the
             5th International Conference on English Historical Linguistics*, S.
             Adamson, V. Law, N. Vincent, and S. Wright (eds.), 537–558. Am-
             sterdam: John Benjamins.
    1993   *English Auxiliaries: Structure and History.* Cambridge: Cambridge
             University Press.
Weinreich, Uriel, William Labov and Marvin I. Herzog
    1968   Empirical foundations for a theory of language change. In *Directions
             for Historical Linguistics*, W. P. Lehmann and Yakov Malkiel (eds.),
             97–195. Austin: University of Texas Press.
Western, August
    1906   Some remarks on the use of English adverbs. *Englische Studien* 36:
             75–99.

Ziegeler, Debra

2003   Redefining unidirectionality: Insights from demodalization. *Folia Linguistica Historica* 14: 225–266.

2004   On the generic origins of modality in English. In *English Modality in Context: Diachronic Perspectives*, D. Hart (ed.), 33–69. Bern: Peter Lang.

Acquisition of modality

Soonja Choi

1. Introduction

Modality is an intriguing topic in child language research because it is a domain that can give us important information about children's semantic development as well as about their social and cognitive development. As Nuyts (this volume) puts it, modality refers to some kind of qualification of state of affairs. This means that by using modal expressions, speakers state more than just what they see: with modal forms speakers can add their own or other people's psychological or mental states regarding the proposition. Accordingly, when children acquire a set of modal expressions, they have grasped at some level the notion that a proposition can be qualified to include their own or other people's assessment about it.

For the last two decades, acquisition of modality in children's language has been approached from several perspectives both in linguistics and developmental psychology. Some of the major issues have been the following:

- The order in which various modal forms and meanings are acquired and the underlying mechanisms that explain such an order.
- The acquisition of epistemic modality and its relation to children's theory of mind.
- The use of modal expressions as part of acquiring competency in discourse interaction.

These issues have been investigated with two types of database: children's spontaneous speech in naturalistic contexts (longitudinally or cross-sectionally collected) and children's responses in various types of experimental conditions. Although English and other Indo-European languages still dominate in the research on acquisition of modality, other languages, such as Japanese, Korean, Chinese, and Turkish, have been examined as well.

The present chapter attempts to provide a coherent review of studies with a focus on issues that relate to four types of modal markers: dynamic, deontic, epistemic, and evidential modal forms (see Nuyts' and de Haan's work in this volume for a full discussion). The first two types, dynamic and deontic modalities, are grouped together as *agent-oriented modalities* (see Gerhardt 1991, for a convincing argument for putting them into one category, particularly in studying child language). *Agent-oriented modality* refers to all modal meanings that predicate conditions on the agent with regard to the completion of an action referred to by the main predicate (Bybee and Fleishman 1995: 6). These conditions include ability, obligation, permission, and root possibility toward the action. The category also includes the agent's desire and intention toward an action.

In contrast to the agent-oriented modality, *epistemic modality* – the third type from the list above – has to do with degree of certainty on the part of the speaker about the truth of the proposition. The speaker may estimate that the events or states expressed in the proposition are possible, probable or certain. In this category, expressions marking different types of information status and source of information, so-called *evidentials* (the fourth type from the above list), can be included. Although it is debatable whether evidentiality is part of epistemic modality (see Nuyts' and de Haan's work in this volume), it is included in this chapter because by specifying, for example, the source of information (e.g., hearsay, or direct evidence), the speaker conveys varying degrees of certainty of the proposition.

This chapter first reviews some general developmental patterns regarding agent-oriented and epistemic modality. It then reviews how the two types of modality are related to children's cognitive development (in particular, to the development of theory of mind). Finally, discourse-pragmatic aspects of modality in early language development are considered, as is the relation between input and acquisition of modality. Overall, it appears that modal expressions are first learned with particular discourse-pragmatic meanings through caregiver-child interactions and later develop into more abstract semantic notions. Also, there is a dynamic interaction between acquisition of modal expressions and the cognitive development in the relevant domain.

2. Developmental pattern of agent-oriented and epistemic modalities

Major findings on the developmental sequence of modality come from longitudinal studies of children's spontaneous speech. Experimental studies of modality began in the early 1980s, and they have mainly examined some detailed aspects of the way children acquire epistemic modal meanings.

2.1. General developmental pattern

Most longitudinal studies on the acquisition of modal auxiliary verbs agree that, in general, children start acquiring agent-oriented modality before epistemic modality (Stephany 1986; Wells 1985; Papafragou 1998; Shatz and Wilcox 1991 review English learners). Stephany (1986) provided a crosslinguistic review of modal development in various languages, with foci on Modern Greek and English. She noted (1986: 398): "deontic meanings are expressed before epistemic ones by children acquiring typologically and genetically quite different languages." In a more recent work, Stephany (1993) reviewed the developmental patterns of modality in German and English, and she drew the same conclusion, namely that agent-oriented modality is acquired before epistemic modality. According to Stephany (1993), one reason for this is that children start out predominantly with non-epistemic acts: i.e., requestive or imperative acts, in social interaction. These acts relate to agent-oriented modals. Epistemic acts (i.e., declarative acts) are developed later, and hence have later development in epistemic modality.

A number of studies have examined in detail the development of modality in English learners. Shatz and Wilcox (1991) report that children learning English acquire modal verbs gradually between 1;10 (1 year; 10 months) and 2;6 (2 years; 6 months). At the beginning, the modal meanings children express are largely agent-oriented: intention, volition/rejection, and inability/ ability. They use *can* or *will* (or quasi-modals (also called *concatenatives*), such as *going to/gonna* or *want to/wanna*) to express ability, intentions and desires as early as 2;0. They also use *can't* to express inability in limited syntactic environments, i.e., mainly in declaratives (Shatz and Wilcox 1991) (see also Choi 1988). Wells' studies (1979, 1985) with a larger sample agree with this general developmental pattern, although the average ages of acquisition are somewhat later. In these studies, Wells sampled 60 children along with their mothers every three months, from 1;3 to 3;6. He found that, overall, the children began expressing agent-oriented modality before epistemic modality. More specifically, the first type of modality that the children (at least 50% of the children in the sample) acquired was the expression of ability/inability (using *can/can't*) at 2;3. This was followed by expression of intention (using *will*) at 2;6 (Wells 1979). By 3;3, an average child produced several types of agent-oriented modality: ability, permission, willingness/intention, obligation, and necessity. In contrast, epistemic modality started slowly from 3;3, when the children began to produce *may* and *might* to express possibility. Furthermore, these epistemic modals were not firmly established until about 5;0. Wells (1985) reports that inferential uses of modals, such as *that will be the postman,* appear even later in development. There is some evidence, however, that children begin to use epistemic modal markers earlier than 3;0. O'Neill and Atance (2000) examined the modal terms *maybe, possibly, probably* and *might* in ten English-learning children recorded longitudinally between 2 and 5 years of age (from the CHILDES (Child Language Data Exchange System) database). The children used these terms productively to denote uncertainty from 2;6 of age. Based on these data, O'Neill and Atance argue that epistemic meanings are acquired earlier than what previous studies had claimed.

The general developmental order from agent-oriented to epistemic modality has also been found in creole languages, such as Antiguan Creole (Shepard 1993). Shepard (1993) studied five children (spontaneous speech at daycare) and found that deontic meanings are acquired earlier than epistemic meanings. Even in the case of *mosa* ('must'), which in Antiguan Creole has only epistemic sense, children used it in a deontic sense before an epistemic sense.

Languages that have a morphosyntactic system similar to English (i.e., modal auxiliary verbs) have shown the same developmental pattern. In Polish, Smoczyńska (1993) studied acquisition of modal verbs in diary data of four children collected from 1;6 to 3;0. She found that the children used various modal verbs (*móc* [may], *musieć* [must], *wolno* [it is allowed], *trzeba* [there is need], *powinien* [should], *da się* [(root) possibility]) in agent-oriented senses, but not in epistemic senses, during this period. In French, Bassano (1996), who followed the language development of a French child from 1;9 to 4;0, reports that the child expressed desires and intentions before 2;0, but that he did not express epistemic meanings (e.g., prediction (*aller* 'go' + *verb*), certainty (*savoir* 'know')) until 2;3.

This developmental progression from agent-oriented to epistemic modality is consistent with the *frequency* data of the early periods in language development. For example, in her study of a French boy, Bassano (1996) reports that during the period from 2;0 to 2;8, agent-oriented modals were predominant and that epistemic modals occupied less than 20% of the child's modal expressions. In English, Wells (1979) also reports a high frequency for the agent-oriented modals, *can* and *will,* expressing ability and intention respectively, but a relatively low frequency for the epistemic modals, *might,* expressing possibility. Wells' data are comparable to Torr's findings (1998). Torr (1998) studied the development of modality in one

English-learning child from 2;6 till 4;2. The data were gathered while the child interacted with her sibling and/or her mother during everyday activities at home. Torr found that from the beginning of the study (i.e., 2;6) expressions of agent-oriented modality were consistently more frequent than those of epistemic modality in the child's speech.

To summarize, studies (of children's spontaneous speech data) on languages where modality is expressed lexically with modal verbs and adverbs, agent-oriented modality is acquired earlier than epistemic modality. (But this pattern may differ for typologically different languages, as later discussion reveals.)

2.2. Acquisition of modality and syntax

In the early stages of acquisition of modality, children's production of modal auxiliary forms seems more lexically than syntactically driven. Shatz and Wilcox (1991: 331) note that "while modal vocabulary growth proceeds fairly rapidly during this early period (e.g., *can/can't, wanna, won't*), the range of syntactic constructions in which the modals appear changes somewhat more slowly." For example, early modals (e.g., *can, will*) are all produced in limited syntactic contexts, mainly in simple declaratives. A few forms are expressed only in the negative (e.g., *can't*) before the respective positive form is acquired. This is probably due to the use of modal forms for pragmatic purposes at an early stage. O'Neill and Atance (2000) report that syntactic growth for modal forms starts at around 3;6. At this age, children's syntax becomes more complex (e.g., use of complement clauses) while they use the same lexical items that they already possess in their repertoire. These findings suggest that a motivation for the early acquisition of modal expressions is the relation of their lexical meanings to discourse functions rather than to their syntactic roles. In fact, after reviewing the development of modality in a large sample, Wells (1985) concludes that acquisition of modality is facilitated by pragmatic properties, such as indication of modulation of action or social regulations. Shatz, Wellman, and Silber (1983), who studied the development of mental verbs (e.g., *think, know*), also note that children produce these verbs first in idiomatic or conversational phrases (e.g., *you know what?*) before using them as mental verbs with clause complements.

Another type of concrete evidence that points to the above conclusion is the limited range of subjecthood in early uses of modal verbs. Several studies converge on the finding that there is a relation between specific type of modality and subjecthood. More specifically, studies have found that children produce agent-oriented modal verbs with the first person pronoun, namely *I*, as the subject. For example, Pea and Mawby (1984), who examined the semantics of modal auxiliary verbs (*can, will, gonna*) in six children aged between 2;4 and 2;10, found that the children used agent-oriented modals with first person to express volition of the self 80% to 95% of the time (e.g., *I will give you a tiny little fork*). This finding is corroborated by other studies: O'Neill and Atance (2000) report that, during the early period, the children in their study used the first person subject to express future intention (e.g., *Maybe I will go away*). There also seems to be a specific relationship between agent-oriented modals and sentence type. Pea and Mawby (1984) report that most of the modals (e.g., *gonna, want*) were used in the affirmative. Negative modal values were used only to express constraints on action or an unwillingness to act (e.g., *can't, won't*) at the time of speaking. On the other hand, for epistemic terms (e.g., *maybe, possibly, might*), children use them mainly with the third person as the subject to express events and states of third-party entities (O'Neill and Atance 2000; Bassano 1996). In O'Neill and Atance (2000), it was not until 4;0 that the expression of uncertainty was used with respect to children's *own* epistemic state in the present, as in *maybe I'm real right*. This specific relationship between subjecthood and modal verbs supports the claim that early modal forms are more semantically and pragmatically based than syntactically based.

2.3. Epistemic modality: Spontaneous speech data

In studies of the acquisition of epistemic modality, the kinds of linguistic forms considered have been diverse. In addition to epistemic modal auxiliaries (*e.g., might, could*), mental verbs denoting speaker's status of knowledge (e.g., *think, know, believe*) as well as modal adverbs and particles (e.g., *probably, possibly, maybe*) have been investigated. Although these forms belong to different grammatical classes (e.g., verbs, auxiliaries, adverbs), they all express different degrees of certainty about the truth of the proposition. Furthermore, children start acquiring these forms across different grammatical classes during the same developmental period. In order to assess the kinds of epistemic meanings children acquire in early periods, then, all these terms that have a modal property need to be examined.

Stephany (1986) reports that a precursor of epistemic modality can be found in children's early uses of tense and aspect markers. In particular, children use past tense or imperfective forms when describing simulated activities or engaging in a pretend play, i.e., an unknown world. For example, two-year-olds learning Turkish used the evidential past form (*-miş*) (e.g., *sen hastay-miş-sin* ('(let's pretend) you are ill') and three-year-olds learning Greek use an imperfective form (e.g., *eγó píjen-a* 'I would be going') to set up scenes in pretend games. This reveals that children are developing modal concepts at this time. Indeed, when children actually start using epistemic modals, they often express possible future events or likely present state of affairs. At around 3;0 or so, children also begin to produce hypothetical statements using conditionals (e.g., *àma kriv-ómuna se mia spiljá, θa me é-vrisk-es?* 'If I hid in a cave, would you find me?' produced by a Greek child aged 3;3 (Stephany 1986)). These conditionals are often about the future domain where the truth is unknown. (See Bowerman 1986 for a semantic analysis of early forms of conditionals.)

In the development of epistemic modality, studies have found a progression from certainty to uncertainty. In a longitudinal study, Bassano (1996) reports a detailed analysis of the development of epistemic meanings of a French child. She investigated the development of various modal expressions including adverbs (e.g., *peut-être* 'maybe') and paraphrastic constructions (e.g., *il se peut que* 'it is possible that'). She found that different types of epistemic modality developed at different times. In this child, the first function to emerge (at around 2;2) was future prediction (e.g., *va venir elsa* 'going to come elsa'). Then, expression of certainty (e.g., *je suis sûr* 'I am sure') emerged along with the expression of ignorance, namely, *sais pas* 'don't know' (at around 2;6). Bassano categorizes the latter (i.e., expression of ignorance) as a subtype of uncertainty. Between 2;6 and 4;0, the child's modal system denoting uncertainty grew richer as he first acquired modal forms for possibility/probability (e.g., *peut-être* 'maybe,' *je crois* 'I believe') and then later hypothetical reference which could be expressed by a conditional (e.g., *si papa il revient, faut pas ouvrir* 'if papa comes back, (we) must not open'). (See also Reilly 1986 for the acquisition of *when* and *if* for a similar developmental pattern within the domain of conditionals.) Thus, overall, certainty was acquired earlier than uncertainty. This finding is corroborated by experimental studies with older French children (aged four to eight years). Bassano and her colleagues (Bassano, Hickmann and Champaud 1992; Champaud, Bassano and Hickmann 1993) tested children's comprehension of stories with a series of questions (such as *Est-ce qu'il est sûr ou pas sûr?* 'Is he sure or not sure?') and found that four- and six-year-olds attributed certainty more often than eight-year-olds did. The late acquisition of uncertainty suggests that it takes some time for the child to acquire the notion that an assertion could be open to question and to consider nonactual references (Bassano 1996: 104).

Shatz, Wellman and Silber (1983) studied the development of early mental verbs, such as *think, know,* and *remember*, in spontaneous speech of one child learning English between 2;4 and 4;0. As already noted, the authors found that these verbs were first found in idiomatic expressions (e.g., *I don't know*) or conversational phrases. For example, the mental verb *know* served at first a conversational function of directing interaction (e.g., *It's a hat, you know*, or *you know what?*). These mental verbs did not express mental states (e.g., *She doesn't know all this*) until 2;8. These longitudinal data were corroborated by a cross-sectional study of 30 children between 2;0 and 3;0, as no children were found to be using mental verbs to express a mental state before the age of 2;6.

Overall, analyses of spontaneous speech data show that children start producing epistemic modals between 2;6 and 3;0. In the next section, a review of experimental studies will reveal that acquisition of full adult-like meanings of epistemic modals takes a number of years in childhood.

2.4. Epistemic modality: Experimental data

In experimental studies, there is converging evidence that four-year-old children are much better than three-year-olds in understanding tasks involving epistemic modal markers. Recall, however, that the findings of the studies on spontaneous speech indicate that children begin producing epistemic modals at around 2;6. Thus, experimental studies show a somewhat later development of epistemic modality than the findings of naturalistic data. The discrepancy is probably due to a certain degree of unnaturalness inherent in experimental tasks. Experimental tasks are artificial in nature as they do not involve children's naturally-occurring psychological states. Thus, the situations presented in experiment tasks are probably more difficult for children to process than those that arise naturally in spontaneous speech contexts. Nevertheless, experimental studies are valuable as they complement the findings of spontaneous speech data. In particular, they give us insight into the extent to which modal meanings are understood at a given developmental period.

Hirst and Weil (1982) examined the extent to which children (of different age groups starting from 3;0 to 6;6) understand the semantic contrasts among various types of epistemic and deontic modal markers. Epistemic modal markers differ in degree of certainty (on the part of the speaker) about the truth of the proposition. For example, concerning the epistemic meanings of *must* and *may* (*John must be home* vs. *John may be home*), the former conveys more certainty than the latter. In the Hirst and Weil study, the experimenter presented the child with a cup and a box and asked the child to indicate where an object (in this case, a peanut) could be hidden based on a pair of modal statements that differed in the degree of certainty, e.g., *The peanut MUST be under THE CUP* and *The peanut MAY be under THE BOX*. The verbs tested were the factual verb *to be*, and the modal auxiliaries *must, should,* and *may*. (Each verb was contrasted with each of the other three.) The rationale was that if the child understood the semantic contrast of the two verbs presented, he/she would perform the task according to the stronger modal meaning. For example, between *The peanut MUST be under the cup* and *The peanut MAY be under the box*, the child will choose the cup following the proposition with *must* since it expresses a higher degree of certainty than *may*. The results showed that the greater the distance between the two modals presented (in terms of the strength of modal meaning), the earlier the contrast was understood. More specifically, the youngest age group (children between 3;0 and 3;6) could only make the contrast between the factual verb *is* and the modal for weak possibility *may*. Four-year-olds could make a number of other contrasts (e.g., *is* vs. *should, must* vs. *may*). Finally, children older than 5;6 could make all types of contrast tested. These results suggest that children first learn the dichotomy (between the two extremes on the continuum), then gradually learn different points in the continuum (*might* vs. *might not*) (see Byrnes and Duff 1989: 386).

Hirst and Weil (1982) also tested the children's knowledge of deontic modality. They asked the children to indicate where the puppet would go based on two statements (made by what the experimenters called *two teachers*) that differed in strength of obligation (*You MUST go to the RED ROOM* vs. *You MAY go to the GREEN ROOM*). Results showed that the children did *not* distinguish the relative strengths of the deontic modals till 5;6! This is unexpected, as naturalistic data have shown that deontic meanings are acquired *earlier* than epistemic meanings (e.g., Wells 1985). Hirst and Weil (1982) point out that, while the epistemic tasks were pretty straightforward (i.e., asking children to pay attention to the sentences and make judgments), the deontic ones were more complex. The task depended on the children's evaluation of the characters presented (i.e., authority figure (teachers)), as well as of their willingness to comply with the commands. For example, the children may have chosen the room that they liked in answering the deontic task rather than following the command with stronger obligation marker (see Byrnes and Duff 1989 for similar results and further discussion).

Several researchers conducted modified versions of Hirst and Weil's study (1982) to examine additional aspects of modality. Byrnes and Duff's study (1989) is worth mentioning here. In Byrnes and Duff (1989), children were not only asked to find the location of an object based on two statements (i.e., the same method as in the Hirst and Weil study) but were also asked to find it based on a *single* statement with a modal marker such as *has to, can't be, might*, or *might not*, e.g., *The penny has to be in the red cup*. Results showed that the three-year-olds did well in the single-statement condition although they did not do well in the two-statement condition. (In fact, all children regardless of age (three-, four-, five-year-olds) performed well in the single-statement condition.) This suggests that three-year-olds do have the "knowledge of how modals are used to indicate a speaker's assessment of what he or she knows" (1989: 387).

Moore, Pure and Furrow (1990) tested children's understanding of a broad range of modal forms: modal verbs, *must, might* and *could*, and modal adjuncts, *probably, possibly*, and *maybe*, as well as mental verbs, *know* and *think*. Following Hirst and Weil's technique, the experimenters gave contrasting pairs of modal sentences (using puppets) as clues to the location of an object. The results showed that while three-year-olds did not differentiate between any of the modal contrasts presented, four-year-olds and older children were able to find the hidden object on the basis of what they heard. As in the Hirst and Weil study, children's performance was better for the pairs of terms with a maximal contrast between them (e.g., *probably* vs. *maybe*) than for the pairs with a relatively minimal contrast (e.g., *possibly* vs. *maybe*). The fact that Hirst and Weil's finding is replicated with a broader range of modal forms suggests that the ability does not come from acquisition of particular lexical items but rather from a more general understanding of the mental state concept of relative certainty (Moore, Pure, and Furrow 1990).

Other studies have shown that a full understanding of epistemic modality takes a few more years. As mentioned earlier in Bassano's experimental studies (Bassano et al. 1992; Champaud et al. 1993) with French children, some epistemic modals were not fully understood till eight years of age.

While modals that express the conditions under which certainty (*je sais que* 'I know that,' *je suis sûr* 'I am sure') is assessed are understood at 4;0, those expressing uncertainty (*je ne suis pas sûr* 'I am not sure,' *je crois* 'I believe,' *je sais si* 'I know if') were not fully understood till 8;0.

Coates' study (1988) revealed that metalinguistic analysis of the modal system is achieved at an even later age. Coates (1988) conducted a classification task with modal markers in English: modal auxiliaries, concatenatives, verb phrases denoting intention (*intend to*), obligation (*be obliged to*), permission (*allowed*), as well as modal adverbs and adjectives. She presented cards each containing a sentence with a modal marker. All sentences had the same core proposition, *I visit my grandmother tomorrow.* Thus, one card, for example, read *I can visit my grandmother tomorrow,* and another card read *I should visit my grandmother tomorrow.* Coates asked eight-year-olds, twelve-year-olds, and adults to sort these cards into piles on the basis of similarity in meaning. Adults classified the modal markers into four distinct categories: epistemic possibility, root possibility/ability/permission, intention/prediction/futurity, and obligation/necessity. Twelve-year-olds' categorization was similar to the adults' with some minor differences. Eight-year-olds, however, did not include a category for epistemic modality and were generally less consistent among themselves in their classification.

The experimental studies reviewed so far can be summarized as follows. There is a gradual development in the level of abstraction in children's understanding of modality. In epistemic modality, children start developing epistemic notions from about three years of age. Initially, children understand individual notions (e.g., certainty, possibility) independent of each other. Also, children acquire the notion of certainty before uncertainty. From about 4;0 children begin to relate one epistemic notion to another. In this process, children start by relating notions at the two ends of a continuum (i.e., notions that are maximally different, e.g., *must* vs. *may*), then gradually relate notions that are in the middle of the continuum. Coates' data suggest that it takes a few more years to reach a high level of abstraction that allows children to classify modal terms into semantic categories.

3. Modal expressions and cognitive development

3.1. Development of modal expressions and theory of mind

Understanding epistemic notions is related to the development of theory of mind in children (Gopnik and Astington 1988). Theory of mind refers to children's ability to assess their own as well as others people's beliefs (i.e., mental states) about a state of affairs. Beliefs and reality are often not the same. For example, upon seeing a pencil case, one may believe that pencils are in the case (without actually seeing them). But if, upon opening it, one sees candies inside the case, he realizes that his previous belief was different from the reality. For developmental psycholinguists the questions have been:

- When and how do children come to have conscious knowledge about changes in their beliefs (i.e., representational change)?
- When do they gain knowledge of the differences between beliefs and reality (i.e., the appearance-reality distinction)?
- When do they understand that other people's beliefs may differ from their own and from reality (called false belief)?

The techniques typically used to investigate young children's mind were developed by Gopnik and Astington (1988). Their basic method was to show children first a "deceptive" object (e.g., pencil case), and then reveal the true nature of the object (e.g., show candies inside the case). The children were then asked what they thought the object was when they first saw it before they opened it (= test of their representational change); what another child would think what the object was (= test of false belief); what the object looked like and really was (= test of appearance-reality distinction). Gopnik and Astington (1988) found that while three-year-olds could not answer the questions correctly, five-year-olds could. The authors concluded that "children begin to be able to consider alternative representations of the same objects at about age 4" (1988: 26).

In this method children's understanding of mental verbs, such as *know, think, believe,* and *guess,* is crucial, as it is with these mental verbs that speakers refer to the content of one's mental states and the varying degrees of certainty on the part of the believer. Recall that in Moore et al.'s (1990) study, it was by age four that children could understand different degrees of certainty in modal terms such as *probably, possibly, maybe.* In the same study, Moore et al. (1990) conducted a second experiment. They tested a group of four-year-olds with both linguistic tasks and theory of mind tasks. For the linguistic task, Moore et al. tested children's understanding of modal and mental terms, *must-might, know-think.* For the theory of mind tasks, following Gopnik and Astington's design (1988), they tested the children's understanding of representational change (*What did you think before you touched the object?*), false beliefs (*What will another person think before touching the object?*), and the appearance-reality distinction (*What does it look like? What is it really?*). The results showed that the two types of tasks (linguistic and nonlinguistic tasks) were positively correlated. Based on this finding, Moore et al. (1990) suggest that both the linguistic and representational abilities shown at around four years of age come from a general development in the representational theory of mind, namely that beliefs can be different from reality, and that beliefs may be held with more or less certainty. Thus, according to Moore et al. (1990) linguistic ability derives from underlying cognitive development.

3.2. Relation between modal expressions and cognitive development

Moore et al.'s study (1990) raises the issue of the relation between language and cognition in the domain of modality. Is the acquisition of modal expressions really a product of general cognitive development? Or can it be the reverse? That is, does acquiring modal expressions actually facilitate the development of cognitive abilities in the relevant domain? A positive answer to the first question would be in line with the traditional Piagetian view, namely that language follows general cognitive development and, therefore, is part of it. A positive answer to the second question would indicate that language is somewhat a separate component from general cognition and that its development is foundational to cognitive development.

Until quite recently, development of modal expressions has often been attributed to the development of underlying cognitive concepts. For example, let's take the findings that children first talk about their own ability and desire before other people's ability and desire, and that they show greater accuracy in self-initiated than other-initiated hypothetical reference (Pea and Mawby 1984; O'Neill and Atance 2000). These developmental patterns have been attributed to children's cognitive decentration process whereby children first look at events and states from their own perspective and only later learn to view them from other people's perspectives. To take another example, children acquire modals for *future* hypotheticals earlier than *past* hypotheticals (e.g., *could/would have* + pp) (Kuczaj and Daly 1979). Kuczaj and Daly point out that the difficulty in acquiring past hypotheticals is not due to the greater syntactic complexity of the past hypothetical form because children already possess the necessary linguistic forms to express past (*have* + pp). It is not a temporal referencing problem either, because children are able to refer to past events at this time. It can only be explained by the cognitive difficulty of processing. Conceptually, hypothesizing something that has not happened in the past is more difficult than hypothesizing a future event: a particular past event has already occurred, so it is hard to hypothesize something against the facts.

Answering questions about the relation between language and cognition requires more than theorizing, however. To understand the relation, it is necessary to conduct investigations that systematically compare linguistic and nonlinguistic abilities in a particular domain. To date, only a handful of studies have looked at this issue systematically (e.g., Aksu-Koç and Didem 2000; de Villers and Pyers 1997; Farrar and Maag 2002; Gonsalves and Falmagne 1999). The studies reported so far suggest that the relationship between language and cognition is dynamic and bi-directional. In some cases, cognitive abilities are foundational to particular linguistic abilities, and in other cases the reverse relation is found.

In recent years, researchers have examined the possibility that specific linguistic ability may actually enhance children's development in theory of mind. One study specifically looked at how linguistic ability in early stages influences the development of theory of mind in later stages. Farrar and Maag (2002) examined the relationship between children's language ability at 2;0 and their theory of mind performance at 4;0. Language ability was assessed by parental report of MacArthur Communicative Development Inventory (MCDI, a checklist of vocabulary acquisition), as well as by analyzing children's speech in naturalistic play session between mother and child. Children were also tested on their verbal memory of sentences of different lengths. Their level of theory of mind was assessed by their performance on understanding of false belief, representational change, and appearance-reality distinction tasks. Results showed a significant interrelation between early language ability and later theory of mind performance. Children who had a high vocabulary level at 2;0 did better in the theory of mind tests at 4;0. This suggests a specific link between early language development and later-occurring theory of mind development. (See also Watson, Painter and Bornstein 2001 for similar results.)

De Villiers and her colleagues (1997, 2000) examined a possible causal link between a specific kind of linguistic ability and the development of theory of mind. In de Villiers and Pyers (1997), the researchers assessed children's ability to use complex sentences, specifically object complementation with main verbs such as *know* and *think* (e.g., *He thinks that he found his ring*) in children's spontaneous as well as elicited production. They also assessed the level of false belief reasoning. These measurements were made at four different times within a year beginning when the children were at the mean age of 3;4. The results showed that the acquisition of sentential complementation is a critical prerequisite (and provides the representational structure) for false belief reasoning in children. De Villiers' studies provide convincing evidence that language is foundational for logical thinking.

Gonsalves and Falmagne's study, however, suggests that certain cognitive abilities may be required for the development of epistemic modality. In Gonsalves and Falmagne's (1999) study, children (aged 2;6 – 5;0) performed both nonlinguistic reasoning and linguistic tasks involving agent-oriented and epistemic modals. In the nonlinguistic task, children were asked to indicate where an object was hidden based on a nonlinguistic cue. In this task, the experimenter presented children with two red and two blue cups. The children were told that two objects were hidden under the cups of the same color. Then the experimenter turned over one of the cups. Sometimes an object was under the cup, but sometimes not. Based on this evidence, the children had to indicate under which of the remaining three cups the object was hidden. In the linguistic tasks, the children were given a modal statement (containing either an agent-oriented or epistemic sense of *can* and *have to*) and were asked to respond to the experimenter's question that measures their comprehension of the statement. The results were that none of the children who failed the nonlinguistic task passed the comprehension task of epistemic modal meanings. From these data, the authors suggest that nonlinguistic reasoning ability is related to and is a *prerequisite* for the comprehension of *epistemic modal meanings*. Concerning the agent-oriented modality, however, there was no significant relation between the nonlinguistic and linguistic tasks. Based on these results, Gonsalves and Falmagne (1999) argue that while epistemic modal meanings are acquired when the conceptual system incorporates the logical distinction between possibility/ impossibility and necessity/non-necessity, agent-oriented modalities are acquired without the support of a full-fledged nonlinguistic reasoning ability. Gonsalves and Falmagne propose that language and cognition provide mutual support to each other in development. "Children's attention to and participation within modal discourse provide an entry point for representing pragmatic modal concepts [= agent-oriented modalities] linguistically, which, in turn, provides the foundation for an eventual linguistic system based on logical and pragmatic meanings" (1999: 213).

Gonsalves and Falmagne's attention to discourse brings us to the topic of the next section, namely, the role of discourse pragmatics in the acquisition of modality. As will be shown below, modals have important discourse functions, and the modal forms young children use convey rich interactional meanings.

3.3. Discourse-pragmatic meanings of modality in children's speech

Several researchers have studied agent-oriented modals from a conversational discourse perspective. In particular, Gerhardt (formerly Gee) conducted detailed analyses of modals in English: *will, gonna, needta,* and *hafta.* Gee (1985; Gee and Savasir 1985) examined linguistic and nonlinguistic contexts of two modal forms, *will* and *gonna,* in the speech of two children while they were playing together. She found that the children used *will* and *gonna* in distinct activity types: *will* was used when children were about to undertake an action (to carry out a joint activity), and where the action was actually performed after the utterance. *Will* thus expressed a commitment to carry out a cooperative activity (i.e., real intention). But *gonna* was used when children were simply organizing their plan linguistically without necessarily acting out (i.e., planning an activity). Gee points out that *gonna* may be considered amodal, because in using *gonna,* children seem to project future events independent of any attitude of commitment of intention to bring about these events.

Gerhardt (1991) also conducted a systematic and detailed analysis of the children's use of *hafta, needta,* and *wanna* (produced by the same two children studied in Gee 1985). Her analyses revealed that *hafta* expresses obligation to act due to the requirement of (long-term) social conventions. For example, during a tea-party pretend play, when her friend began to eat some cookies, the child said, "But *first you HAFTA put them on a plate.*" It is a social convention in the western culture to first put food on a plate and eat it from the plate. *Needta,* on the other hand, expresses obligation (i.e., a strong volition) to act due to the child's internal force which is beyond his control, e.g., *I NEEDTA go to the bathroom.* Finally, *wanna* expresses a weaker volition that is personal, which may not always be in accord with the demand of the outside world. Thus, these three quasi-modals are associated with distinct semantic meanings as well as particular discourse pragmatic functions.

It should be noted that in Gerhardt's analysis, the dynamic meaning of future planning, such as *will* and *gonna,* leads to the epistemic meaning of prediction. Gerhardt argues that the "agent-based modalities [=dynamic and deontic meanings] gradually shade into epistemic modality when the event referred to loses its anchoring in the speaker's agency and control, and begins to be the content of the speaker's beliefs. Eventually, the story of modality will have to be rewritten to acknowledge the non-discrete multi-dimensional meaning space which is involved" (1991: 536). In this modal system, then, dynamic and epistemic meanings are at different points on one continuous scale.

The same conclusion is drawn in Guo's study (1995) on the use of *néng* 'can' in children learning Mandarin Chinese. *Néng* 'can' in Mandarin Chinese expresses ability and permission (and it extends to epistemic modality expressing possibility). Guo examined the uses of this form during peer plays in children aged three, five, and seven years (using a similar method of analysis as in Gee 1985). His analysis convincingly has shown that children learning Mandarin Chinese use *néng* 'can' for an interpersonal function that can be characterized as 'challenge to the addressee.' For example, the children in his sample used *néng* when they tried to show off their special abilities (e.g., building a Lego structure) to their peers. Guo argues that "this discourse function is the primary factor motivating the semantic change of *néng* 'can' from the three year olds' physical abilitative meaning through the five year olds' deontic meaning, to the seven year olds' epistemic-like meaning" (1995: 235). In other words, the process involved in this semantic change is hypothesized as semanticization of discourse function.

These discourse analyses of lexical modals in English and Mandarin Chinese suggest children are very sensitive to the discourse functional aspects of modal forms. In the next section, we will find out that when a language provides a set of verbal suffixes to convey epistemic/evidential meanings with significant discourse functions embedded in them (e.g., taking the addressee's view into account), children acquire them from very early on.

3.4. Sentence-ending suffixes as modal expressions: Early acquisition of evidential markers in discourse interaction

In languages where modality is expressed lexically, we find a clear picture of epistemic modality emerging later than agent-oriented modalities. However, when we look at languages such as Japanese, Korean, and Turkish that mark modality in bound morphemes (in addition to lexical forms), the picture of developmental sequence in modality becomes more complex. In these languages, a set of verbal suffixes (bound morphemes) expresses a special kind of modality. These suffixes express the speaker's assessment of the information status (e.g., whether the information is new or old, or shared or not shared with the listener) and source of information (e.g., whether the event/state of affairs is directly or indirectly perceived). These markers are typically termed *evidentials*. As discussed earlier, evidentials are epistemic to the extent that there is a component of degree of certainty in the semantics of these markers. For example, by specifying the source of information (for example, hearsay, or direct evidence) the speaker can convey different degrees of certainty of the proposition. Acquisition studies of Korean, Japanese, and Turkish have consistently shown that children begin acquiring the evidential markers of their language from early on.

3.4.1. Korean

Korean (an SOV language) has a set of verbal suffixes that occur at the end of a sentence (1–4 below). These sentence-ending (SE) forms belong to an obligatory class of verbal suffixes (i.e., a sentence must end with an SE form that is suffixed to the final verb), and they occur in informal interactions and are used to mark the status of the speaker's (and listener's) knowledge about the proposition and the source of information (Choi 1991; Lee 1991). More specifically, the suffix *-ta* indicates new/unassimilated knowledge in the speaker's mind, whereas *-e* marks old/assimilated information. The suffix *-ci* (or a stronger form, *-cyana*) indicates that the information is certain and is shared by both the speaker and the listener. The suffix *-tay* introduces indirect evidence (e.g., hearsay or reported speech). *Tay* is also used in story-telling:

(1)   Younghi-ka   Seoul-ul   ttena-ss-e.
      Younghi-SUBJ Seoul-OBJ leave-PAST-SE   (old /assimilated)
      'Younghi left Seoul.'

(2)   Younghi-ka   Seoul-ul   ttena-ss-ta.
      Younghi-SUBJ Seoul-OBJ leave-PAST-SE   (new/unassimilated)
      'Younghi left Seoul and I just realized it.'

(3)   Younghi-ka   Seoul-ul   ttena-ss-ci.
      Younghi-SUBJ Seoul-OBJ leave-PAST-SE   (shared/certain)
      'I know that Younghi left Seoul.'

(4)   Younghi-ka   Seoul-ul   ttena-ss-tay.
      Younghi-SUBJ Seoul-OBJ leave-PAST-SE (reported speech/story-telling)
      'I heard that Younghi left Seoul.'

In an earlier paper (Choi 1991), I traced the acquisition of these markers, and found that this set of evidential suffixes is acquired between 1;9 and 2;6, roughly in the order mentioned above. The first two (*-ta* and *-e*) are acquired before 2;0, and the other two between 2;1 and 2;6. These results are corroborated by other studies (Kim 1997; Zoh 1981). The data suggest that Korean children acquire these forms by 2;6, the period when English-learning children are reported to just begin acquiring epistemic modals.

It should be noted, however, that not all the meanings expressed in the adult grammar for these suffixes were present in the early-acquired SE forms. For example, in adult grammar, the suffix *-ci* also expresses certainty of a proposition based on inference. But this meaning did not appear in children's speech during the period studied (Choi 1995).

In previous work (Choi 1995), I also traced the acquisition of four agent-oriented modals encoding obligation, desire, ability and permission: *-ya twayta* 'must,' *-ko siphta* 'want,' *-su issta* 'can,' and *-to twayta* 'are allowed to' (*-ta* is a citation form in Korean). As shown in (5), these agent-oriented modal markers (in fact, all agent-oriented modal markers in Korean) consist of connectives (suffixed to the main verb) and free-standing auxiliary verbs:

(5)   Younghi-ka   Seoul-ul   ttena-ya   tway-e.
      Younghi-SUBJ Seoul-OBJ leave-CONN AUX-SE
      'Younghi must go to Seoul.'

Specific auxiliary verbs must co-occur with specific connectives to express particular deontic meanings. For example, the connective *-ya* plus the auxiliary verb *twayta* together mean 'obligation' (*must* in English). Thus, agent-oriented modal markers are morphologically more complex than SE verbal suffixes. Korean children begin to acquire these markers later than the early-acquired SE evidential suffixes (i.e., *-ta, -e, -ci, -tay*), as these markers are not productive in children's speech until around 2;6.

3.4.2. *Japanese*

Japanese children also acquire their sentence-ending forms early (Clancy 1985). These forms, like Korean, express various statuses of knowledge of the proposition that are closely related to conversational discourse interactions. Clancy notes that "these sentence-final particles are essential in face-to-face interaction in Japanese" (Clancy 1985: 427). Clancy reports that

Japanese children begin to acquire five to seven different sentence-ending particles (e.g., *-ne, -yo, -no*) between 1;6 and 2;0. Some of these particles have semantic and discourse functions close to the Korean sentence-ending forms. For example, the particle *-ne*, which children acquire from early on, is similar to *-ci* in Korean (but they are by no means translation equivalents! see below). *Ne* expresses information which children assume to be shared with the listener. *Ne* also expresses information that the child has repeatedly heard, i.e., assimilated knowledge:

(6)   Pointing to a very large boat in a picture, a boy aged 1;11 says:

ookii-ne?
big-SE
'(It's) big, isn't it?' (Clancy 1985: 429)

Ne contrasts with *yo*, which is used when children provide new information to the listener. "*Yo* and *ne* thus express two basic contrasting attitudes of a speaker communicating information to a listener" (Clancy 1985: 430). Another interesting particle is *-no*, which has a number of functions of which one is to express that the speaker believes the proposition is true based on some inference. Clancy (1985) reports that children use these forms correctly from their earliest occurrences.

It is intriguing that children acquire seemingly abstract meanings like those of SE suffixes from such an early age. Choi (1991) offered some explanations for the early acquisition of SE suffixes in Korean:

–   The forms are perceptually salient as they occur in the sentence-final position.

–   They belong to an obligatory grammatical class, which means that the input frequency for these forms is high.

–   They have a high degree of semantic transparency (Slobin 1973) since they only express evidential/epistemic meanings (i.e., they do not convey deontic meanings, nor do they incorporate tense or aspectual meanings).

–   They have rich discourse-interactional functions. In particular, these suffixes marking the status of information (in the speaker's and the addressee's mind) contribute to the construction of shared knowledge between the caregiver and child.

An affective component in producing these forms may also enhance the acquisition of such abstract concepts in ways similar to what Akatsuka and Clancy (1993) describe in relation to the early acquisition of conditionals in Japanese and Korean children. In the adult grammar of Japanese and Korean, a conditional meaning is expressed by a connective, *–tara* and *–myen* respectively, on the main verb of the conditional clause. An example is given in Korean in (7):

(7) pi-ka   o-myen   sanpo   an   ka-lkke-ya.
     rain-SUBJ come-COND promenade NEG go-FUT INTENTION-SE
     'If it rains, (I) won't go for a walk.'

In their insightful analysis, Akatsuka and Clancy (1993) point out that, in Japanese and Korean, conditional sentences express deontic notions such as 'permission,' 'necessity,' and 'obligation' (equivalent to *may, should,* and *must* in English), and that these sentences pragmatically express desirability/ undesirability of the action (see also Clancy, Akatsuka and Strauss 1997). For example, in (8), a Korean mother uses a conditional construction to tell the child not to eat:

(8) Mek-umyen an-tway.
     Eatt-COND   Neg-go.well
     'If you eat, it is not good.' (=(You) must not eat.)

In this example, the mother expresses prohibition by resorting to her evaluation that it is not good (= undesirable) for the child, and showing an emotional concern for the child. In this way, the utterance contains an affective component in the mother's speech. Akatsuka and Clancy (1993) show that in Japanese and Korean, this type of deontic conditional emerges early in children's speech (between 2;0 and 2;6), and that this is because deontic conditionals are strongly related to a pragmatic and affective meaning, namely, desirability/undesirability of the action.

Using this insightful analysis, I would argue that Korean and Japanese children acquire epistemic/evidential SE particles early also because these particles are charged with affective meanings. More specifically, using these particles appropriately, the child and the mother create a bond where new information is exchanged and a domain of shared knowledge is constructed (cf. Choi 1995).

3.4.3. Turkish

Aksu-Koç (1988, 1998; Aksu-Koç and Slobin 1986) has reported extensively on Turkish children's acquisition of two types of past tense: *-dI(/Iyor)* and *-mIş*. These two past tense markers have specific modal meanings incorporated in them, namely, different degrees of assimilation of a proposition in the speaker's mind. Aksu-Koç (1988) found that Turkish children acquire these verbal suffixes from early on, using them appropriately in conversation. Between 1;8 and 2;6, Turkish children first acquire *-dI* and shortly afterwards *-Iyor* to express direct experience (marking immediate past/completed action vs. ongoing events, respectively). They then acquire *-mIş* to refer to new information (that the child has not realized before) or to events in story-telling and pretend plays. Well before the age of three, Turkish children also learn to distinguish between events from direct experience (with *-dI*) and those from nonwitnessed process (with *-mIş*). Using *-mIş* to indicate nonwitnessed events means that children are acquiring the notion of inference, thus marking source of evidence (as well as past reference) (Aksu-Koç 1988).[1]

Choi and Aksu-Koç (1996) compared acquisition of SE verbal suffixes in Korean- and Turkish-learning children. What is similar between the two languages is the general developmental patterns of modal meaning, and the kinds of notions the two groups of children encode with modal markers between 1;6 and 3;0. In both Korean and Turkish, direct experience is expressed early marking immediate past and on-going events (*-dI/-Iyor* in Turkish and *-ta* in Korean). Both groups also distinguish between new and old information from early on. Toward the end of the third year, both groups begin to express indirect speech. Within this common developmental pattern, however, from a very early age children in each language are remarkably sensitive to the language-specific meanings of modality. It should be noted here that in the adult grammar, the two systems differ in significant ways: whereas in Korean the sentence-ending modal suffixes express purely modal meanings, in Turkish, modal markers are fused with tense and aspectual meanings (e.g., Korean *-ta* vs. Turkish *-dI/-Iyor*). The two systems also differ in the kinds of epistemic/evidential meanings each form expresses. In fact, none of the forms in the two languages can be matched as having equivalent meanings. In our data, from the beginning of modality acquisition, Korean and Turkish children produced modal forms that conform to the language-specific semantic pattern. For example, Korean children used the *-ta* form with both telic and stative verbs, but Turkish children differentiated between -*dI* and -*Iyor* based on the aspectual properties of the verb types (i.e., -*dI* with telic verbs and -*Iyor* with activity and stative verbs). Also, in congruence with the adult grammar, Turkish children used -*mIş* to signal both novelty of information and a past event inferred from present state. In contrast, Korean children used -*ta* for novelty of information but not for the inference function (Choi and Aksu-Koç 1996).

Language-specificity can also be seen in the acquisition of the SE particles in Japanese and Korean. In the adult grammar, although on the whole, the particles in Japanese and Korean express similar types of notions, these notions are carved up differently in each language for semantic purposes. For example, -*ne* in Japanese expresses shared information, like -*ci* in Korean, but also expresses assimilated knowledge, which is separately expressed by -*e* in Korean. Acquisition data show that Japanese and Korean children acquire the language-specific form-function relations from the onset of their acquisition of these particles.

Looking at Japanese, Korean, and Turkish data, it is truly remarkable that children learning these languages acquire the language-specific semantic categories in this domain of modality from such an early age. These data suggest that children attend to the semantic and pragmatic contexts of the forms as well as their morphological properties (i.e., salience of verbal suffixes). Thus, to fully understand the development of modality, it is necessary to consider the extent to which caregiver input affects the acquisition of modality.

4. Caregiver input and acquisition of modality

Shatz and Wilcox (1991: 320) propose that "acquiring a language of modality in part involves a process of socialization of cognition" and that "an appropriate model of the acquisition may be a dynamic, interactive one of mutual influence between language and thought" (1991: 320). Indeed, there is evidence for both the influence of input and of universal cognitive development in the acquisition of modality. First, studies have shown that maternal speech has important bearings on modal forms and meanings children learn and use frequently at an early stage. In English, the modals *can* and *will*, the two forms acquired first in many children, are the modals that English-speaking mothers use frequently when talking with their children (Wells 1979; see also Shatz and Wilcox 1991 for a report of a study of the relation between input and acquisition of modals in English and German).

Furthermore, epistemic modals, which English-learning children acquire late, are observed to be quite infrequent in mothers' speech: Shatz and Wilcox (1991) report that maternal input to young children consists of few epistemic modals (10% of all modals in mothers' speech to children aged 2;5). Thus, the developmental pattern of acquiring agent-oriented modals earlier than epistemic modals is at least in part related to the frequency of input in mothers' speech.

However, high frequency does not always explain children's early modal development. Shatz and Wilcox (1991) note that children *can* acquire modals that are relatively rarely used by the mothers. For example, in their study, young German children expressed necessity with modal forms although their mothers used it quite rarely (once or a few times). This suggests that there is more than linguistic input that determines the child's developmental pattern of modality.

In my own studies (Choi 1991, 1995), I looked at the relation between mothers' input frequency and the order of acquisition of the SE suffixes in Korean. Recall that in the modal development in Korean, children acquire the SE evidential/epistemic suffixes in the order of -*ta* (new/unassimilated information), -*e* (old/assimilated information), -*ci* (shared information/certainty), -*tay* (indirect/reported speech). In Choi (1991), I counted the frequency of these four modal markers in mothers' speech prior to the time the children began to use them productively, and examined whether the rate of frequency relates to the order of acquisition. I found only a partial relation between input frequency and acquisition order. Korean mothers used the suffix -*e* most frequently followed by -*ci*, -*ta*, and -*tay*, in that order. The difference in frequency between -*e* and -*ta* was quite large, 35% vs. 8%, respectively, on average in mothers' speech. In their children's speech, however, -*ta* was first acquired followed by -*e*. The forms -*ci* and -*tay* were acquired third and last, respectively. The early acquisition of -*ta*, despite a low frequency in mothers' speech, can be explained by its salience in semantic and pragmatic properties. It marks new information that is perceptually salient in the here-and-now and is of interest to the child. On the other hand, the relatively early acquisition of -*e* and the late acquisition of -*tay* may be attributed at least in part to the differences in the rate of input frequency for the two terms in mothers' speech. Based on these data, I have suggested that both input frequency and the child's own cognitive abilities at the time of acquisition contribute to the early acquisition of modal suffixes in Korean (Choi 1991). In addition, the discourse contexts (both linguistic and nonlinguistic) constructed by the mother and the child together serves as a scaffold within which children can grasp abstract concepts of modality from an early age (Choi 1995). Furthermore, as Akatsuka and Clancy (1993) propose, an affective component existing in the uses of these modal forms constitutes another enhancing element for the acquisition of SE particles.

Similar conclusions are made in Aksu-Koç (1998), who examined in detail the relation between input and acquisition of sentence-ending verbal suffixes in one Turkish mother-child pair. Aksu-Koç (1998) found only a partial relation between the caregiver input and the child's acquisition pattern. On the one hand, the distribution of verb types the child used for their early-acquired verb suffixes corresponded to the distribution pattern in the mothers' speech. For example, following the pattern of her mother, the child used the tense/aspect/modal marker *-dI* predominantly with achievement verbs (e.g., *bit-* 'finish,' *ol-* 'become'). On the other hand, the order of acquisition of the modal markers did not correspond entirely to input frequency in the mother's speech. For example, the child acquired *-dI* before *-Iyor*, whereas *-Iyor* was much more frequent than *-dI* in the mother's speech. The author explains that the early acquisition of *-dI* may be due to its semantic and pragmatic salience, namely that *-dI* expresses changes of state in the here-and-now, which the child can process cognitively at a young age. Aksu-Koç (1998) concludes that input and universal cognitive-processing strategies, as well as discourse contexts, play an interactive role in the acquisition of Turkish tense/aspect/modal morphology.

5. Conclusion

This chapter provided a review of research over the last two decades on the acquisition of modality in children learning different languages. A general finding is that children begin to acquire modality toward the end of the second year. Children acquire agent-oriented modalities before epistemic modalities, particularly in the case of languages where modality is expressed by auxiliary verbs (e.g., English, German, French). In the case of agent-oriented modalities, studies have shown that children use them first to express what they (i.e., first person) want and need before they talk about what others (i.e., third persons) want or need. In the case of epistemic modalities, children express certainty (of the truth of proposition) before uncertainty and inferences. Studies suggest that these early modal forms and meanings are more semantically and pragmatically motivated than syntactically driven. No relation has been found between the development of modal forms and the growth of syntax, i.e., there was no syntactic growth (e.g., MLU length) as children's repertoire of modal forms grew. On the other hand, the development of modal forms across languages shows a consistent semantic pattern that can be explained by cognitive and pragmatic factors.

Studies of children learning typologically different languages show that children are sensitive to a special kind of modal system from early on. Specifically, children learning languages like Korean, Japanese, and Turkish acquire a sophisticated system of modal forms that denote various types of knowledge state, such as new or old information, shared or non-shared information. Discourse analyses reveal that these markers have rich interactional meanings that take into account what the speaker and the listener know at the time of interaction. These meanings are cognitively within reach from a young age, particularly when these meanings are exchanged within emotionally positive and rich interactions between the caregiver and child. Indeed, a review of the relation between caregiver input and acquisition of modality shows that acquisition of modality involves "a process of socialization of cognition" (Shatz and Wilcox 1991) where children's cognitive understanding of modal notions is enhanced by their meaningful conversations with the caregiver.

Studies on the relation between modal expressions and cognition suggest that the relation is a dynamic one. On the one hand, there is evidence that some general cognitive development is necessary for acquiring modality (particularly in the epistemic domain). On the other hand, studies of theory of mind suggest that the acquisition of modal terms and mental verbs is crucial in understanding representational change and false beliefs. In fact, it has been demonstrated in English learners that linguistic capacity in this particular area may be a prerequisite for conceptual development related to the theory of mind.

In order to understand the exact nature of the interaction between modal expressions and cognition, more studies need to be conducted in typologically different languages detailing the input and the acquisition patterns of modality and examining the relationship between specific type of modality and specific type of cognitive capacity. Findings from such studies will shed light not only on the relation between modality and cognition but also between language and thought in general.

Note

1. Early acquisition of epistemic/evidential particles has been reported in Cantonese and Turkish as well. Lee and Law (2000) studied spontaneous speech of three children longitudinally for a year with the starting ages (of observation) ranging from 1;7 to 2;8. They report that children learning Cantonese begin to produce the particle wo^4, expressing new and unexpected information, and contrast it with the particle lo^1, expressing obviousness, from 2;0.

References

Akatsuka, Noriko and Patricia Clancy
    1993   Conditionality and deontic modality in Japanese and Korean. *Japanese/Korean Linguistics* 2: 177–192.

Aksu-Koç, Ayhan
    1988   *The Acquisition of Aspect and Modality: The Case of Past Reference in Turkish.* Cambridge: Cambridge University Press.
    1998   The role of input vs. universal predispositions in the emergence of tense-aspect morphology: Evidence from Turkish. *First Language* 18: 255–280.

Aksu-Koç, Ayhan and Didem M. Alici
    2000   Understanding sources of beliefs and marking of uncertainty: The child's theory of evidentiality. In *The Proceedings of the Thirtieth Annual Child Language Research Forum*, E. V. Clark (ed.), 123–138. Stanford: Center for the Study of Language and Information.

Aksu-Koç, Ayhan and Dan I. Slobin
    1986   A psychological account of the development and use of evidential in Turkish. In *Evidentiality: The Linguistic Coding of Epistemology*, W. Chafe and J. Nichols (eds.), 159–167. Norwood: Ablex.

Bassano, Dominique
    1996   Functional and formal constraints on the emergence of epistemic modality: A longitudinal study on French. *First Language* 16: 77–113.

Bassano, Dominique, Maya Hickmann and Christian Champaud
    1992   Epistemic modality in French children's discourse: 'to be sure' or 'not to be sure'? *Journal of Child Language* 19: 389–414.

Bowerman, Melissa
    1986   First steps in acquiring conditionals. In *On Conditionals*, E. C. Traugott, A. ter Meulen, J. Reilly, and C. Ferguson (eds.), 285–307. Cambridge: Cambridge University Press.

Bybee, Joan and Suzanne Fleischman
    1995   Modality in grammar and discourse: An introductory essay. In *Modality in Grammar and Discourse*, J. Bybee and S. Fleischman (eds.), 1–14. Amsterdam: Benjamins.
Byrnes, James and Michelle Duff
    1989   Young children's comprehension of modal expressions. *Cognitive Development* 4: 369–387.
Champaud, Christian, Dominique Bassano, and Maya Hickmann
    1993   Modalité épistémique et discours rapporté chez l'enfant français. In *Modality in Language Acquisition*, N. Dittmar and A. Reich (eds.) 185–210. Berlin/New York: Mouton de Gruyter.
Choi, Soonja
    1988   The semantic development of negation: A cross-linguistic longitudinal study. *Journal of Child Language* 15: 517–531.
    1991   Early acquisition of epistemic meanings in Korean: A study of sentence-ending suffixes in the spontaneous speech of three children. *First Language* 11: 93–119.
    1995   Early acquisition of epistemic sentence-ending modal forms and functions in Korean children. In *Modality in Grammar and Discourse*, J. Bybee and S. Fleischman (eds.), 165–204. Amsterdam: Benjamins.
Choi, Soonja and Ayhan Aksu-Koç
    1996   Development of modality in Korean and Turkish: A crosslinguistic comparison. In *Perspectives in Language Acquisition: Selected Papers from the VIIth International Congress for the Study of Child Language*, A. Aksu-Koç, E. Erguvanli-Taylan, A. Ozsoy and A. Kuntay (eds.), 123–138. Istanbul: Bogazici University Printhouse.
Clancy, Patricia
    1985   The acquisition of Japanese. In *The Crosslinguistic Study of Language Acquisition, vol. 1*, D. I. Slobin (ed.), 373–524. Hillsdale: Lawrence Erlbaum Associates.
Clancy, Patricia, Noriko Akatsuka, and Susan Strauss
    1997   Deontic modality and conditionality in discourse: A cross-linguistic study of adult speech to young children. In *Directions in Functional Linguistics*, A. Kamio (ed.), 19–57. Amsterdam: Benjamins.
Coates, Jennifer
    1988   The acquisition of the meanings of modality in children aged eight and twelve. *Journal of Child Language* 15: 425–434.
De Villiers, Jill and Jennie Pyers
    1997   Complementing cognition: The relationship between language and theory of mind. *Boston University Conference on Language Development* 21: 136–147.

De Villiers, Jill and Peter de Villers
　2000　　Linguistic determination and the understanding of false beliefs. In *Children's Reasoning and the Mind*, P. Mitchell and K. J. Riggs (eds.), 191–228. East Essex: Psychology Press.
Farrar, Jeffrey and Lisa Maag
　2002　　Early language development and the emergence of a theory of mind. *First Language* 22: 197–213.
Hirst, William and Joyce Weil
　1982　　Acquisition of epistemic and deontic meaning of modals. *Journal of Child Language* 9: 659–666.
Gee, Julie
　1985　　An interpretive approach to the study of modality: What child language can tell the linguist. *Studies in Language* 9: 197–229.
Gee, Julie and Iskendar Savasir
　1985　　On the use of *will* and *gonna*: Toward a description of activity-types for child language. *Discourse Processes* 8: 143–175.
Gerhardt, Julie
　1991　　The meaning and use of the modals *hafta*, *needta* and *wanna* in children's speech. *Journal of Pragmatics* 16: 531–590.
Gonsalves, Joanna and Rachel J. Falmagne
　1999　　Cognitive prerequisites for modal verb acquisition. *Boston University Conference on Language Development* 23: 204–215.
Gopnik, Alison and Janet Astington
　1988　　Children's understanding of representational change in its relation to the understanding of false belief and the appearance-reality distinction. *Child Development* 59: 26–37.
Guo, Jiansheng
　1995　　The interactional basis of the Mandarin Modal *néng* 'can.' In *Modality in Grammar and Discourse*, J. Bybee and S. Fleischman (eds.), 205–238. Amsterdam: Benjamins.
Kim, Y. J.
　1997. The acquisition of Korean. In *The Crosslinguistic Study of Language Acquisition, Vol. 4*, D. I. Slobin (ed.), 335–443. Mahwah: Lawrence Erlbaum Associates.
Kuczaj, Stan and Mary Daly
　1979　　The development of hypothetical reference in the speech of young children. *Journal of Child Language* 6: 563–579.
Lee, Hyo Sang
　1991　　Tense, aspect, and modality: a discourse-pragmatic analysis of verbal affixes in Korean from a typological perspective. Unpublished doctoral dissertation. University of California at Los Angeles.

Lee, Thomas Hun-Tak and Ann Law
    2000   Evidential final particles in child Cantonese. In *The Proceedings of the Thirtieth Annual Child Language Research Forum,* E. V. Clark (ed.), 131–138. Stanford: Center for the Study of Language and Information.

Moore, Chris, Kiran Pure and David Furrow
    1990   Children's understanding of the modal expression of speaker certainty and uncertainty and its relation to the development of a representational theory of mind. *Child Development* 61: 722–730.

O'Neill, Daniela and Cristina Atance
    2000   'Maybe my daddy give me a big piano': The development of children's use of modals to express uncertainty. *First Language* 20: 29–52.

Papafragou, Anna
    1998   The acquisition of modality: Implications for theories of semantic representation. *Mind and Language* 13: 370–399.

Pea, Roy and Ronald Mawby
    1984   Semantics of modal auxiliary verb uses by preschool children. *Proceedings of the International Congress for the Study of Child Language* 2: 204–219.

Reilly, Judy
    1986   The acquisition of temporals and conditionals. In *On Conditionals,* E. C. Traugott, A. ter Meulen, J. S. Reilly and C. A. Ferguson (eds.), 309–332. Cambridge: Cambridge University Press.

Shatz, Marilyn, Henry Wellman and Sharon Silber
    1983   The acquisition of mental verbs: A systematic investigation of the first reference to mental state. *Cognition* 14: 301–321.

Shatz, Marilyn and Sharon Wilcox
    1991   Constraints on the acquisition of English modals. In *Perspectives on Language and Thought: Interrelations in Development,* S. Gelman and J. Byrnes (eds.), 319–353. Cambridge: Cambridge University Press.

Shepard, Susan
    1993   The acquisition of modality in Antiguan Creole. In *Modality in Language Acquisition,* N. Dittmar and A. Reich (eds.), 171–184. Berlin/ New York: Mouton de Gruyter.

Slobin, Dan I.
    1973   Cognitive prerequisites for the development of grammar. In *Studies of Child Language Development,* C. A. Ferguson and D. I. Slobin (eds.), 175–208. New York: Holt, Rinehard and Winston.

Smoczyńska, Magdalena
   1993   The acquisition of Polish modal verbs. In *Modality in Language Acquisition*, Dittmar and A. Reich (eds.), 145–170. Berlin/New York: Mouton de Gruyter.

Stephany, Ursula
   1986   Modality. In *Language Acquisition*, P. Fletcher and M. Garman (eds.), 375–400. Cambridge: Cambridge University Press.
   1993   Modality in first language acquisition: The state of the art. In *Modality in Language Acquisition,* N. Dittmar and A. Reich (eds.), 133–144. Berlin/New York: Mouton de Gruyter.

Torr, Jane
   1998   The development of modality in the pre-school years: Language as a vehicle for understanding possibilities and obligations in everyday life. *Functions of Language* 5: 157–178.

Watson, Anne, Kathleen Painter, and Marc Bornstein
   2001   Longitudinal relations between 2-year-olds' language and 4-year-olds' theory of mind. *Journal of Cognition and Developmet* 2: 449–457.

Wells, Gordon
   1979   Learning and using the auxiliary verb in English. In *Language Development*, V. Lee (ed.), 250–270. London: Croom Helm.

Wells, Gordon
   1985   *Language Development in the Pre-School Years*. Cambridge: Cambridge University Press.

Zoh, M. H.
   1981   *Hankwuk Atong-uy Ene Whoyktuk Yenkwu* [A Study of Language Acquisition in Korean Children]. Seoul: Seoul National University Press.

Modal expression in Valley Zapotec

Pamela Munro

1. Introduction

Tlacolula Valley Zapotec (or, as I will call this language here, *Valley Zapotec*)[1] aptly illustrates de Haan's contention (this volume) that there are many disparate ways that modal concepts may be expressed, since Valley Zapotec expresses basic modal concepts through verb inflection, by auxiliary verbs, and with a second-position adverbial clitic. In this paper I will first survey the ways in which modality is expressed in Valley Zapotec. I will then look more briefly at the systems of core modality in English, the Yuman language Mohave, and the Muskogean language Chickasaw, in each of which there is a core group of morphemes that express both deontic and epistemic modality. In contrast to these languages, Valley Zapotec displays an unusual asymmetry, since deontic and epistemic modality are expressed with separate grammatical mechanisms, and there does not seem to be a single isolable category of core modal morphemes.

In identifying the expressions of modality within the grammar of Valley Zapotec, I will adopt the broad view of modality, or mood,[2] of Chung and Timberlake (1985: 241), for whom

> mood characterizes the actuality of an event by comparing the event world(s) to a reference world, termed the actual world. An event can simply be actual (more precisely, the event world is identical to the actual world); the event can be hypothetically possible (the event world is not identical to the actual world); the event may be imposed by the speaker on the addressee; and so on. Whereas there is basically one way for an event to be actual, there are numerous ways that an event can be less than completely actual.

For Chung and Timberlake, then, mood "is concerned principally with different types of non-actuality" (1985: 241).

Arguably, one might also include simple negative sentences in this survey, since clearly any negative sentence is also concerned with events that occur or states that hold in a world that is different from the actual world.

While I will discuss some negative structures here, my main concern in this paper will be with what one might call *independent modality*: non-actuality expressed without any overt operator to determine that modality. In a negative sentence, the negative morpheme determines the non-actuality of its complement, so any explicit mark of non-actuality on that complement can be argued to be dependent rather than independent: ordinary negated clauses are not independently modal. Similarly, in an English sentence like *I want to go*, the infinitival complementizer could certainly be analyzed as a marker of non-actual clausal modality. However, I will consider that any modality attached to the infinitive in this English sentence is dependent on the semantics of the verb *want*.

A further distinction that I will be concerned with in this paper is that between deontic modality and epistemic modality. I follow Chung and Timberlake (1985: 247) in using *deontic* to include both dynamic modality and the more restricted category of deontic modality defined by Nuyts (this volume), since the distinction between the latter two categories is not relevant to the data I consider here.

Below I first survey modal expressions in Valley Zapotec and then present the systems of core modality in three other unrelated languages, English, Mohave, and Chickasaw. Finally, I return to the position of Valley Zapotec within a typology of modal systems.

2.   Expressions of modality in Valley Zapotec

2.1. Modality in the Valley Zapotec "aspect" system

As in other Zapotec languages, verbs in Valley Zapotec consist minimally of a base plus an inflectional prefix, typically referred to in the literature as an *aspect prefix*. But such markers are used to show not only aspect, but also modality. Further, as Lee (1999) argues, their syntactic distribution also indicates tense. Most Valley Zapotec verbs have either six or seven different "aspects," exemplified in the paradigms in (1), using the terminology of Munro and Lopez et al. (1999); the aspect prefixes are in bold:[3]

(1) Habitual: **rzh**:ùu'nny 'runs'   **ra**'ahcw   'puts on (a shirt)'
     Perfective: **bzh**:ùu'nny 'ran'   **gwu**'aht   'put on…'
     Progressive: **ca**zh:ùu'nny 'is running' **ca**ya'ahcw 'is putting on…'
     Neutral: —   **n**aa'cw   'is wearing…'

Irrealis: **y**zh:ùu'nny 'will run'   **ga**'acw 'will put on…'
Subjunctive: **n**zh:ùu'nny '(if...) had run' **n**ya'ahcw '(if...) had put on...'
Definite: **x**:ùu'nny 'will surely run' **za**'ahcw 'will surely put on...'

(1) illustrates the fact that both prefixes and verb bases can display considerable irregularity. In most analyses the Habitual stem is taken as basic in some sense (this is the form usually listed in dictionaries, for example).[4] Verb stems like these can be used without change with noun subjects in sentences like those in (2):[5]

(2)   a. Ca-zh:ùu'nny bèe'cw.
          prog-run   dog
          'The dog is running.'

      b. Gw-u'aht   Jwaany cotoony.
          perf-put.on Juan   shirt
          'Juan put on the shirt.'

      c. Y-tòo'oh Gye'eihlly ca'rr.
          irr-sell Mike   car
          'Mike will sell the car.' (Lee 199: 14, ex. 41)[6]

Valley Zapotec is a VSO language, although most constituents can appear in a focus position before the verb. Because Valley Zapotec has no case marking, an initial focused noun phrase (identified in the translation with small capitals) in many transitive sentences is ambiguous:

(3)   Jwaany gw-àa'izy Beed.
      Juan   perf-hit   Pedro
      'JUAN hit Pedro'; 'Pedro hit JUAN.'

2.2. Modals vs. non-modals in Valley Zapotec

The Habitual, Perfective, Progressive, and Neutral aspects have been considered non-modal aspects, while the Irrealis, Subjunctive, and Definite are modal aspects, following Lee (1999).[7] Specifying exactly what *modal* and *non-modal* mean within this system presents a certain challenge. The non-modal aspects are used to describe events "taken to occur in the actual world of the speaker and listener" (Lee 1999: 14). Lee characterizes the Habitual as "used to denote ongoing or regularly repeated states or events," the Progressive as "immediately ongoing events or states," and the Perfective as "used to denote completed actions" (1999: 13). The Neutral is used with a restricted number of verbs, and generally indicates a state resulting from the action of those verbs. The translations in (1) illustrate these meanings of the non-modal aspects.

As Lee points out, a completed action shown by the Perfective may actually be located in the future, as in (4):

(4)   Yzh:ii   chih   y-zëhnny=a', al   **b**-da'uh Gye'eihlly.
      tomorrow when irr-arrive=1s already **perf**-eat Mike.
      'When I arrive tomorrow, Mike will have already eaten.'

(Lee 1999: 13, ex. 38)

As example (4) illustrates, pronominal subjects are expressed with clitic pronouns such as first person singular =*a* ' following the verb.

Lee adopts a somewhat different definition of what constitutes modality from the one I outlined earlier. She identifies modal readings as "expressing the relationship between an event and the actual world of the speaker and listener" (1999: 14), distinguishing two types of readings of the Valley Zapotec modal aspects, which she terms *modal* and *non-modal* readings. She considers as non-modal interpretations of currently unrealized events that the speaker nonetheless believes will certainly occur in his own actual world. Thus, (2c), even though it is in the Irrealis, refers to "an event assumed to take place at a later time in the actual world containing Mike and the speaker. The proposition of Mike selling the car at a later time is presumed to be a real event in the real world: the speaker would not have uttered this sentence if she or he did not believe it would be true that Mike would sell his car" (Lee 1999: 14). Thus it is technically non-modal, even though unrealized (cf. also (4); I return to the meaning of future sentences like (2c) below.) Lee (1999: 14) cites examples such as (5), in which the Irrealis is used on a complement of matrix Habitual 'want': this illustrates what she would call a modal reading of the Irrealis aspect, because the "truth value is not fixed in the actual world" (Lee 1999: 215):

(5)   R-càa'z   Gye''eihlly **y**-tòo'oh ca'rr.
      hab-want Mike   **irr**-sell car
      'Mike wants to sell the car.'

Here,

> the event of Mike selling the car does not take place the actual world in
> which Mike exists (since it's a potential, rather than actual, event) but rather
> in the set of possible worlds denoted by Mike's desire. In contrast to [(2c)]
> above, in which the event of Mike selling the car at some future time is pre-
> sumed to be true, in this case, the event is expressed as possible, but the
> speaker and listener are not committed to believing it will (or won't) actually
> take place. (Lee 1999: 15)

My task is to describe grammatical devices for expressing non-actuality in
Valley Zapotec, and so I will not distinguish modal (5) and non-modal (2)
uses of the Irrealis aspect, because both concern non-actual events. But, in
this task, we nonetheless must respect, as Lee does, that there is not a precise overlap between modal interpretation and modal aspect. In (4), the act
of eating by Mike is not yet actual and is expressed in the Perfective because it is completed with respect to another event, but neither is an event
the speaker could actually have observed.

2.3. Irrealis in Valley Zapotec

Lee notes (1999: 15) that the Irrealis is used not only in the complements of
intensional verbs, such as *rcàa'z* 'wants' (5), but also in the complements
of modal verbs such as *nàa pahr* 'must, has to' in (6):

(6) Nàa pahr **ch**-a'=a'.
     cop to **irr**-go=1s
     'I have to go'; 'I should go.'

Another important use of the Irrealis is in plural and various types of formal
imperatives (including negative imperatives). The Valley Zapotec pronominal system distinguishes four second persons, singular vs. plural and informal
vs. formal. The latter opposition is merged in plural imperatives such as
(7), however, which begin with the plural hortative particle *u'all*, followed
by an Irrealis verb:

(7) U'all **y**-nnìi'zh(-làa')   li'ebr nàa'.
     hort.p **irr**-give.to.non.3(-please) book pron.1s
     '(Please) give me the book [plural].'

Greater politeness can be shown in many cases with the verb suffix *-làa'*, roughly 'please.'

Singular formal imperatives, as in (8), look like future sentences with a second person singular formal subject:

(8)   **Y**-nnìi'zh-làa'=yuu'   li'ebr nàa'.
      irr-give.to.non.3-please=2s.form book pron.1s
      'Please give me the book [formal].'

An even more deferential imperative begins with a formal imperative of the verb *rsaguehll* 'is so good as to,' followed by another imperative form:[8]

(9)   a. **Y**-saguehll=yuu'   **y**-nnìi'zh-làa'=yuu'   li'ebr
         irr-be.so.good=2s.form **irr**-give.to.non.3-please=2s.form book
         nàa'.
         pron.1s
         'Would you be so good as to please give me the book [formal].'

      b. **Y**-saguehll=yuu'   **m**-nnìi'zh-làa'   li'ebr nàa.'
         irr-be.so.good=2s.form **perf**-give.to.non.3-please book pron.1s
         'Would you be so good as to please give me the book[formal].'

The Irrealis is also used for expressions of wishes following particles, such as *u'c*, as in (10a); this may be a shortened form of the conventionalized wish in (10b):

(10) a. U'c   cwìi'=a'   rrie'f.
         hopefully **irr**.get=1s raffle
         'Hopefully I'll win the raffle.'

      b. U'c   nnah   Dyooz cwìi'=a'   rrie'f.
         hopefully neut.say God   **irr**.get=1s raffle
         'Hopefully I'll win the raffle.' ('Hopefully God says I'll win the raffle.')

2.4.   Definite in Valley Zapotec

In contrast to the Irrealis, the Definite is used in matrix clauses to specify futures that the speaker is certain will occur, as in (11):

(11) **S**-tòo'oh Gye'eihlly ca'rr.
       def-sell Mike   car
      'Mike will surely sell the car.'

Lee claims that Definites are "licensed by Mood features defining these events as necessarily true – that is, in all possible worlds imagined by the speaker, it is true that the event described by the Definite-marked verb will occur" (1999: 240). She regards Definites as encoding "a different type of modality: that of necessity, rather than possibility" (1999: 242). I return to the meaning of the Definite future below.

Definite verbs, unlike verbs in other aspects, do not allow subjects or objects to be contrastively focused (Lee 1999: 16). Compare (12a), which shows focus on the subject of an Irrealis clause, with (12b), which demonstrates that focus is not possible in a Definite clause:

(12) a. Gye'eihlly **y**-tòo'oh ca'rr.
          Mike   **irr**-sell car
          'MIKE will sell the car'. (cf. (2c))

      b. *Gye'eihlly **s**-tòo'oh ca'rr.
          *Mike   **def**-sell car
          'MIKE will surely sell the car'. (cf. (11))

Lee argues that the Definite verb raises to the focus position itself, and thus blocks any other element from occupying this position and "contributes to the emphatic reading of the sentence" (1999: 235).

Definite verbs are often degraded or ungrammatical when negated (Lee 1999: 235–36), which Lee argues follows from the status of the Definite as "necessarily true" (1999: 240). Moreover, only Definite verbs can be used in questions introduced by the particle *uu*, generally used when speakers are expecting a positive response (1999: 18): thus, (13a), with the Definite, is a felicitous *uu* question, while (13b), with the Irrealis, is not.

(13) a. Uu   **z**-a'uw=ùu'   beèe'l?
          Q.aff **def**-eat=2s.inf meat
          'Will you eat meat?' (Lee 1999: 18; ex. 56)

      b. *Uu **g**-a'uw=ùu'   beèe'l?
          Q.aff **irr**-eat-2s.inf meat
          'Will you eat meat?' (Lee 1999: 18; ex. 57)

2.5. Subjunctive in Valley Zapotec

The third modal aspect is the Subjunctive. This form is rare to non-existent in matrix clauses. Lee (1999) cites simple sentence uses of the Subjunctive such as (14), but in fact my collaborator invariably characterizes such sentences as "incomplete":

(14) **N**-tòo'oh Gye'eihlly c'arr.
      subj-sell Mike   car
      'Mike was going to sell the car (but didn't).' (Lee 1999: 19, ex. 62)

Whether or not (14) is complete as a full sentence, however, it clearly has a non-actual, thus modal, reference. One Subjunctive verb that is conventionally used in main clauses for the expression of wishes is *nyu'clàaa'z* 'would have liked, wanted to (but couldn't),' but even in examples such as (15), it is most common for such sentences to be complex, including a reason or other background:

(15) Benito Juarez b-zhùu'nny la'ahzh:=nìi'   Me'ijy
      Benito Juarez perf-run   native.pueblo=anap Mexico

      chih **ny-u'clàa'z**=rëng n-guhty=rëng lài'.
      when **subj-want**=3p.prox subj-kill=3p.prox pron.3s.dist

      'BENITO JUAREZ fled his native country of Mexico when they wanted to kill him.'

The most common use of the Subjunctive may be in negative past statements such as (16a), which are, however, reported as synonymous with negative Perfectives like (16b) (though, as Lee reports (1999: 19–20), speakers appear to volunteer Subjunctive past negatives more often than Perfective ones):[9]

(16) a. Que'ity **n**-tòo'oh=di' Gye'eihlly ca'rr.
          neg   **subj**-sell=pt Mike   car
          'Mike didn't sell the car.'

      b. Que'ity **b**-tòo'oh=di' Gye'eihlly ca'rr.
          neg   **perf**-sell=di' Mike   car
          'Mike didn't sell the car.'

If the use of the Subjunctive here reflects older usage, it is easy to see why less conservative speakers might assume a Perfective could be used in a negative sentence, since all other aspects can freely occur negated.

Simple conditional sentences in Valley Zapotec use *bàall* 'if' and, with non-present reference, the Irrealis in both clauses, as in (17):

(17) Bàall **g**-àann=a' lòo'=ng   **gu**-e'ipy=a' la'anng.
     if   **irr**-see=1s face=3s.prox **irr**-tell=1s pron.3s.prox
     'If I see him I'll tell him.'

In contrast, counterfactual conditionals use hypothetical *ballnah* 'if,' frequently with the Subjunctive in both the 'if' and 'then' clauses, as in (18):

(18) Ballnah **ny**-àann=a' lòo'=ng   **ny**-e'ipy=a' la'anng.
     if.hyp **subj**-see=1s face=3s.prox **subj**-tell=1s pron.3s.prox
     'If I had seen him I would have told him.'

However, just as the Perfective may replace the Subjunctive in negative sentences such as (16b), counterfactuals may also have Perfective in the 'then' clause (19a) or in both clauses (19b) (though not, apparently, only in the 'if' clause):

(19) a. Ballnah **ny**-a'c-gài' ny-iia Gye'eihlly loh wnyààa',
        if.hyp **subj**-be-five subj-go Mike   to healer

        a   **b**-ya'ahc   Gye'eihlly.
        already **perf**-get.cured Mike

        'If Mike had gone to the curandero a fifth time, he would have been cured.'

     b. Ballnah **g**-uhcgyèiny x:-mu'ully Gye'eihlly, a   **b**-èèi'ny
        if.hyp **perf**-accumulate poss-money Mike   already **perf**-do

        Gye'eihlly gaan a   **b**-cweeby x:-carre'ed=e'eh Gye'eihlly.
        Mike   gain already perf-renew poss-wagon=dim Mike

        'If Mike's money had accumulated (i.e., if Mike had accumulated more money), he would have been able to replace his little wagon.' [10]

This occurrence of the Perfective rather than the Subjunctive in both clauses of counterfactuals, then, is another use of the Perfective that is clearly non-actual, like the Perfective's appearance in future completive clauses such as (4).

The final use of the Subjunctive is in complements of intensional verbs and certain modal auxiliaries with past reference. The 'kill' complement of the Subjunctive verb *nyu'clààa'z* 'would have liked' in (15) illustrates the first case; (20) illustrates the second:

(20) Nàa pahr **ny**-a'=a'.
     cop to   **subj**-go=1s
     'I should have gone.'

As Lee observes, the Subjunctive often seems to be "a past-tense analogue to the Irrealis" (Lee 1999: 230). Past negatives and counterfactual conditionals present alternations between Subjunctive and the usual past expressed by the Perfective. These last suggest that in replacing Subjunctives with Perfectives, Valley Zapotec may be following the path of English, where subjunctive forms are all but defunct, with past subjunctive occurring exclusively in singular counterfactual constructions like *if I were*, which is regularly produced by many speakers as *if I was* (since all other past subjunctives are indistinguishable from the past).[11]

2.6. Deontic vs. epistemic in Valley Zapotec

The uses of the Perfective and Irrealis aspects to express imperatives and the Irrealis in wishes are clearly deontic. It is harder to classify the future uses of the Definite and Irrealis on a deontic-epistemic scale, however.

Out of context, speakers usually translate English simple futures with Irrealis rather than Definite verbs: thus, a future car sale by Mike might be more likely to be mentioned with (2c) rather than (11). When questioned about such pairs of sentences, however, speakers report that Irrealis future statements such as (2c) are relatively uncertain (you would like to believe it will happen, but you do not know for sure), whereas, just as Lee says (1999: 240), they describe Definite future statements as absolutely certain. Since Definite futures express the speaker's assessment of the necessity or certainty of a future event, this use must be epistemic. The Irrealis future does not represent a wish or the expression of capability, however, but is simply a weaker degree of epistemic modality, that of possibility rather than necessity. Although the modal aspects thus have both deontic and epistemic uses, there seems to be no case in which any of the Valley Zapotec aspects is ambiguous between epistemic and deontic readings in any particular discourse or syntactic context.

2.7. The expression of deontic modality with Valley Zapotec auxiliary verbs

The principal way in which independent deontic modality is expressed in Valley Zapotec is with auxiliary verbs, such as *rquìii'ny* 'must' (21), *nàa pahr* 'must, have to, should' (22) (already exemplified in (20) above), or *rìi'lle'eh* 'can, may' (23):

(21) **R-quìii'ny** g-àa'p bùunny mùuully tye'nn ch-iia bùunny
     hab-need irr-have person money so.that irr-go person
     làad=ih.
     side=dem.dist
     'One [a person] must have money in order for one to go to the States [to that side].'

(22) **Nàa pahr** gy-ii'ah Rrube'ng rmùudy.
     cop to   irr-drink Ruben   medicine
     'Ruben has to take the medicine.'

(23) **R-ìi'lle'eh** r-ùa'll   Rrube'ng Dìi'zhtiily.
     hab-can   hab-read Ruben   Spanish
     'Ruben can read Spanish.'

2.8. Auxiliary status

Expressions such as *nàa pahr*, *rquìii'ny*, and *rìi'lle'eh* are auxiliaries for two reasons.[12] First, in contrast to the normal Valley Zapotec pattern, the subject in sentences (22–23) or the first clause of (21) follows the second, main (complement) verb rather than the first modal verb. Thus, sequences like *nàa pahr gyìi'ah*, *rquìii'ny gàa'p*, and *rìi'lle'eh rùa'll* work like matrix verb phrases. Second, and perhaps more strikingly, the subject or another clausal element in auxiliary sentences can appear in sentence initial focus position, before the whole auxiliary-plus-complement phrase, as in (24–25): focus movement is often facilitated by the presence of the focus particle *làa'*:

(24) a. (Làa') Rrube'ng **nàa pahr** gy-ìi'ah   rmùudy.
       (foc) Ruben   cop to   irr-drink medicine
       'RUBEN has to take the medicine.'

   b. (Làa') rmùudy   **nàa pahr** gy-ìi'ah Rrube'ng.
       (foc) medicine cop to   irr-drink Ruben
       'Ruben has to take the MEDICINE.'

(25) a. (Làa') Rrube'ng **r-ìi'lle'eh** r-ùa'll   Dìi'zhtiily.
       (foc) Ruben   hab-can   hab-read Spanish
       'RUBEN can read Spanish.'

   b. (Làa') Dìi'zhtiily **r-ìi'lle'eh** r-ùa'll   Rrube'ng.
       (foc) Spanish   hab-can   hab-read Ruben.
       'Ruben can read SPANISH.'

The data in (24–25) contrast with the situation with non-auxiliary two-verb constructions, in which it is impossible to focus an element from the lower (second) clause. Thus, consider the three types of complement structures in (26–28):

(26) a. **M-nàa** Gye'eihlly gw-àa'izy Jwaany Beed.
       perf-see Mike   perf-hit   Juan   Pedro
       'Mike saw Juan hit Pedro.'

   b. (Làa') Gye'eihlly **m-nàa** gw-àa'izy Jwaany Beed.
       (foc) Mike   perf-see perf-hit   Juan   Pedro
       'MIKE saw Juan hit Pedro.'

   c. *(Làa') Jwaany **m-nàa** Gye'eihlly gw-àa'izy Beed.
       *(foc) Juan   perf-see Mike   perf-hit   Pedro
       *'Mike saw JUAN hit Pedro.'; *'Mike saw Pedro hit JUAN.'
       (OK as 'JUAN saw MIKE hit Pedro' or 'JUAN saw Pedro hit MIKE.')

(26a) is a normal complex structure with a perception verb (Valley Zapotec has very few overt complementizers). It is fine to focus the subject of the higher verb *mnàa* 'saw' (26b), but impossible for either the subject or the object of the lower clause to appear at the beginning of the sentence (26c) (although, as the acceptable readings of (26c) show, such elements may be focused within their own clause).

   Examples (27a) and (28a) are same and different subject complement structures with the higher verb *rcàa'z* 'wants.' The corresponding (b) sentences show, again, that it is fine to focus the subject of 'wants,' but, as the remaining examples indicate, an element of the Irrealis clause following *rcàa'z* may not be focused:[13]

(27) a. **R-càa'z** Rrube'ng g-acbèe Dìi'zhtiily.
       hab-want Ruben   irr-know Spanish
       'Ruben wants to learn Spanish.'

   b. (Làa') Rrube'ng **r-càa'z** g-acbèe   Dìi'zhtiily.
      (foc)   Ruben   hab-want irr-know Spanish
      'RUBEN wants to learn Spanish.'

   c. *(Làa') Dìi'zhtiily **r-càa'z** Rrube'ng g-acbèe.
      *(foc) Spanish   hab-want   Ruben   irr-know
      *'Ruben wants to learn SPANISH.'

(28) a. **R-càa'z** Emily g-acbèe   Rrube'ng Dìi'zhtiily.
       hab-want Emily irr-know Ruben   Spanish
       'Emily wants Ruben to learn Spanish.'

   b. (Làa') Emily **r-càa'z**   g-acbèe   Rrube'ng Dìi'zhtiily.
      (foc)   Emily hab-want   irr-know Ruben   Spanish
      'EMILY wants Ruben to learn Spanish.'

   c. *(Làa') Rrube'ng **r-càa'z**   Emily g-acbèe   Dìi'zhtiily.
      *(foc) Ruben   hab-want Emily irr-know Spanish
      *'Emily wants RUBEN to learn Spanish.'
      (OK as 'RUBEN wants EMILY to learn Spanish.')

   d. *(Làa') Dìi'zhtiily **r-càa'z**   Emily g-acbèe   Rrube'ng.
      *(foc) Spanish   hab-want Emily irr-know Ruben
      *'Emily wants Ruben to learn SPANISH.'

Although *rquìii'ny* and *nàa pahr* 'must,' on the one hand, and *rìi'lle'eh* 'can,' on the other, are all auxiliary verbs that express independent modality, they represent two quite different classes of auxiliaries,[14] generally reflecting the distinction between modal necessity (or obligation) and modal possibility (or capability). Necessity auxiliaries like *rquìii'ny* and *nàa pahr* must have complements in one of the modal aspects, either Irrealis, as in (21–22), or Subjunctive. Possibility auxiliaries like *rìi'lle'eh* work quite differently, since with them the auxiliary and complement must agree (or be compatible) in tense[15] (for example, in (22) *rìi'lle'eh* and its complement *rùa'll* are both Habitual).

2.9. Necessity auxiliaries

Here are some additional examples of necessity auxiliaries (which express 'must,' 'should,' 'has to,' 'is supposed to'), each with an Irrealis complement:

(29) **R-yàall**   y-càa'ah Gye'eihlly te'ihby da'   yuhuh.
     hab-deserve **irr**-get   Mike   one   piece land
     'Mike should get a plot of land.'

(30) **R-uhny-gaan ch**-iia bùunny scweel chih   nàa bùunny mnìi'iny.
     hab-do-gain   **irr**-go person school when cop person child
     'One should go to school when one is a child.'

(31) **Nàa cwe'eenn g**-a'uw=ëhmm   tyo'p gweell te'ihby zh:ih.
     cop account   **irr**-eat=3s.anim two   time   one   day
     'He [an animal or small child] is supposed to eat two times a day.'

As noted above, auxiliary verbs of the necessity class may be used in a past sense with their complement in the Subjunctive:

(32) **R-quìii'ny ny**-a'uw=a'.
     hab-need **subj**-eat=1s
     'I should have eaten.'

(33) Que'ity **nàa**=di' **pahr** ny-a'uw=a'.
     neg   cop=pt   to   **subj**-eat=1s
     'I shouldn't have eaten.'

(34) **R-uhny-gaan ny**-iia   Gye'eihlly scweel chih   g-uhc Gye'eihlly
     hab-do-gain **subj**-go Mike   school when perf-be Mike
     mnìi'iny.
     child
     'Mike should have gone to school when he was a child.'

Only the use of the Subjunctive complement locates the reference of the modal verb in the past. Modal auxiliary verbs such as *rquìii'ny* 'needs to, must,' *ryàall* 'deserves to, should,' *ruhnygaan* 'should' (literally 'succeeds'), *nàa cwe'eenn* 'is supposed to, has to' (literally 'is the account'), and *nàa pahr* 'must' (literally 'is to') are close to fixed forms. Those that look like normal verbs, such as the first words in (23–25), only occur in the Habitual (*r-* aspect), while other auxiliary expressions have some other invariant structure (*nàa pahr* and *nàa cwe'enn*, for example, are copular in form).

Necessity verbs have several other special characteristics. Many of them have more basic non-modal uses (in which they may occur with an unrestricted set of aspectual prefixes); their modal uses are metaphorical or lexically derived. Also, although I have called this the *necessity class of auxiliaries*, there are other verbs in the same structural class that have an aspectual rather than modal sense,[16] such as *rahclu'ch* 'struggles to,' *rìe'ddihzy* 'just starts to,' and *a gùall* 'is just about to,' as in (35):

(35) **A   gù-all   ch**-iia Maar.
     already perf-reach **irr**-go Bulmaro
     'Bulmaro is just about to go.'

2.10. Possibility auxiliaries

The two main possibility auxiliaries besides *rìi'lle'eh* 'can, be able to, be allowed to' (23) are *rahc* (36), a verb whose meaning in this construction is identical to that of *rìi'lle'eh*, but which in non-auxiliary uses means 'be,' and *rahcgaan* 'be able to, succeed in, manage to' (36):

(36) **R-ahc r**-bèe'b Beed gùu'ann.
     hab-be **hab**-ride Pedro bull
     'Pedro can ride the bull.'

(37) Chi'cy **r-ahc-gaan r**-uny=a'   ecsplicaar xi   behll=ih nàa mejoor...
     then   hab-be-gain **hab**-do=1s explain what fish=dist cop best
     'So I was [habitually] able to explain which of those fish were best...'

Each of these auxiliaries may occur in different aspects, as in (38–40), with the following complement verb agreeing in tense:

(38) Zi'cy.nàa estaad rèe' a'xta' nih que'ity r-àaly   rèe'
     in   state this even rel neg   hab- be.born here
     z-alle'eh g-a'c[17] gobernadoor.
     def-can **irr**-be governor
     'In this state, even someone who wasn't born here can be governor.'

(39) Que'ity=di' bentaan **ch-ìi'lle'eh** y-zhye'illy.
      neg=pt   window **irr**-can   **irr**-open
      'The window can't open [i.e., the window won't be able to be opened].'

(40) Chih   b-zee'nny=ëhnn Tijwa'ann **g-uhc.gaan**   m-nnìi'-nèe=nn
      when   perf-arrive=1p Tijuana   **perf**-be-gain **perf**-say-with=1p
      Lu'c   steeby pohr tele'fonoh.
      Lucas again   by   telephone
      'When we arrived in Tijuana, we were able to talk with Lucas again
      by telephone.'

As with the necessity auxiliaries, the class of possibility auxiliaries has
some members whose meaning is aspectual rather than modal, such as
rgàa'ah 'happens to,' *rluhahzh* 'finishes,' and *rzalloh* 'begins,' as in (41):[18]

(41) A   g-uhc   x:o'p iihahz nih **b-zalloh**   **ca**-cwaa'=nn
      already perf-be six   year   rel **perf**-begin prog-write=1p
      dìi'zh   rèe'.
      language this
      'It was six years ago that we began writing this language.'

All the modal auxiliaries discussed in this section express deontic modality.
We can identify the necessity and possibility auxiliaries themselves as the
modal operators in their clauses, used with modal aspect complements in
the Irrealis and Subjunctive referring to current and past unaccomplished
events and states. In contrast, complements of the possibility auxiliaries are
only rarely marked as non-actual. This sort of weak (dynamic) possibility
modality is comparable to English *Do you see that?*, meaning 'Can you see
that?', or *The baby is walking*, meaning 'The baby can walk.'

2.11. Epistemic modality in Valley Zapotec

As with many languages, Valley Zapotec employs a number of grammatical
devices to express epistemic modality. Some epistemic notions are coded
by adverbs, such as *seguuar* 'surely' in (42):

(42) **Seguuar** bzyaàa'n   Li'eb lìu'.
      surely   opposite.sex.sibling Felipe pron.2s.inf
      'You must be Felipe's sister'; 'Surely you are Felipe's sister.'

There is also one Valley Zapotec auxiliary with epistemic modal content, *ràa'izybahg*, illustrated in (43):

(43) **R-àa'izy=bahg** zhyàaa'g   Jwaany loh ra wbwàaa'n.
     hab-hit=just   **neut**.associate Juan   in pl thief
     'Juan must be associated with the thieves.'

Ràai'izybahg, literally 'just hits,' expresses an epistemic 'must' reading, and is unusual in several ways. First, the Habitual-Neutral construction seen in (43) is characteristic of the possibility class of auxiliaries rather than the necessity class: 'must' auxiliaries otherwise require a complement in either the Irrealis or Subjunctive aspect. Second, this is the only case I know of in which an epistemic modal meaning is expressed with an auxiliary in Valley Zapotec. All the other modal auxiliaries discussed above express deontic modality. But *ràa'izybahg* cannot express deontic modality.

Still, the most common means of expressing epistemic modality is by the second position clitic *=zhyi'*, a member of one of several different classes of postclitics, including a group of "second position" (Wackernagel) clitics, as seen in (44). The clitic *=zhyi'* follows the first element of the sentence, regardless of its lexical class, whether that constituent is the verb (44a), the subject (44b), the object (44c), or an adverb (or something else) (44d), indicating the speaker's evaluation of the likelihood of the event of Mike's having eaten the grasshopper:

(44) a. B-da'uh=**zhyi'** Gye'eihlly bx:àady.
        perf-eat=epis Mike   grasshopper
        'Mike must have eaten the grasshopper.'

     b. Gye'ihlly=**zhyi'** b-da'uh bx:àady.
        Mike=epis   perf-eat grasshopper
        'MIKE must have eaten the grasshopper.'

     c. Bx:àady =**zhyi'**   b-da'uh Gye'eihlly.
        grasshopper=epis perf-eat Mike
        'Mike must have eaten the GRASSHOPPER.'

     d. Nài'=**zhyi'**   b-da'uh Gye'eihlly bx:àady.
        yesterday=epis perf-eat Mike   grasshopper
        'Mike must have eaten the grasshopper YESTERDAY.'

The second-position clitics generally express the speaker's evaluative comment on or reaction to a situation. In addition to *=zhyi'* (and its variant

=zhya'), they include *=bahg* 'just, really,' *=ihzy/=dihzy* 'only,' *=ga'* 'instead,' *=la'* 'usually,' *=za'* 'unexpectedly,' and *=zyu'* 'wow,' as well a few longer clitics (or, possibly, clitic combinations) that function as units, such as *=ahgza'* 'also, again.' These clitics are both simple and special, in the sense of Zwicky (1977), meaning both that they are phonologically dependent and that their position is morphosyntactically rather than lexically determined.

Second-position clitics precede certain other classes of Valley Zapotec clitics, such as pronominal clitics (45) and demonstrative clitics (46):

(45) B-da'uh-**zhy**=ëng   bxàady.
      perf-eat=epis=3s.prox   grasshopper
      'He must have eaten the grasshopper.'

(46) Bùunny=**zhy**=ahg   r-àa'p   mùully.
      person-epis=dem.prox   hab-have   money
      'This person might have money.'

Possessed phrases (47), prepositional phrases (48), and quantified noun phrases (49) are among the types of focused constituent that allow clitics like *=zhyi'* to appear in more than one position:[19]

(47) a. Behts=**zhyi'**   Gye'eihlly ca-yùa'll.
          brother.m.s.=epis Mike   prog-sing
          'MIKE'S BROTHER must be singing.'

      b. Behts   Gye'eihlly=**zhyi'** ca-yùa'll.   = (47a)
          brother.m.s. Mike=epis   prog-sing

(48) a. Cwe'eh=**zhyi'** Jwaany   zuga'=ng.
          beside=epis   Juan   neut.stand=3s. prox
          'He must be standing NEXT TO JUAN.'

      b. Cwe'eh Jwaany=**zhyi'** zuga'=ng.   = (48a)
          beside Juan=epis   neut.stand=3s.prox

(49) a. Chòonn=**zhyi'** bùunny m-nàa   lòo'=ng.
          three=epis   person perf-see face/to=3s.prox
          'THREE MEN must have seen him.'

      b. Chòonn bùunny=**zhyi'** m-nàa   lòo'=ng. = (49a)
          three   person=epis   perf-see face/to=3s.prox

Normally speakers report no difference in meaning between such variants.[20]

In the cases in (47–49), the two positions for the epistemic clitic are after the first word of the constituent (a) or at the end of the constituent (b) (following a cross-linguistic trend; cf., e.g., Anderson and Zwicky 2004). When a relative clause follows an initial focused noun, as in (50), however, the clitic may either follow that noun or the verb of the relative clause:[21]

(50) a. Bùunny=**zhyi'** nih m-nò=o'   loh=nìi'   r-àa'p mùully.
       person=epis   rel perf-see=2s.inf face=anap hab-have money
       'Maybe THE PERSON YOU SAW has money.'

   b. Bùunny nih m-nò=**zhy**=ùu'   loh=nìi'   r-àa'p mùully. =(50a)
       person rel perf-see=epis=2s.inf face=anap hab-have money

As the examples presented suggest, the meaning of epistemic *=zhyi'* is quite variable: it is very commonly translated with epistemic 'must,' but may also express epistemic 'might' or 'could' or adverbs like 'maybe,' 'probably,' or 'perhaps.' In every case, however, its meaning is not deontic: in a statement, it gives an indication of the speaker's confidence in the truth of the sentence. Thus, *=zhyi'* is very frequently used to indicate hesitancy (or politeness) in questions, as below:

(51) R-ùa'll=**zhyi'** Gye'eihlly èee?
     hab-sing=epis Mike   Q
     'Does Mike sing, by any chance?'

(52) X:a=**zhyi'** mo'od b-èi'ny=rëng?
     how=epis way   perf-do=3p.prox
     'How might they have done it?'

The *=zhyi'* clitic is apparently never used to indicate deontic modality in Valley Zapotec.

3.   Core modality

Nuyts (this volume) observes that "there is a significant crosslinguistic trend for languages to have a category of grammatical expression forms… which expresses precisely the set of [modal] meanings…and…that there is, again crosslinguistically, a systematic developmental relationship between these meanings in these forms." Thus, the expression of modality is often, or quite possibly usually, systematic, with an isolable category of core modal morphemes that share syntactic and morphological features with no other elements and can be used (at least in some cases) to express epistemic as well as deontic modality. The position of Valley Zapotec in this patterning of modality comes clearer in a comparison of the foregoing with what might be understood as *core modality* in three other languages: English, the Yuman language Mohave, and the Muskogean language Chickasaw. Each of these three languages has a set of modal morphemes that constitute a separate morphological category. These morphemes – usually, a rather restricted number – may combine with each other or with tense and aspect morphemes to express various modal concepts. Some or all of these morphemes may be used to express epistemic as well as deontic or modality. Certainly each language also has other elements with modal value as well, but the core of modal expression uses this isolable group of morphemes. Interestingly, both the Mohave and Chickasaw core modals present intriguing – but different – similarities to English, and both systems do include some evidence for earlier separate auxiliary status of their modal elements. These comparisons provide a nice context for a return to Valley Zapotec.

3.1. Core modality in English

The modal system of English is well known. English has a syntactically unified set of modal auxiliaries (*can, could, may, might, must, shall, should, will,* and *would*) that have a number of morphological and syntactic features shared with no other group of verbs. (There are, of course, other modal elements whose distribution is more restricted, such as *need*, as well as quasi-modals like *have to, ought to,* and *be able to*, and numerous adverbs and other elements with modal content, but I will not consider these to be part of the core modal group, since they do not share all the syntactic features of the modal auxiliaries.) Unlike other matrix verbs or other auxiliaries, the core modals do not show subject agreement, have no participial forms, do not occur in non-finite contexts, and show no *do* support in negative, question, or emphatic contexts.

Oppositions of the *shall-should* and *will-would* type have been identified with earlier preterite inflection, although none of these pairs of modals shows a present-past difference except for some uses of *can* vs. *could.* More often, past modal reference is shown with the perfect auxiliary *have.*

Most of the modal auxiliaries can be used to express either deontic or epistemic modality, often in opposing versions of the same sentence, as in *He must go to bed very early...he's so cranky this evening* (deontic) versus *He must go to bed very early...I always see his light go out before nine o'clock* (epistemic).

Most dialects of English do not allow combinations of the modal auxiliaries in the same clause, but double modal constructions such as *might could* or *may will* are allowed in some non-standard regional dialects. In each of these cases, the first modal is interpreted as an epistemic modifier of the second.

Occasional uses of the English modal auxiliaries do not seem to refer to non-actual events. This is particularly true of the use of *would* to indicate a past habitual, as in *Every summer we would go to the mountains.*

3.2. Core modality in Mohave

Mohave,[22] a Yuman language of Arizona and California, expresses core modality with various combinations of one or more of the following elements:

(53) p   ly   s   u   m   a

Independent modality, including references to the future, may also be expressed by the irrealis morpheme -*h/-th* (Munro 1976: §1.223), the augment vowel verb suffixes -*a* and, especially, -*i* (Munro 1976: §1.416), and the auxiliary use of the verb '*i* 'say' (Munro 1976: §1.7); imperatives are shown with a special verb form (Munro 1976: §1.123). But clearly the elements listed in (53) express core modality.

These formatives combine with some degree of freedom in the order given to express various modal concepts. *Ly* and *s* are the basic indicators of modality. "Every modal string must include one of these two elements... [which] do not cooccur" (Munro: 1976: 112-113), with *ly* indicating a weaker and *s* a stronger modal force; it is harder to propose a meaning for the other elements in (53).

Mohave is a pro-drop language with SOV order in which sentences often consist of a single verb. Here are some examples of *ly* modals, with the modal suffixes boldfaced but not given specific glosses, since the meanings of the individual modal suffixes often cover a fairly wide semantic range.[23] The *ly* suffixes express wishes, wonderings, permission, and weak obligation.

(54) 'aha-ly   '-a'oop-**lya**.
      water-loc 1-swim-mod.lya
      'I wish that I could swim.'   (Munro 1976: 119, ex. 579)

(55) Isma-m   iduu-**lyu**.
      sleep-ds be-mod.lyu
      'I wonder if (it could be that) he's sleeping.'
                                                     (Munro 1976: 120, ex. 588)

(56) Modiily   m-amaa-**plyu**.
      bread   2-eat-mod.plyu
      'You can have some bread.'   (Munro 1976: 117, ex. 568)

(57) Pith   m-iyem-**plyum**.
      now   2-go-mod.plyum
      'You'd better go now'   (Munro 1976: 118, ex. 571)

Next, here are some *s* modals, expressing strong obligation:

(58) M-iyem-**psa**.
      2-go-mod.psa
      'You have to go.'   (Munro 1976: 114, ex. 552)

(59) Nyany-ch a'we-**psum**.
      he-nom   do-mod.psum
      'He's the one who's got to do it.'   (Munro 1976: 115: 558)

The *–psum* suffix in (59) can also have epistemic force, either in a strong
future or as epistemic 'must,' as below:

(60) Mahwat-ny-ch   m-tapuy-**psum**.
      bear-dem-nom   3>2-kill-mod.psum
      'That bear's surely going to kill you.'   (Munro 1976: 115, ex. 60)

(61) Makhaav-ch   ido-**psum**.
      Mohave-nom   be-mod.psum
      'She must be a Mohave.'   (Munro 1976: 115, ex. 561)

Although I have written the Mohave modal suffixes as attached directly to
the verb, like other suffixes, there is some evidence that they may, in fact,
be incorporated verbal elements. For example, at least one modal suffix has

an ablauted form used when the subject of the preceding verb is plural, and ablaut is a standard way of indicating that a verb has a plural subject in Mohave (cf. (62a–b)):

(62) a. M-a'aav-**psum**.
    3>2-hear-mod.psum
    'He will surely hear you.'   (Munro 1976: 116, ex. 564a)

    b. M-a'aav-ch-**paysum**.
    3>2-hear-pl-pl.mod.psum
    'They will surely hear you.'   (Munro 1976: 116, ex. 564b)

The modal suffix *-suma* does not indicate non-actual events or states but rather, just like English *would*, shows a habitual meaning:

(63) 'anyaa-m nyakupay modiily ichoo-**suma**?
    day-with all   bread   make-hab
    'Does she make bread every day?'   (Munro 1976: 125, ex. 606)

-Suma is not used to express any more conventional modal meaning, but I identify it with the core modals because it includes elements from (53) and because, like all the preceding modal sentences, it does not include any indication of realis verbal aspect. However, ordinary habitual sentences are not non-actual, and in fact *–suma* may combine with the Mohave perfective suffix *-pch*, as below:

(64) 'anyaa-m nyakupay Hor-ly   '-iyem-**suma**-pch.
    day-with all   Ehrenburg-loc 1-go-hab-perf
    'I go to Ehrenburg all the time.'   (Munro 1976: 126, ex. 602)

In various constructions perfective *-pch* may be discontinuous, with *-p* following a first verb and *–ch* after a second verb, or with *-p* between the main verb and one of a few suffixes with arguably more independent status, with *-ch* following that suffix. Just this structure may appear with habitual *-suma*, providing further support for the idea that the Mohave modal suffixes have some independent (possibly auxiliary) characteristics:

(65) 'alytomink 'asent-ch Hor   '-iyem-p-**suma**-ch.
    week   one-pl   Ehrenburg 1-go-p-hab-ch
    'I go to Ehrenburg every week.'   (Munro 1976: 126, ex. 607)

As this quick sketch shows, the Mohave core modal system follows Nuyts' description, with a restricted group of modal morphemes that indicate both deontic and epistemic modality and provide several types of support for the idea that modals may originally have been separate words, revealing some intriguing similarities between Mohave and English.

3.3. Core modality in Chickasaw

In Chickasaw,[24] a Muskogean language of Oklahoma most closely related to the better described language Choctaw (and unrelated to Mohave, Valley Zapotec, or English), core modality is expressed through combinations of the basic modal suffixes and various tense/aspect morphemes. (Chickasaw also has evidential suffixes, as well as adverbs and other elements that can indicate various other types of non-actuality that I will not discuss here.)

All the Chickasaw modal suffixes begin with a sequence of *a* followed by glottal stop. The two most basic ones are incompletive *-a'chi* and potential *-a'ni*, as below:[25]

(66) Hilh-**a'chi**.
      dance-inc
      'He will dance.'

(67) Hilh-**a'ni**.
      dance-pot
      'He can dance'; 'He may dance.'

Like Mohave, Chickasaw is an SOV language in which many sentences consist simply of an inflected verb. Munro and Willmond (1994: xliv) report that the third important modal suffix, "convictional" *-a'hi*, "is relatively uncommon in simple sentences but is used on statements reflecting the speaker's firm belief rather than sure knowledge, generally about the future." An important use of *-a'hi* is in combination with the auxiliary verb *bíyyi'ka* (which independently means 'be all over' or 'be eternally') to express ability:

(68) Shiiki   yamm-at im-alikch-**a'hi** bíyyi'ka.
      buzzard   hat-nom dat-doctor-cvc   be.all.over
      'That Buzzard can doctor him.'

These three basic modal elements can be combined with a tense/aspect suffix such as perfective *–tok*, as in (69)–(71), each of which refers to different sorts of past deontic modality:

(69) Hilh-**a'chi**-tok.
      dance-inc-pt
      'He would have danced (but he didn't get the chance)';
      'He was supposed to dance.'

(70) Hilh-**a'n**-tok.
      dance-pot-pt
      'He could have danced (but he didn't show up).'

(71) Hilh-**a'hi**-tok.
      dance-cvc-pt
      'He should have danced (it was his duty).'

These modal suffixes appear following a verb stem inflected for subject, object, and negation and before tense/aspect markers like *-tok*, as shown below:

(72) Yappa-kílla   aash-l-**a'chi**.
      this-only   say-1sl-inc
      'This is all I'm going to say'; 'I'm going to say only this.'

(73) Hilha-l-**a'n**-tok.
      dance-1sl-pot-pt
      'I could have danced.'

(74) Ak-hi'lh-ok-**a'chi**.
      1sN-dance-neg-inc
      'I won't dance.'

All three of these modal suffixes cause a deletion of any preceding vowel: thus, the first person singular agreement suffix in (72)–(73) and the complex negative suffix in (74) both end in *i*, but this vowel deletes before the modal suffix.

Several other less common modal suffixes also begin with *a'* but cannot combine with a following tense/aspect marker. These include *-a'cho*, a stronger version of incompletive *-a'chi'*, and *-a'shki*, a hortative suffix used especially in formal or sacred contexts:

(75) Chi-holhchifo-at   holiitó'p-**a'shki**.
      2sII-name-nom   be.precious-hort
      'Hallowed be thy name.'[26]

(76) Kil-imp-**a'chi**-k<u>a</u> himmaka' nittak nanna   ish-po-pihínt-**a'shki**.
      1pI-eat-inc-ds   now   day   something 2sI-1pII-feed.hn-hort
      'Give us something today for us to eat.'

Chickasaw future statements like (66) may be variably epistemic and deontic.
As we have noted earlier, non-volitional simple future predictions seem to
be epistemic in status; however, the past form of (66), (69), suggests past
volitionality, a deontic quality. The type of epistemic statement that indicates
the speaker's assessment of the likelihood of an event or state is normally
expressed with an extra occurrence of potential -*a'ni* following a statement
(after a tense/aspect suffix, if one is present). Unlike the modal suffixes discussed so far, -*a'ni* does not cause deletion of a preceding vowel, and in fact
is generally preceded by a linking *h* when it follows a vowel. This -*(h)a'ni*
expresses epistemic 'must' or 'might,' as in the following examples:

(77) Hilha-**ha'ni**.
      dance-epis
      'He must be dancing (I can hear the music).'

(78) Hilha-tok-**a'ni**.
      dance-pt-epis
      'He must have danced.'

(79) Hilh-**a'chi-ha'ni**.
      dance-inc-epis
      'He must be going to dance (I see everything set up ready).'

(80) Hilh-**a'chi**-tok-**a'ni**.
      dance-inc-pt-epis
      'He must have been supposed to dance.'

(81) Ak-hi'lh-ok-ísh-**a'chi-ha'ni**.
      1sN-dance-neg-yet-inc-epis
      'I might not have danced yet (at that future time).'

Although in synchronic Chickasaw the sequence *hilha-ha'ni*, as in (77), or
-*a'chi-ha'ni*, as in (79) or (81), is segmented so as to end with -*ha'ni*, it is

likely that originally the *h* was a suffix on the first element rather than the initial element of the second. This -*h* suffix would have been cognate to the general Choctaw tense or predicative suffix -*h* (Broadwell to appear; Nicklas 1972), which is not used in Chickasaw (cf. Munro and Willmond 1994: xxxvii), thus suggesting that epistemic *(h)a'ni*, at least, might well have originally been a separate (auxiliary) verb.

The brief description of Chickasaw core modality presented here shows that Chickasaw also follows Nuyts' description, containing a restricted, morphosyntactically distinguished core group of modal morphemes that again may provide support for the idea that modals may originally have been separate words. Most epistemic modality in Chickasaw is indicated with one of the normal (primarily deontic) modal morphemes, but in a different position from those modals, offering a striking similarity to the English double modal construction.

4. The status of Valley Zapotec in a typology of modality

I began this paper by noting that the extreme diversity of modal expression in Valley Zapotec helps to validate the suggestion in de Haan's paper (this volume) that there are many ways in which modality is expressed cross-linguistically; the paper was devoted to an extended description of the Valley Zapotec system. However, there seem to be two important ways in which the Valley Zapotec system for the grammatical expression of modal concepts is different from the notion of core modality as described by Nuyts (this volume).

First, Valley Zapotec does not have a core set of modal morphemes with a unique syntax and morphology. Modality is expressed morphologically within the system of verbal aspect, lexically with modal auxiliary verbs, and syntactically with a second position clitic. Of these, the most basic notions of modality semantically seem to be expressed by the auxiliary verbs, but these do not constitute a unique class. There are two groups of modal auxiliary verbs, which might be called *necessity auxiliaries* and *possibility auxiliaries*, each with a distinct syntax, but each of these groups also includes aspectual auxiliaries whose syntax is indistinguishable from that of the modal auxiliaries but which do not express modal meaning.

Second, the expression of deontic and epistemic modality is almost completely distinct in Valley Zapotec. While the aspect prefixes have both deontic and epistemic uses, these are fairly clearly distinguished by construction type. The necessity and possibility auxiliaries have only deontic uses. There is one epistemic auxiliary, but its syntax is anomalous in several ways, and it has no deontic uses. The main expression of epistemic modality is with the second position clitic *=zhyi'*, which has no deontic uses.

Both of these observations run counter to Nuyts' observed significant cross-linguistic trend. But what this shows, of course, is that cross-linguistic trends are only trends, and there are many more types of modal systems than we might guess just by looking at English!

Notes

1. Tlacolula Valley Zapotec (*Ethnologue* code ZAB, 2003) is spoken in the northwest Tlacolula District of Oaxaca, about an hour's drive southeast of the capital, Oaxaca City, as well as by perhaps 5000 immigrants to the Los Angeles area. For some ethnographic background on this language, see Lopez and Munro (1999) and Munro (2003); for additional linguistic background, see Munro and Lopez et al. (1999), Lee (1999), and Munro, Lillehaugen, and Lopez (in preparation). The names *Valley Zapotec* and *Tlacolula Valley Zapotec* are potentially confusing, since the Valley of Oaxaca and even the smaller Tlacolula Valley cover a considerably wider area than that where the Valley Zapotec language referred to is spoken. However, the *Ethnologue*'s name *Guelavía Zapotec* seems inappropriate, since it singles out just one of many pueblos where the language is spoken.

    My work on this language has concentrated on the variety of the language spoken in the pueblo of San Lucas Quiaviní, and all examples presented here come from this dialect, but the basic description here is valid for the whole language group as a whole. I am grateful to my collaborator Felipe H. Lopez and to Rodrigo Garcia and all the other speakers of Valley Zapotec who have helped me learn about their language, as well as to other linguists who have worked on the language, especially Felicia Lee, Aaron Broadwell, Mike Galant, Ted Jones, Brook Lillehaugen, and Olivia Martínez, as well as Cynthia Walker, whose initial work convinced me of the interest of Valley Zapotec modality, and John Foreman, Carson Schütze, and other participants in the UCLA American Indian Seminar, who offered very helpful suggestions. This research has been supported by the Department of Linguistics, Academic Senate, and Institute for American Cultures of UCLA; by the National Science Foundation; and by Department of Education, Title VI Funds granted to Charles Briggs of UC San Diego.

2. The term *mood* is often used to refer to explicit marking within the verbal morphology. I will not pursue the distinction between mood and modality here.

3. The names for these aspects are mine, and probably should be reevaluated. Researchers on other Zapotec languages (e.g., Black 2000 and many others in the SIL tradition) have called aspects cognate to the Perfective *completive*, those cognate to the Irrealis *potential*, and those cognate to the Neutral *stative*. I chose the name Perfective, in part following a Slavic tradition, because *completive* seems inappropriate, given the use in imperatives described below; Irrealis, because main clause uses of this form have a future rather than potential meaning; Subjunctive, because of that form's use in counterfactuals and other subordinate clauses (Adam 2003 calls this Contrafactive). I remain unsatisfied with the name Neutral, but *stative* seems unacceptable because of the use of this form for the verb *nnah* 'says,' as I argue in Munro (2002b).

4. Habitual stems are often translated in dictionaries with third person singular verb forms (as in (1)), because they can be used without further modification with noun subjects, as in (2).

5. All examples are in the orthography of Munro and Lopez et al. (1999). The abbreviations are as follows: aff : affirmative, anap : anaphoric, anim : animal, cop : copula, def : definite, dem : demonstrative, dist : distal, epis : epistemic, foc : focus, form : formal, hort : hortative, hyp : hypothetical, inf : informal, irr : irrealis, m.s. : male speaking, neg : negative, neut : neutral, perf : perfective, pl : plural, pt : point, prog : progressive, pron : independent pronoun, prox : proximate, Q : question, rel : relative, subj : subjunctive. 1, 2, 3 and s, p are used in pronominal glosses. (Valley Zapotec distinguishes a number of different categories of third persons, such as San Lucas Quiaviní proximate, distal and animal (among others); cf. Munro 2002a.) Clitic boundaries are indicated with =. A period separates elements of a complex gloss. Note that many morphemes have more than one phonological realization; I will not discuss these alternations here.

6. I have slightly adapted the glosses and spelling of some examples cited from Lee (1999) to conform with the data in the rest of this paper.

7. I do not consider an additional puzzling aspectual form, the "non-future Definite," which both Munro and Lopez et al. (1999) and Lee (1999) consider to be another form of the Definite, but which seems to me now to be a separate entity. Although this aspect, which only occurs with two or three verbs of motion and their derivatives, is marked with a prefix homophonous to the Definite prefix, it differs crucially from the Definite proper in three important ways: it refers to a non-future event; it is pronounced slightly differently from the future Definite; and it lacks the structural peculiarities of the Definite (for instance, as Lee (1999: 236) notes, it allows focus fronting; cf. the discussion of (13) below). If the non-future Definite is a separate aspect, then it is a non-modal rather than a modal aspect (as I use these terms), so it need not concern us here.

8. (9a) might suggest that *rsaguehll* is like 'wants' (5) in selecting an Irrealis complement. But the second verb in (9a) is actually identical to that of the formal imperative in (8), while in (9b) what follows *ysaguehllyuu'* is a normal subjectless imperative with a Perfective verb. (Although this form normally

can only be used informally, in this construction it is appropriate even when addressing a formal 'you.') Thus, the verb after *ysaguehllyuu'* in both versions of (9) actually seems to be an imperative.

9. The "point" clitic =*di'* follows the verb of many negated clauses.

10. This example illustrates one of the most unusual typological features of Valley Zapotec, the use of repetition rather than pronominalization or reflexivization in same-clause coreference (see Lee 2003).

11. Indeed, English present subjunctives are also often interpreted as past. Consider Ray Charles's famous version of "America the Beautiful," in which he says, "God done shed His grace on thee" (past), for Katharine Lee Bates's "God shed His grace on thee" (subjunctive).

12. Broadwell (2003) presents a similar argument for three auxiliaries in San Dionisio Ocotepec Zapotec (a language fairly similar to Valley Zapotec) which, as he notes, belong to the class Munro and Lopez et al. (1999) somewhat misleadingly identify as "non-modal auxiliaries," identified in the current analysis as members of the possibility class of auxiliaries and aspectual auxiliaries with similar behavior.

13. These data (and similar data with pronouns rather than noun arguments) thus suggest that Valley Zapotec 'want' is not a restructuring verb in the sense of Rizzi (1976) and Cinque (2003), since aside from the difference in the aspect of their complements, 'want' is otherwise structurally the same as 'see.'

14. Munro and Lopez et al. (1999) label verbs like *rquìii'ny* and *nàa pahr modal auxiliary verbs* and verbs like *rìi'lle'eh non-modal auxiliary verbs*, because of the association of the first group with the modal auxiliaries. However, this terminology is confusing, since both types of auxiliary clearly can be used to express modal concepts, with the auxiliary acting as the modal operator, so I will not use it here. Regrettably, Munro and Lopez et al. are incorrect about several features of this system. First, they claim that a modal auxiliary may also have a Definite complement; this appears not to be correct (probably appropriately, given Lee's (1999) analysis of the semantics of the Definite). Second, Munro and Lopez et al. mistakenly identify *rìi'lle'eh* as a modal auxiliary.

15. I say *tense* rather than *aspect* (as might be expected given the Valley Zapotec system) because there are several cases of possibility auxiliary plus complement constructions with different aspects, such as Definite auxiliary and Irrealis complement or Habitual auxiliary and Neutral complement, as well as cases of several auxiliaries with ongoing complements marked as Habitual or Progressive. The aspects of both the auxiliary and the complement must be compatible with the tense reference of the clause.

16. In addition, a surprisingly large number of these expressions contain portions that are borrowed from Spanish (*gaan* (30) from *ganas*, *cwe'eenn* (31) from *cuenta*, *pahr* (22) from *para*, etc.). This observation raises the question of how such notions were expressed in earlier forms of Zapotec, which I cannot consider here.

17. Speakers report that there is little difference between the Habitual plus Habitual use of *rìi'lle'eh* (23) or the Definite plus Irrealis use (38); both can express either ability, possibility, or permission, given the proper context.

18. *Rahcgài'* 'does for a fifth time.' (19a) and other similar verbs also work like possibility auxiliaries.

19. Strangely, however, noun-plus-adjective sequences allow the clitic only following the adjective:

    (i) Bùunny zyùal=**zhyi'** gw-àa'izy=ùu'.
        person tall=epis   perf-hit=2s.inf
        'You must have hit THE TALL MAN.'

    (ii) *Bùunny=**zhyi'** zyùal gw-àa'izy=ùu'.
         person=epis   tall perf-hit=2s.inf.

    At least in some cases, noun-plus-adjective sequences seem almost like compounds, as discussed for Isthmus Zapotec by Pickett (1997). This rather startling idea is supported by native speaker intuition in many cases, as well as by the fact that many Valley Zapotec adjectives have special postnominal attributive forms that cannot be used alone (Munro 2002b).

20. The main indications I have seen that such variation might be linked to difference in scope involve the clitic *=ihzy* 'only'; I have seen no such differences with epistemic *=zhyi'*.

21. Perhaps this suggests that the relative pronoun *nih* does not count as an element of the relative clause. A similar question might be raised about the *o* question marker in examples like the following:

    (iii) O   b-ìi'lly=**zhyi'** Gye'eihlly?
          Q.aff perf-sing=epis   Mike
          'Did Mike perhaps sing?'

22. I am forever grateful to my Mohave (Mojave) teachers, especially the late Nellie Brown and the late Robert S. Martin. My current understanding of the data here owes a lot to the work of Margaret Langdon and Lynn Gordon. The data here are presented in the practical orthography and spelling of Munro, Brown, and Crawford (1992) rather than in the phonetic system used in Munro (1976). I have slightly adapted some translations and glosses for consistency. The name of the language is also spelled *Mojave*.

23. Abbreviations used in the Mohave glosses include dem : demonstrative, ds : different subject, hab : habitual, loc : locative, mod : modal, nom : nominative, perf : perfective, pl : plural. 1, 2, 3 indicate pronominal person. Portmanteau subject-object agreement prefixes are indicated with Subject>Object; thus, *3>2* means 'third person subject, second person object.'

24. I am very grateful to Catherine Willmond and the other Chickasaw speakers who have taught me, especially the late Lizzie Frazier. A basic overview of the language and explanation of the orthography is included in Munro and Willmond (1994) (note in particular that underlined vowels are nasalized). I am particularly

indebted to Lynn Gordon, Charles Ulrich, and Aaron Broadwell for discussion and other input about Chickasaw.

25. The following abbreviations are used in glosses of the Chickasaw examples: cvc : convictional, dat: dative, ds : different subject, epis : epistemic, hn : HN grade, hort : hortative, inc : incomplete, nom : nominative, pot : potential, pt : perfective. Person and number are indicated with 1, 2, s, p. Chickasaw has a complex active agreement system: series I usually shows the subject of an active or transitive verb; series II the subject of a non-active verb, the object of a transitive verb, or an inalienable possessor; and series N the subject of a negated active or transitive verb.

26. Both (75) and (76) are from Mrs. Willmond's translation of the Lord's Prayer, which uses *-a'shki* at the end of every line.

References

Adam, Christopher C.
    2003   A Beginning Morphophonology of Dihidx Bilyáhab (Santo Domingo Albarradas Zapotec). M.A. thesis, California State University, Northridge.

Anderson, Stephen R. and Arnold M. Zwicky
    2003   Clitics. In *International Encyclopedia of Linguistics, vol. 1*, William Frawley (ed.), 325–328. Oxford: Oxford University Press.

Black, Cheryl A.
    2000   *Quiegolani Zapotec Syntax*. Dallas: SIL International-University of Texas at Arlington.

Broadwell, George A.
    2003   Optimality, complex predication, and parallel structures in Zapotec. In *Proceedings of the LFG03 Conference*, M. Butt and T. Holloway King (eds.), 75–91. Stanford: CSLI Publications.

Chung, Sandra and Alan H. Timberlake
    1985   Tense, aspect, and mood. In: *Language Typology and Syntactic Description, vol. III: Grammatical Categories and the Lexicon*, T. Shopen (ed.), 202–258. Cambridge: Cambridge University Press.

Cinque, Guglielmo
    2003   Restructuring: A minicourse. UCLA class lectures.

Grimes, Barbara F. and Joseph E. Grimes
    2004   *Ethnologue: Languages of the World*. Dallas: SIL International. (www.ethnologue.com)

Lee, Felicia A.
    1999   Antisymmetry and the syntax of San Lucas Quiaviní Zapotec. Ph.D. dissertation, UCLA.
    2003   Anaphoric R-expressions as bound variables. *Syntax* 6: 84–114.

Lillehaugen, Brook Danielle
  2003   The Categorial Status of Body Part Prepositions in Valley Zapotec. M.A. thesis, UCLA.
Lopez, Felipe H. and Pamela Munro
  1999   Zapotec immigration: The San Lucas Quiaviní experience. *Aztlan* 24: 129–149.
Munro, Pamela
  2002a   Hierarchical pronouns in discourse: Third person pronouns in San Lucas Quiaviní Zapotec narratives. *Southwest Journal of Linguistics* 21: 37–66.
  2002b   Aspects of stativity in Zapotec. Paper presented at the LASSO Annual Meeting, Pasadena.
  2003   Preserving the language of the Valley Zapotecs: The orthography question. Paper presented at the conference on Language and Immigration in France and the United States: Sociolinguistic Perspectives, Austin.
Munro, Pamela, Natalie Brown and Judith G. Crawford
  1992   *A Mojave Dictionary. UCLA Occasional Papers in Linguistics* 10. UCLA Department of Linguistics.
  2002   Hierarchical pronouns in discourse: Third person pronouns in San Lucas Quiaviní Zapotec narratives. *Southwest Journal of Linguistics* 21: 37–66.
Munro, Pamela and Catherine Willmond
  1994   *Chickasaw: An Analytical Dictionary.* Norman: University of Oklahoma Press.
Munro, Pamela and Felipe H. Lopez, with Olivia V. Méndez [Martínez], Rodrigo Garcia, and Michael R. Galant
  1999   *Di'csyonaary X:tèe'n Dìi'zh Sah Sann Lu'uc (San Lucas Quiaviní Zapotec Dictionary / Diccionario Zapoteco de San Lucas Quiaviní).* Los Angeles: UCLA Chicano Studies Research Center Publications.
Munro, Pamela, Brook Danielle Lillehaugen and Felipe H. Lopez
  forthc. *Cali Chiu? A Course in Valley Zapotec.*
Nicklas, T. Dale
  1972   The Elements of Choctaw. Ph.D. dissertation, University of Michigan.
Pickett, Velma
  1997   When is a phrase a word? Problems in compound analysis in Isthmus Zapotec. Paper presented at the UCLA American Indian Linguistics Seminar.
Rizzi, Luigi
  1976   Ristrutturazione. *Rivista di grammatica generativa* 1: 1–54.
Zwicky, Arnold M.
  1977   *On Clitics.* Bloomington: Indiana University Linguistics Club.

Modality in American Sign Language

Sherman Wilcox and Barbara Shaffer

1. Signed languages

Signed languages are natural human languages used by deaf people throughout the world as their native or primary language[1]. Although there has been no formal survey of the world's signed languages, linguists generally assume that they number in the hundreds. The 13th edition of the Summer Institute of Linguistics *Ethnologue* lists 114 signed languages (Grimes 1996), but we believe that this significantly underestimates the number. The gestural-visual modality of signed languages is reflected in their linguistic structure. Signed languages make extensive use of space, for example by incorporating spatial locations to indicate verbal arguments. In addition to the hands, the face plays a critical role in signed language grammar, expressing a range of information such as questions, topic, adverbials, and so forth.

The modern era of linguistic research on signed language began in the late 1960s with the pioneering work of the American linguist William C. Stokoe. He was a professor of English at Gallaudet College (now Gallaudet University) in Washington, DC, the only liberal arts university for deaf people. Stokoe began to apply linguistic techniques borrowed from the structuralist tradition prevalent at the time to study the language that he saw deaf students using in his classroom – ASL. His research eventually led to a broad interest in the structure of ASL by linguists and initiated research worldwide to analyze the world's signed languages.

Over the past 40 years, linguists have demonstrated that signed languages such as American Sign Language (ASL) may be analyzed and described using the same units as spoken language. While differences in structure attributable to modality (spoken versus signed) have been noted (Klima and Bellugi 1979), the overwhelming conclusion is that signed languages share important characteristics with spoken languages.

A common misunderstanding is that signed languages are merely representations of spoken languages – that ASL, for example, is a signed representation of spoken English. Signed languages are independent languages with their own lexicons and grammars. Like spoken languages, signed languages have genetic and historical relations with other signed languages. ASL's closest genetic relative, for example, is French Sign Language (LSF).

2.   A brief sketch of ASL

2.1. Phonology

One of the pioneering discoveries made by Stokoe was that ASL can be described phonologically. Before this, it was assumed that the signs – that is, the words – of a signed language were unanalyzable. Stokoe showed that a sign consists of analyzable units of structure and coined the term *chereme* for these sublexical units (Stokoe 1960).

Stokoe analyzed the phonology of signs into three major classes: handshape (the configuration that the hand makes when producing the sign), location (the place where the sign is produced, for example on the head, or in the neutral space in front of the signer's body), and movement (the motion made by the signer's hands in producing the sign, for example upward or towards the signer's body). Stokoe called these the *aspects* of a sign. Later linguists called these aspects the *parameters* of a sign and added a fourth parameter (Battison 1978): orientation (the direction which the palm of the hand faces when producing the sign). The psychological reality of parameters is demonstrated by the existence of minimal pairs, signs differing only in one parameter which have different meanings (Klima and Bellugi 1979).

2.2. Morphology

ASL, like many signed languages, is highly synthetic with tendencies towards polysynthesis. ASL allows morphemes indicating action, person agreement, aspect, and adverbial information to be combined into a single, multimorphemic ASL word; for example, 'I very carefully gave [one] to each [person]' would be expressed with a single sign in ASL.

2.3. Syntax

Research on the syntax of signed languages has examined issues of word class, word order, relations among constituents (such as relative clauses), question formation, topic-comment structure, the flow of information in discourse, and the grammatical use of space. ASL discourse is characterized by a high degree of topic-comment structure (Janzen et al. 1999). Topics are marked grammatically, with the topic phrase accompanied by raised eyebrows, a slightly backward head tilt, often with a pause between the topic and comment phrases, and with the final sign of the topic phrase held slightly longer. Topic-comment structure has been described for ASL as a basic sentence type along with others, such as interrogatives, imperatives, and assertions, but the frequency with which topic-comment structures appear in discourse suggests that it is more basic. Thus, topics can appear as part of any given sentence type.

2.4. Grammaticization

Grammaticization is the linguistic process by which grammatical material (for example, future markers or modal auxiliaries) develops historically out of lexical material (Bybee et al. 1994; see also the papers by Nuyts, de Haan, and Traugott in this volume). Grammaticization operates much the same in signed languages such as ASL as in spoken languages. For example, modals in ASL develop historically out of lexical material with concrete, embodied meanings. Thus, the ASL modal auxiliary meaning 'can,' even when used for mental ability (as in *He can read*), developed historically from the ASL sign STRONG 'having physical strength.'

A similar example comes from the development of the agentive suffix (similar to the English *-er*) in ASL. Historically, this suffix originated as a full lexical form meaning 'body.' Over time, the orientation and location parameters changed and the movement became greatly reduced. Semantically, the sign changed from meaning 'strictly body' to become 'one who does something [as specified by the verb].' It also became a bound form obligatorily attached to a verb. The current sign TEACHER is thus the free lexical form TEACH and the reduced agentive suffix which developed from the sign for body.

2.5. Fingerspelling

A common misunderstanding is that signed languages are merely (or largely) comprised of fingerspellings. This is not the case. Fingerspelling makes use of handshape configurations that correspond to the alphabet of the majority written language. Fingerspelling is often used for proper names or technical terms, and is used for loan words in signed languages; for example, *of, all, sure,* and several other English words have been borrowed into ASL through fingerspelling. A variety of fingerspelling systems exists among the world's signed languages. ASL and many other signed languages use a one-handed system. British Sign Language (BSL) and some other signed languages use a two-handed fingerspelling system. The amount of fingerspelling used in a signed language varies greatly. ASL and BSL rely extensively on fingerspelling; the use of fingerspelling in most other signed languages is more restricted.

Fingerspelling is more than a sequence of canonical handshape configurations, since the articulatory movements within the fingerspelled word influence each other. Perseverative and anticipatory coarticulation affects the actual shaping of fingerspelled words, creating a fluid transition between letters (Wilcox 1992).

2.6. Classes of articulators

It is possible to divide the articulators used to produce signed languages such as ASL into two broad classes: manual and nonmanual. Signs produced with the manual articulators may be lexical or grammatical. Thus, in addition to lexical signs such as GO, STRONG, or MIRROR, the modals discussed in this chapter, such as CAN, MUST, and POSSIBLE, are manually produced signs.

Two striking features characterize nonmanual articulators. First, nonmanual articulators, particularly facial gestures, are used predominantly to code grammatical functions such as topic, interrogatives, and imperatives. Nonmanual articulators rarely if ever are used to produce lexical morphemes.[2] Second, the forms that these markers take for specific functions are remarkably similar across a wide range of genetically and areally unrelated languages. For example, in a typological study of interrogatives in more than 30 signed languages, Zeshan (2004) found that all used nonmanual marking for polar questions. In addition, she reported that nonmanual signals marking polar questions tend to be quite similar across signed languages, typically involving a cluster of facial gestures including eyebrow raise, eyes wide open, eye contact with the addressee, head forward position, and forward body posture (Zeshan 2004: 19).

The significance of these facts for the expression of modality relates to the connection between subjectivity and facial markers on the one hand,

and between subjectivity and modality on the other. Langacker (1991) describes subjectivity in a way that reveals how this semantic notion can also be used to characterize the difference between manual and nonmanual articulators. Using an example based on visual perception, he says (1991: 316):

> Consider the glasses I normally wear. If I take my glasses off, hold them in front of me, and examine them, their construal is maximally objective, as I will understand the term: they function solely and prominently as the OBJECT OF PERCEPTION, and not at all as part of the perceptual apparatus itself. By contrast, my construal of the glasses is maximally subjective when I am wearing them and examining another object, so that they fade from my conscious awareness despite their role in determining the nature of my perceptual experience. The glasses then function exclusively as part of the SUBJECT OF PERCEPTION – they are one component of the perceiving apparatus, but are not themselves perceived.

When we consider the hands as articulators of a signed language, they naturally lend themselves to a maximally objective construal because they are available as objects of our perception. The face, on the other hand, invites a subjective construal because our face is not normally available as an object of our own perception.

In addition to these characteristics of hands and faces as articulators, we note that facial markers in signed languages are used to indicate the speaker's attitude towards the propositional information on the hands, or to otherwise modify the manual meaning; for example, facial markers also function as adverbial and adjectival markers which co-occur with manual signs.

It is worth noting that the face is regarded as a signal of our stance towards what we are saying, such as when we say of a person's statement that "in spite of what he said, *his face gave him away.*"

We also use the term *subjectivity* in its more traditional, pragmatic-semantic sense to describe the asymmetry between an utterance's proposition content, the information that speakers supposedly share when they converse and that is the focus of linguistic analysis, and the speakers' attitudes, evaluations, and opinions (Scheibman 2002). Subjectivity, as Lyons (1995) notes, is simply the expression of self, or the speaker's viewpoint, in language. Our point is that the asymmetry of facial versus manual articulators in signed languages, where the face is predominantly used to comment on or modify the manual content, mirrors the asymmetry noted by Lyons which is inherent in semantic subjectivity.

A number of linguists have commented on the connection between subjectivity and modality. Palmer (1986: 16) notes:

> Modality in language, especially when marked grammatically, seems to be essentially subjective. ... Modality in language is, then, concerned with subjective characteristics of an utterance, and it could even be further argued that subjectivity is an essential criterion for modality. Modality could, that is to say, be defined as the grammaticalization of speakers' (subjective) attitudes and opinions.

We will return to these concepts later when we discuss epistemic modality, and in the final section on modality and intensification.

3. Modality in ASL

The expression of modal notions in signed languages has not been extensively explored. The most extensive work to date on modals comes from ASL, although Ferreira Brito (1990) conducted a pioneering study of modality in Brazilian Sign Language. The classic text *The Sign Language: A Manual of Signs* by J. Schuyler Long (1918) describes ASL auxiliary verbs, including the form and meaning of the following modals: CAN, CAN'T, MAY (MAYBE, PERHAPS), SHOULD (OUGHT), MUST (NEED, HAVE TO), HAVE (FINISHED), WILL (SHALL), WON'T. Fischer and Gough (1978) mention modals in their discussion of ASL verbs but do not discuss their semantics or discourse function. Padden (1988) also discusses the modals CAN, WILL, SHOULD, and MUST but likewise does not discuss in any depth the semantics of these words, instead focusing on the types of nominals that precede modals. The semantics of modals is typically discussed in only a cursory way in ASL textbooks.

Wilcox and Wilcox (1995) presented a functional analysis of ASL modals. Their study focused on the gestural basis of modal notions, proposing that certain common gestures become lexicalized as ASL modals and examining an iconic relation between strong and weak modal forms. Janzen and Shaffer (2002) further explored the developmental path that leads from gesture to lexical form, and the grammaticization of these lexical forms into modals. Shaffer (2004) provided a detailed analysis of ASL modal notions and the relation between their discourse function and information ordering.

The sections to follow describe the meaning and discourse functions of ASL modals; their grammaticization from lexical sources; and, when appropriate, their hypothesized origins in gestural sources. Regarding the latter, we will suggest that two distinct routes lead from gestural sources to modal forms. One route leads from manual gestural forms to lexical signs, which then grammaticize to modal verbs. The second starts with certain distinct types of manual markers such as manner of movement, as well as non-manual gestural forms. These gestures do not enter the linguistic system as lexical signs; rather, they appear as prosodic markers which then develop directly into grammatical forms such as markers of modal strength.

For our discussion we will draw upon the classification scheme proposed by van der Auwera and Plungian (1998). The key elements of this model are that it describes modality as the semantic domain that involves necessity and possibility. The expression of necessity and possibility plays out in four domains: participant-external, participant-internal, deontic, and epistemic. Participant-external refers to those situations where the source of the condition is external to the participant engaged in the state of affairs, such that the conditions make this state of affairs either necessary or possible. Participant-internal refers to those situations where the source of the condition is internal to the participant engaged in the state of affairs. Deontic modality is classified as a subdomain of participant-external modality, which "identifies the enabling or compelling circumstances external to the participant as some person(s), often the speaker, and/or as some social or ethical norm(s) permitting or obliging the participant to engage in the state of affairs" (1998: 81). Epistemic modality indicates the degree of certainty with which one makes an assertion (see also the papers by Nuyts and de Haan in this volume).

We use this classification scheme because it captures the motivation for the grammaticization paths seen in our data. We also prefer this scheme because in our ASL data, the forms for necessity and possibility are the same across all domains – participant-external, participant-internal, deontic, and epistemic. Finally, we find that this scheme, when applied to signed languages, motivates the search for gestures that likely served as language-external sources for these modal forms.

3.1. Necessity

The modal notion of necessity in ASL is predominantly expressed with the word MUST/SHOULD. Long (1918: 61) describes the ASL word expressing 'necessity': "*Must*, indicating *Necessity* and *Need*. – Crook the forefinger of 'G' hand, then turn it so the end points down; push the hand downward;

the downward motion is often repeated several times." The sign is illustrated in Figure 1:

Figure 1. Long MUST.

In his section on auxiliary verbs, Long (1918: 26) also notes that this sign may be produced "with more or less force," perhaps indicating weak and strong variants. In this same section Long notes that the form used to express 'should' and 'ought' also means 'duty': "*Should, Ought,* indicating duty. – Press the crooked forefinger of the right 'G' hand against the lips and then move toward side and downward as in 'must.'"

Note that ASL SHOULD/OUGHT in 1913 was a two-part sign, the first part corresponding in form to that of MUST. The sign described by Long as SHOULD/OUGHT is no longer attested in ASL; in modern ASL, SHOULD/OUGHT is the less forceful variant of MUST. We will discuss the relation between these more and less forceful variants subsequently.

3.1.1. Participant-external

A classic *deontic obligation* modal use in ASL is given in Shaffer (2004):

(1)   a.   [POSS.1 BAD EXPERIENCE THAT SCHOOL WHAT-gesture]-topic
           EVERY MORNING DEAF LINEUP-2h.
           'My worst experience with that school was that every morning the
           deaf (kids) lined up.'

b. [BEFORE CLASS]-TOP MUST LINEUP-2h.
   'Before class we had to line up.'

c. TOILET A-L-L SIT-2h TOILET SIT.
   'and then all sit on the toilet in unison.'

d. [FINISH]-topic, DUTY, WOMAN MUST WIPE CLEAN BEHIND ALL.
   'When we were finished the woman had to wipe all our bottoms.'

e. PRO.1 DISGUST THAT ORAL SCHOOL DETEST!
   'I hated that oral school. Hated it!'

In this example, the signer is saying that an external authority (presumably a school official) obligated the woman to perform an action on the children; in turn, the woman obligated the children to perform an action. While the source of obligation in (1d) is not stated overtly (the woman on duty likely did not make the rules regarding toileting), it is clear that it is external to the agent (the woman) performing that action.

Participant-external *advisability* refers to those discourse contexts where the speaker offers advice about a current state of affairs but does not include herself in the situation:

(2) (leaning back) SHOULD COOPERATE, WORK TOGETHER, INTERACT
     FORGET (gesture)) PAST PUSH-AWAY NEW LIFE FROM-NOW-ON
     [SHOULD]-bf.
     'They (the deaf community) should cooperate and work together,
     they should forget about the past and start anew.'

(3) YOU SHOULD WRITE ORDER [WRITE]-topic PRO.1 WANT PLEASE
     eye gaze to addressee PUT-DOWN (on paper) M-E-D MEDIUM CHILE
     PRO.2-SHOULD WRITE PRO.3 DON'T KNOW POSS.2 ORDER.
     'You should write it out with your order. Write, "I want medium
     chile." You should write it, otherwise they don't know what you want.'

The speakers in (2) and (3) are imposing the condition described by SHOULD, but they are external to the situation being discussed. The speaker in (2) is stating what the deaf community (the participants) should do. The participant in (3) is being told by the speaker how she should order chile in a restaurant.

Participant-external *root necessity* describes those situations where general circumstances compel the action named in the proposition. Root necessity is strongly tied to the lack of an overt or salient obligator. The sense of

MUST in (4) is best described as 'it is necessary' or 'the situation makes it necessary.' In this case the absence of a front seat made it necessary for the speaker and his friends to sit in the back seat:

(4)   (looks at watch) MUST LEAVE, HARD FIND EXIT, BIG PARK cl:1 (walk hurriedly) FIND T-A-X-I cl:3 (car pull up) SMALL VW. LOOK-AT, [DRIVER]-topic SIT (left front seat) [PRO.3 CHAIR]-topic, EMPTY. MUST WE-THREE cl;bent-3 (back seat) [PRO.1]-topic (sit behind driver).

'We had to leave but it was hard to find the exit, it was a big park. We walked quickly and found a taxi. It was a small VW. When I looked closely I saw that the driver was sitting in the front left seat but there was no passenger seat. The three of us had to sit in the back, and I sat right behind the driver.'

Another example of participant-external *root necessity* is seen with the final production of MUST in (5). In (5a) and (5b) the signer is explaining that the only way to catch what the teacher was fingerspelling was to look at the entire sentence, to not look away when the subject of the sentence (the train) was spelled. If one looked away, one would miss important information.

(5)   a.   POSS.1 MOTHER MUST WATCH(2h) FINGERSPELL++ "T-H-E T-R-A-I-N I-S N-O-T C-O-M-I-N-G."

'My mother had to watch fingerspelling. "The train is not coming."'

b.   POSS.1 MOTHER WON'T LOOK$_A$ BECAUSE PRO.3 center SAY N-O-T ALL LOOK-2h$_b$ PRO.3 SAY NOT COMING LOOK(ctr) SENTENCE MUST.

'My mother didn't look (to the train) because the teacher had said "not." All (the other kids) looked. But she said "not coming." They needed to watch the whole sentence.'

While it could be argued that this use is deontic necessity, we claim that the sense of MUST in this case is one of root necessity: in order for B to occur, A must occur. The source of the condition is understood to be the situation itself, which is a highly abstracted and thus more subjective use of MUST.

3.1.2. *Participant-internal*

In contrast to those uses of modals where the condition is imposed by an external source, in participant-internal uses the participant is the source of the condition described by the modal. In (6) the speaker is stating the *physical necessity* for green chile. No external source obligates him to eat chile. His perceived physical need is the source of the condition:

(6) a. [KNOW SOUTH COUNTRY]-topic (waits for attention) [KNOW SOUTH COUNTRY SPANISH FOOD]-topic STRONG CHILE MUST PRO.1. (leans back)
'You know how it is in the southern part. You know how it is with Spanish food. In the southern part, there's a lot of hot chile. I have to have chile.'

   b. MUST WITH CHILE MUST PRO.1 (leans back, turns head) FEEL, WITH CHILE.
'I have to have chile. I have to.'

In participant-internal *advisability*, the speaker is a participant in the situation being described and is imposing a limiting condition upon himself/herself (as well as others). Participant-internal advisability typically uses *we* as the semantic agent, while participant-external advisability commonly uses *you* or *they* as the semantic agent.

In (7) the speaker is discussing politics and comments on the plight of poor people. He uses *we* as the agent, suggesting that he sees himself as part of the problem, and proposed solution:

(7) THAT ONE B-I-G P-R-O-B-L-E-M PRO.1p PROBLEM [gesture WHAT]-topic ECONOMY PRO.1p SHOULD HELP POOR LOW PEOPLE AREA SHOULD.
'One big problem is the economy. We should help poor people.'

3.1.3. Gestural sources of necessity

For spoken languages, grammaticization typically leads from lexical morphemes to grammatical morphemes. Such grammaticization has been documented for ASL and other signed languages (Janzen 1995; Sexton 1999; Wilbur 1999; Meir 2003; Zeshan 2003). Recent studies of ASL grammaticization (Janzen 1995; Wilcox and Wilcox 1995; Janzen and Shaffer 2002; Shaffer 2002) have expanded on the notion by claiming that the grammaticization path in many cases can be extended back to include gestural sources of lexical and grammatical morphemes.

When searching for the lexical sources of ASL modal forms, we turn to French Sign Language (LSF) because it is the closest genetic relative of ASL. The ASL necessity form is illustrated in Figure 2:

Figure 2. ASL sign MUST.

It is clearly related to the LSF form IL FAUT 'it is necessary' in Figure 3:

Figure 3. Modern LSF sign IL FAUT (from Girod 1997).

The LSF form is also attested in mid-nineteenth century LSF, as in Figure 4:

Figure 4. Old LSF sign IL FAUT (from Brouland 1855).

Related forms in LSF include DEVOIR 'duty' and DEVOIR L'ARGENT 'owe.' Wilcox and Wilcox (1995) and Shaffer (2000) speculated that the source of necessity forms may be a pointing gesture indicating monetary debt, citing the modern ASL word OWE and the fact that it is not uncommon cross-linguistically to find verbs indicating monetary debt grammaticize to mean general obligation (Bybee et al. 1994).

   In both ASL OWE and LSF DEVOIR de L'ARGENT, the forms consist of two components: a finger pointing downward at the palm of a flat, upward-oriented hand. The gestural source of the pointing finger appears to be a gesture described by de Jorio (1832: 308) and used as far back as classical antiquity to indicate 'in this place' and 'insistence.' Dodwell (2000) discusses this gesture, illustrated in Figure 5. He calls this an imperative (2000: 36): "It consists of directing the extended index finger towards the ground." According to both de Jorio and Dodwell, the gesture was described by Quintillion in the first century AD: "when directed towards the ground, this finger insists" (Dodwell 2000: 36).

   The upward-oriented hand gesture is also described by de Jorio as indicating "a request for a material object" (2000: 128). Thus, the combination of these two gestures seems to indicate an insistence or demand that a material object – in this case money – be placed in the hand.

Figure 5. Roman gesture meaning 'insist' (from Dodwell 2000, plate XVb).

Janzen and Shaffer (2002) suggested that the composite gesture of pointing at the upturned palm entered the LSF lexicon as a verb indicating monetary debt and that the form then underwent semantic generalization, which resulted in uses where no monetary debt was intended, only a general sense of obligation. We would clarify this analysis slightly. We now believe what likely happened was that the composite gesture of pointing to the upturned palm did enter the old LSF lexicon as a verb meaning 'to owe money.' It seems likely, however, that the downward-pointing finger, one component of this composite gesture, entered the LSF lexicon as a necessity form.[3]

3.2. Possibility

The semantic domain of possibility includes all notions of physical and mental ability, skills, root possibility, permission, and epistemic possibility. We begin with participant-internal possibility and work outward because it is assumed that the source of all possibility meanings is physical strength, an internal attribute.

Long (1918: 62) describes the ASL word expressing 'possibility' as follows: "*Can*, indicating *Ability, Power.* – Extend 'S' hands forward from the sides, thumb sides up with elbows against sides; bring both hands down with a jerking motion." It is illustrated in Figure 6:

Figure 6. Long CAN.

Figure 7. Long STRONG.

Long (1918: 62) also describes the difference between CAN and STRONG: "The sign for '*strong*' is very similar. The difference lies in the way the hands are moved. For 'strength' they are moved somewhat sidewise with a slight circular motion." (Figure 7).

3.2.1. Participant-internal

A common meaning of participant-internal possibility is *physical ability*. In (8) the speaker states his physical ability to lift 100 pounds. In (9) the speaker is discussing his experiences in a school for the deaf that taught speech-reading skills, and, to a lesser extent, speech skills. The participant is a hypothetical 'one' but it is understood that the speaker is included.

(8) PRO.1 CAN LIFT-WEIGHT 100 POUNDS.
     'I can lift one hundred pounds.'

(9) a. [ORAL SCHOOL TEACH HOW SAY WORDS]-topic
         NOT PRO 3 INTERESTING PRO.3.
         'What was interesting about my oral school was that it didn't emphasize speech articulation.'

     b. [CAN LIP-READ R-E-A-D-L-I-P-S EMPHASIZE LIP-READ]-topic LATER
         CAN PICK-U-P SPEAK, SOUND.
         'If you can read lips (they emphasized lip-reading), then you can learn to talk.'

Root possibility refers to those discourse uses where the enabling condition is present in the situation itself. Often there is no salient agent, and therefore no condition on the agent. The condition is more generalized to the situation being discussed. In (10) the speaker is relating to a friend her experience buying a new house. She tells the friend about a conversation she had with her husband concerning the benefits of the new house, describing what is possible in the new house and its yard.

(10)   PRO.1 TELL HERE BIG Y-A-R-D, G-A-R-D-E-N, POSSIBLE HAVE PLAY
        VOLLEYBALL CAN PEOPLE GATHER CAN MORE INTERACT, NICE.
        'I told (my husband) that (this house) has a big yard, and garden. It has
        a lot of potential. We could play volleyball, have people over. It would
        be better for social events.'

3.2.2. Participant-external

Permission is often considered to be a type of deontic possibility and a counterpart to deontic obligation. Pragmatically, permission typically is granted to the agent by an external source.

A bit of background information is necessary before we can discuss (11). When schools for the deaf were founded in the United States, signed language was the mode of instruction. Later, beginning around the turn of the twentieth century, there was a 50–75 year period when schools banned the use of signs in favor of oral methods of instruction. In (11), the signer is describing her mother's schooling and states that while the teachers were permitted (presumably by an external authority) to use signs, most spelled out each word using the manual alphabet instead:

(11)   POSS.1 MOTHER TIME TEACH, TEACH CAN SIGN BUT ALWAYS FINGER-
        SPELL+++.
        'In my mother's time the teachers were allowed to sign, but they al-
        ways fingerspelled.'

Participant-external *root possibility* describes those modal uses where a condition inherent in a situation that is external to the main clause agent enables the agent to perform the action described by the verb. In (12) the speaker is discussing the use of American TTYs (a type of text telephone) by deaf people in Iceland. He states that while the Icelandic alphabet contains two additional letters, it is still possible for the deaf people there to use American TTYs:

(12) AMERICAN POSS.3 PRO.3p, AMERICAN C-O-M. LETTER TWO, ADD, MEAN CAN LIVE WITHOUT. THAT TWO LETTER DON'T-CARE.[PRO.1p]-topic 26. (left hand) [PRO.3]-topic 28. BUT CAN LIVE WITHOUT TWO.

'They (people in Iceland) used American (TTYs). They have two more letters, but they can live without the two letters, it doesn't matter. We have 26, they have 28, but they can live without the two.'

3.2.3. Gestural sources of possibility

In a discussion of markers of possibility, Bybee et al. (1994) note that while English *can* likely began as a verb meaning 'to know,' there are several known cases of words predicating physical ability that come to be used to mark general ability as well. Two cases are cited. English *may* was formerly used to indicate physical ability and later came to express general ability. Latin *potere* 'to be able,' which is related to the adjective *potens,* meaning 'strong' or 'powerful,' provided the source for French *pouvoir* and Spanish *poder*, both meaning 'can' (1994: 190).

Wilcox and Wilcox (1995) and Janzen and Shaffer (2002) have suggested a similar grammaticization path for markers of possibility in ASL. As we saw in Figure 6 and Figure 7, there is a clear phonological and semantic relation between the ASL forms CAN and STRONG. This connection can be seen in film data from a 1913 lay sermon:

(13) PRO.3 KNOW EACH OTHER BETTER AND PRO.3 CAN UNDERSTAND EACH OTHER BETTER AND FEEL BROTHER.
'We know each other better and are able to understand each other better and feel like brothers.'

(14) OUR FATHER STRONG OVER MOON STARS WORLD.
'Our father is strong over the moon, and stars and world.'

(15) SELF CAN GET-ALONG WITHOUT OUR HELP.
'He can get along without our help.'

In the above examples, STRONG and CAN are signed in an identical manner. In (14) it is unclear whether the signer was intending a strength or ability reading.

The original development from gestural source to lexical sign surely occurred several centuries ago in LSF. The LSF signs FORT (in Figure 8) and POUVOIR (in Figure 9) are also phonologically related, and we suggest that the source is a gesture indicating upper body strength:

Figure 8. LSF lexical sign FORT.

Figure 9. LSF grammatical sign POUVOIR.

We further suggest that the old LSF lexical sign FORT 'to be strong' gram-maticized into POUVOIR 'can,' which is used in constructions expressing physical ability, mental ability, root possibility, as well as permission and epistemic possibility.

In order to understand the relation between the LSF forms FORT and POUVOIR and their ASL counterparts STRONG and CAN, we must digress a bit and describe the nature of the relation between these two languages. The mechanism by which LSF and ASL came into contact, so-called *methodical signs*, is unique to signed languages. Originally developed at the Paris Insti-tute for the Deaf in the late 18th century, methodical signs were invented sign forms, typically composed of a base lexical sign borrowed from LSF to which various modifications were made to reflect the structure of spo-ken/written French. For example, Lane (1980: 122) cites Epée's description of the methodical sign aimable 'lovable': "I make the radical sign [for love], then the sign for an adjective, but of one terminating in able formed from a verb: To this I must subjoin the sign for possible or necessary."

Methodical signs were adapted by Thomas Gallaudet and Laurent Clerc, a former student at the Paris Institute, to reflect English structure and were used in the deaf education classroom at the newly established American Asylum for Deaf-Mutes in Hartford, Connecticut in 1817. Gallaudet soon noted that an existing signed language was already in use, and in fact he came to advocate that teachers of the deaf should know both methodical signs and this natural language.

Thus, it is clear that deaf people in America were communicating with each other, and that the language they used would likely have been related to signed languages from nations which contributed settlers to the colonies at this time, including Britain, France, and Spain. Groce (1985) reports that a population of deaf people on Martha's Vineyard around this time used a signed language related to a regional dialect used in Britain. Beyond this, we have very little idea what that language looked like.

Specific to this study and to modal forms, the implication is that the LSF forms FORT and POUVOIR were brought into American education when Gallaudet and Clerc established deaf education in this country. We have virtually no clue as to what existing forms might have been used in the deaf community at that time. We do know that by shortly after the turn of the 20th century, when the films that we cite here were made and when Long wrote his description of ASL, STRONG and CAN were still closely related phonologically. Example (14) suggests that they were also somewhat poly-semous.

We also know that these forms in contemporary ASL are clearly distinct phonologically and semantically. While CAN is still made in roughly the same location and with the same handshape as described by Long, the orientation of the hands has changed so that the palms face downward, and the movement often has reduced to a flexing of the wrist rather than a full downward stroke of the forearm. STRONG is now made with the same handshape, but the location has moved up considerably, and the sign moves outward, away from the signer, rather than downward as it did in the earlier form.

3.3. Epistemic modality

Epistemic modality in ASL is expressed by a combination of manual signs, and manual and nonmanual markers. The particular combination of manual and nonmanual markers indicates the degree of speaker certainty. In addition, the position of a modal in an utterance corresponds to the modal's scope and to its role in the discourse (Shaffer 2004). Modals with scope over only the verb appear near the verb, while modals with clausal scope appear near the end of the clause, in the comment of topic-marked constructions. Position also corresponds to the modal's degree of grammaticization. In deontic obligation, for example, which is a less grammaticized meaning, the modal appears in a position immediately preceding the verb. In epistemic necessity, the most grammaticized meaning, the modal typically appears at the end of the utterance, as in (16):

(16)   [LIBRARY HAVE DEAF LIFE]-top [SHOULD]-bf/hn.
       'The library should have Deaf Life/I'm sure the library has Deaf Life.'

Because of the weak, reduplicated articulation, nonmanual marking (brow furrowing and a head nod), and information ordering, (16) indicates the speaker's positive commitment to the truth of the proposition. The same utterance with the modal produced without nonmanual markers and in preverbal position would be grammatical and felicitous, but it would have a non-epistemic, participant-external advisability meaning.

Epistemic modality also is expressed with possibility, as in (17):

(17) [SAME SIGN BECAUSE BAD TRANSLATION FALSE C-O-G-N-A-T-E]-topic
      [DOUBT]-bf/hs (pause) (gesture "well") [POSSIBLE]-hn.

      'I doubt the two concepts share the same sign (now) because of a
      problem with translation, or because of a false cognate, but, well, I
      suppose it's possible.'

In describing the expression of epistemic modality in ASL, Wilcox and
Wilcox (1995) and Shaffer (2004) discuss a set of words including FEEL,
SEEM, and OBVIOUS. We now prefer to classify these words as inferential
evidentials. Van der Auwera and Plungian (1998) regard inferential evidentiality, which identifies the evidence as based on reasoning, as an overlap
category between epistemic modality and evidentiality. The following examples demonstrate these uses:

(18) a. [FEEL SOMEONE CL:1 NOTICE GO-INTO SWIPE YOU]-yn?
          'Do you suppose someone walked by, noticed it, and just went in
          and stole it?'

      b. [NOT-KNOW]-hs [SEEM+]-hn.
          'I don't know, apparently that's what happened.'

(19) [TIM, JENNIFER]-topic [DIVORCE SEEM]-brow furrow/slow head nod.
      'It looks like Tim and Jennifer are going to get a divorce/think Tim
      and Jennifer are going to get a divorce.'

(20) [MAN PRO.3 RICH]-topic [OBVIOUS]-bf/hn.
      'That man is obviously rich.'

One way that epistemic modality is expressed in ASL is with 'future.'
When the sign FUTURE is combined with a constellation of manual and
nonmanual gestures, the sense is one of future certainty indicating that the
speaker is strongly convinced that the event will come about (see Bybee et
al. 1994: 248). In example (21), the speaker uses FUTURE twice, first in
preverbal position indicating temporal reference, then in clause final position indicating his certainty that the event will take place:

(21) RT 29 THINK-LIKE PRO.3 R-O-C-K-V-I-L-L-E P-I-K-E PRO.3 BUILD+
PRO.3 [FUTURE]-topic/wg DEVELOP [FUTURE]-bf/hn S-O WHY MUST
$_a$MOVE$_b$ NEAR COLUMBIA MALL?

'(I live off) route 29, the Rockville Pike area. In the future I'm sure
they will develop that area. So why do I have to move all the way up
near Columbia Mall?'

In (22) the speaker indicates his certainty that he will win the lottery:

(22) [SUPPOSE PRO.1 SEND+++ PCH]-topic RECEIVE MONEY [FUTURE]-bf/hn.
'If I keep sending in the Publisher's Clearing House sweepstakes, I'm
sure I'll rake in the money.'

Thus, the constellation of manual and nonmanual markers are what distinguish the epistemic and the temporal readings of FUTURE. Note that in example (21) the brow furrow and head nod only occur on the epistemic
FUTURE. In addition, this form of FUTURE is signed with a short, sharp
movement. The nonmanual markers that co-occur with the temporal
FUTURE indicate topic, and the manual (wiggle) markers, which also result
in a longer, softer movement, add a temporally distal meaning to FUTURE.

The same manual and nonmanual markers that we have just described
for epistemic commitment are also used to indicate the speaker's degree of
certainty with the inferential evidentials SEEM, FEEL, and OBVIOUS. Wilcox
and Wilcox (1995) report an example showing both weak and strong inferential evidential senses of SEEM. In a discussion about which of two possible translations would be more appropriate for a particular ASL utterance,
one speaker asks, "Which do you think she said, this or that?" The second
speaker responds:

(23) SEEM++ index$_i$
'I think she said this...'[4]

(The two study the videotape of the
utterance under discussion some more)

SEEM index$_i$!
'Yes, this has to be what she said!'

In this transcription, the double plus symbols after the first instance of
SEEM represent slow reduplication, which contrast with the sharp, short
movement of the second instance. The first form indicates weak speaker

commitment; the second indicates strong commitment. Wilcox and Wilcox (1995: 156) suggest that an iconicity principle is involved in this contrast: "In epistemics, possibility is expressed with reduced gestural substance; probability or certainty is expressed with strong gestural substance."

In summary, epistemic commitment is typically indicated by both manual and nonmanual means. The manual marking consists of an alternation of the manner in which a sign's movement is articulated: a sharp, brisk movement and a slower, softer movement indicating strong and weak commitment, respectively. The nonmanual marking consists primarily of brow furrow and head nod, indicating strong commitment. These markers as a group function to indicate a special type of intensification, the strength or intensity of epistemic commitment.

4. Modality and intensification

A number of scholars discuss how modal strength is expressed across a range of semantic domains (Palmer 1986; Bybee et al. 1994). As we have just seen, modal strength plays an important role in the epistemic domain, where it signals the speaker's degree of epistemic commitment, from tentative to fully confident. Modal strength also is important across the entire domain of modality; for example, in participant-internal possibility, it indicates degrees of ability, and in participant-external necessity, it indicates degrees of deontic obligation.

We propose that modal strength is a specialized expression of the more general notion of intensification. We do this for two reasons. First, it seems appropriate to discuss the semantics of modal strength as a matter of degree of intensification – that is, as variation along a scale of intensification of necessity, possibility, and speaker's epistemic commitment. Modal strength in ASL is formally related to other types of intensification, such as intensity of color. Second, the way that intensification is expressed in ASL is by phonetic variations in gestural strength, that is, by changes in the strength of a sign's movement. Thus, the expression of modal strength in ASL is iconic: semantically weak modality such as weak deontic obligation is expressed with weak gestural forms, while semantically strong modality such as strong deontic obligation is expressed with a strong gestural form (Wilcox and Wilcox 1995).

It is well known that languages use different means to express modal strength. In some languages these distinctions are expressed lexically, as

English does with *must* and *should* for expressing strong and weak deontic obligation respectively. Similarly, Spanish has several different forms to express degrees of necessity:

(24) Ella necesita quedarse en casa para cuidar a los niños.
      'It is necessary for her to stay home to take care of the children.'

(25) Ella tiene quedarse en casa para cuidar a los niños.
      'She has to stay home to take care of the children.'

(26) Ella debe quedarse en casa para cuidar a los niños.
      'She should stay home to take care of the children.'

Other languages use morphological means to express modal strength. For example, Palmer (1986: 65) cites data from Hixkaryana (Derbyshire 1979) in which the intensifier *ha* is used to mark degree of epistemic certainty:

(27) a. nomokyaha   ha.
          he come+NONPAST INT
          'He must certainly come.'

      b. nomokyan   ha.
          he come+NONPAST UNCERT INT
          'He may come.'

ASL indicates modal strength with the addition of markers such as those described above. In the remainder of this paper, we describe the way in which intensification is expressed in ASL, intensification across a range of modal uses, and the nature of the marker of modal intensification in ASL.

4.1. Intensification in ASL

Intensification is indicated by a change in the manner of movement of the sign: the weak forms exhibit a soft, reduplicated movement, while the strong forms are produced with a single, forceful stroke. Weak and strong forms also are accompanied by a set of nonmanual, facial markers including brow furrow and head nod. The manual intensification devices were first described by Frishberg (1972: n.p.):

The difference between the signs for DEEP-YELLOW and YELLOW is a differ-ence in intensity of movement. The first sign is made with a single, tense, brisk motion of one hand, whereas the second sign has a rocking motion of the same hand configuration. We can also make a distinction between the kinds of motion in the signs for YELLOW and YELLOWISH. YELLOWISH moves in the same general direction as YELLOW but with smaller, gentler, and more soft motion.

Frishberg called these movement alternations *sharp* and *soft*, respectively, and argued that they were morphological forms bound to lexical roots. In addition to the color examples just given, examples include the alternations of HOT/VERY-HOT, SMART/VERY-SMART, FAST/VERY-FAST. Frishberg also described sharp and soft modal forms: "For example, the sign MUST can express any degree of obligation or necessity from 'must' through 'should,' 'ought to,' and 'have to,' depending on the manner in which the movement is made." In an extension of Frishberg's work, Gorbet (2003) identified allo-morphs of the SHARP morpheme related to the general meaning of intensifi-cation, such as amplification (DIRTY/FILTHY), spatial or temporal compres-sion (STUDY/CRAM), selection within a domain (YELLOW/REALLY-YELLOW), and, somewhat less prototypical but still in the semantic range of intensifi-cation, inceptive (BURN/BURST-INTO-FLAMES).

These markers of intensity in ASL thus show great semantic range, from lexical uses such as the distinction between 'hot' and 'very hot' to more grammatical uses such as inceptive and the expression of epistemic com-mitment. Whether a grammaticization path from the more lexical to the more grammatical meanings can be identified remains for now an open question. As for the other modal forms, however, we might ask whether a gestural source can be identified, and here an answer suggests itself.

4.2. The second route

Wilcox (2004) has proposed that the facial and manner of movement markers such as those that signal intensification constitute a second route by which gesture becomes incorporated into signed languages. According to this pro-posal, these markers are prosodic or intonational components of signed languages derived from gestural sources which ultimately have their source in the expression of emotion or the speaker's personal, subjective response to some state of affairs. Their link to the expression of modal strength should come as no surprise, since prosody is one of the resources languages have available for the expression of subjectivity. Discussing epistemic modality, Lyons (1995: 331) ties subjectivity and modality to prosody, remarking that "All natural languages provide their users with prosodic resources – stress and intonation – with which to express the several distinguishable kinds of qualified epistemic commitment."

Manner of movement is analogous to prosody and intonation in yet another way. Writing of intonation, Bolinger (1986) noted that people often remark, "I don't mind what she said, but I don't like the way she said it." This distinction between the propositional *what* and the subjective *way*, which, as Bolinger points out, is often dismissed "as a mere manner of saying, an accompaniment to the message rather than an inseparable part of it" (Bolinger 1986: 3), mirrors the distinction between the *what* of a sign's movement and the *way* it is produced, its manner of movement.

Bolinger (1986: 195) regarded intonation as part of a "gestural complex whose primitive and still surviving function is the signaling of emotion" and asked, "How far has intonation come on the road to the arbitrary and conventional?" (1986: 198). Our claim is that manner of movement in the expression of intensification provides a glimpse at how we might answer this question. For signed languages, gesture seems to have entered the language system, the realm of the arbitrary and conventional, and in the case of epistemic modal forms has travelled some distance towards becoming fully grammatical. Interestingly, this also seems to be the conclusion reached by Fónagy (1983: 341) for spoken languages, who notes that "modal intonation patterns represent undoubtedly the highest level of semantic organization which can be reached by tonal means. … Intonation had to cover nonetheless a long distance in semantic space to become, from a mere reflection of emotional states, a denotation of modal categories."

When we turn to the nonmanual markers associated with intensification and modal strength, the situation is much the same. In this case, however, the evidence is much clearer in support of the gestural source of these markers. Wilcox and Wilcox (1995: 146–148) point out that head nod and brow furrow are not only used to mark modal forms, especially epistemic modals, but also wh-questions and imperatives. Looking only at intonation in spoken language, Bolinger (1986: 208) also points out a relationship between wh-questions and imperatives mediated by gesture:

> Even wh-questions that appear to be only for eliciting information are affected by gesture to the extent of being more question-like or more command-like. Wh-questions straddle the line between interrogative and imperative: they use interrogative inversion but freely use an intonation that is

more typical of commands – continuous down motion plus a terminal fall. So if a speaker asks, 'Where did you put it?' with nothing arched up ('with a solemn expression') and with lips tightly close at the end of the utterance, the assumption of authority is manifest. But if the usual question cues are added – smile, raised eyebrows, and mouth open at end of utterance – the authority is softened.

Once again, when these gestures enter the signed language system, they do so first as prosodic devices that accompany and modulate the more propositional portion of the linguistic message. Like manner of movement, however, they too travel along the route from gesture to grammar, eventually functioning to distinguish between a statement and an interrogative, or, as we saw in (21), between temporal future and future certainty meanings. In some cases, such as when they serve to indicate degree of obligation or ability, these forms exhibit almost continuous variation and thus appear more prosodic. In other cases, they seem to have moved much farther along the path to fully grammatical and obligatory. This is the case for the expression of epistemic commitment. The ASL necessity form can only be used in an epistemic sense when it appears in the soft, reduplicated form, glossed as SHOULD:

(28) [PRO.1 SEND LETTER ASK TRANSLATE SPANISH]- topic, [RECEIVE THIS WEEK SHOULD]-bf/hn.
'I sent a letter to the Spanish translator and asked them to translate it. I should receive it this week.'

We suggest that the soft marking in this case has achieved morphological status.

5. Conclusions

We have described a range of modal forms in ASL and suggested that their semantics are best described, following van der Auwera and Plungian (1998), by using the semantic domains of necessity and obligation, participant-external and participant-internal, and epistemic modality. We have also documented that, as for spoken languages, modal forms often develop from lexical sources.

Unlike spoken languages, for signed languages such as ASL, we can often trace the ultimate source of these lexical forms to gestures outside the language system. Here, we have provided evidence of two routes leading from gesture to grammar: one in which manual gestures go through a lexical stage before developing into more grammatical forms, and a second which leads from gesture to prosodic device and then directly to grammar.

Notes

1. Many authors refer to *sign languages*. We prefer the term *signed language*, parallel to *spoken language* and *written language*.
2. Dively (2001) describes a small set of non-manually produced signs. None, however, appears to be strictly lexical. Most are nonmanual grammatical signs or discourse markers.
3. Two points need further study. First, we can find no purely lexical predecessor for IL FAUT. This may be because the gesture meaning 'insist' already had a grammatical sense to it. Second, we do not here explore the further development of the upward-facing palm gesture, except to note that it occurs in certain classifier forms for 'flat object,' one of which is a component of the ASL word MONEY.
4. We have slightly changed the translation from Wilcox and Wilcox (1995) to better reflect the meaning of this utterance.

References

Battison, R.
   1978   *Lexical Borrowing in American Sign Language.* Silver Spring, MD: Linkstok Press.
Bolinger, D.
   1986   *Intonation and its Parts: Melody in Spoken English.* Stanford: Stanford University Press.
Brouland, J.
   1855   *Langage mimique: Spécimen d'un dictionnaire des signes.* Washington, DC: Gallaudet Archives.
Bybee, J., R. Perkins and W. Pagliuca
   1994   *The Evolution of Grammar: Tense, Aspect, and Modality in the Languages of the World.* Chicago: University of Chicago Press.
de Jorio, A.
   1832   *Gesture in Naples and Gesture in Classical Antiquity: A Translation of La mimica degli antichi investigata nel gestire napoletano, Gestural Expression of the Ancients in the Light of Neapolitan Gesturing* (transl. A. Kendon, 2000). Bloomington: Indiana University Press.

Derbyshire, D. C.
1979   *Hixkaryana*. Lingua Descriptive Series, 1. Amsterdam: North Holland.
Dively, V. L.
2001   Signs without hands: Nonhanded signs in American Sign Language. In *Signed Languages: Discoveries from International Research*, V. L. Dively, M. Metzger, S. F. Taub and A. M. Baer (eds.), 62–73. Washington, DC: Gallaudet University Press.
Dodwell, C. R.
2000   *Anglo-Saxon Gestures and the Roman Stage*. Cambridge: Cambridge University Press.
Ferreira Brito, L.
1990   Epistemic, alethic, and deontic modalities in a Brazilian Sign Language. In *Theoretical Issues in Sign Language Research, vol. 1: Linguistics*, S. D. Fischer and P. Siple (eds.), 224–260. Chicago: University of Chicago Press.
Fischer, S. D. and B. Gough
1978   Verbs in American Sign Language. *Sign Language Studies* 18: 17–48.
Fónagy, I.
1983   Preconceptual thinking in language (An essay in paleontology). In *Glossogenetics: The Origin and Evolution of Language*, E. de Grolier (ed.), 329–353. New York: Harwood Academic Publishers.
Frishberg, N.
1972   Sharp and soft: Two aspects of movement in sign. Unpublished ms.
Girod, M.
1997   *La langue des signes: Tome 2. Dictionnaire bilingue élémentaire*. Vincennes: International Visual Theatre.
Gorbet, L.
2003   The semantics of SHARP in American Sign Language. Paper presented at the annual meeting of the Linguistic Association of the Southwest (LASSO), Los Angeles, California, October 2003.
Grimes, B.
1996   *Ethnologue*. Dallas: Summer Institute of Linguistics.
Groce, N. E.
1985   *Everyone Here Spoke Sign Language: Hereditary Deafness on Martha's Vineyard*. Cambridge: Harvard University Press.
Janzen, T.
1995   The polygrammticization of FINISH in ASL. Manuscript, University of Manitoba.
Janzen, T. and B. Shaffer
2002   Gesture as the substrate in the process of ASL grammaticization. In *Modality and Structure in Signed and Spoken Languages*, R. Meier, D. Quinto, and K. Cormier (eds.), 199–223. Cambridge: Cambridge University Press.

Janzen, T., B. Shaffer and S. Wilcox
    1999   Signed language pragmatics. In *Handbook of Pragmatics*, J. Verschueren, J.-O. Östman, J. Blommaert and C. Bulcaen (eds.), 1–20. Amsterdam: Benjamins.
Klima, E. and U. Bellugi
    1979   *The Signs of Language*. Cambridge: Harvard University Press.
Lane, H.
    1980   A chronology of the oppression of sign language in France and the United States. In *Recent Perspectives on American Sign Language*, H. Lane, and F. Grosjean (eds.), 119–161. Hillsdale: Lawrence Erlbaum.
Langacker, R. W.
    1991   *Concept, Image, and Symbol: The Cognitive Basis of Grammar*. Berlin/New York: Mouton de Gruyter.
Long, J. S.
    1918   *The Sign Language: A Manual of Signs*. Washington, DC: Gallaudet College Press.
Lyons, J.
    1977   *Semantics*. Cambridge: Cambridge University Press.
    1995   *Linguistic Semantics*. Cambridge: Cambridge University Press.
Meir, I.
    2003   Grammaticalization and modality: The emergence of a case-marked pronoun in Israeli Sign Language. *Journal of Linguistics* 39: 109–140.
Padden, C.
    1988   *Interaction of Morphology and Syntax in American Sign Language*. New York & London: Garland Publishing, Inc.
Palmer, F. R.
    1986   *Mood and Modality*. Cambridge: Cambridge University Press.
Pélissier, P.
    1856   *Iconographie des signes*. Paris: Imprimerie et Librarie de Paul Dupont.
Sexton, A. L.
    1999   Grammaticalization in American Sign Language. *Language Sciences* 21: 105–141.
Scheibman, J.
    2002   *Point of View and Grammar: Structural Patterns of Subjectivity in American English Conversation*. Amsterdam: Benjamins.
Shaffer, B.
    2000   A syntactic, pragmatic analysis of the expression of necessity and possibility in American Sign Language. Unpublished Ph.D. dissertation, University of New Mexico.

2002   CAN'T: The negation of modal notions in ASL. *Sign Language Studies* 3: 34–53.

2004   Information ordering and speaker subjectivity: Modality in ASL. *Cognitive Linguistics* 15: 175–195.

Stokoe, W. C.
1960   *Sign Language Structure*. Silver Spring: Linstok Press.

van der Auwera, J. and V. A. Plungian
1998   Modality's semantic map. *Linguistic Typology* 2: 79–124.

Wilbur, R.
1999   Metrical structure, morphological gaps, and possible grammaticalization in ASL. *Sign Language and Linguistics* 2: 217–244.

Wilcox, P., and S. Wilcox
1995   The gestural expression of modality in American Sign Language. In *Modality in Grammar and Discourse*, J. Bybee, and S. Fleischman (eds.), 135–162. Amsterdam: Benjamins.

Wilcox, S.
1992   *The Phonetics of Fingerspelling*. Amsterdam: Benjamins.

2004   Gesture and language: Cross-linguistic and historical data from signed languages. *Gesture* 4: 43–75.

Zeshan, U.
2003   'Classificatory' constructions in Indo-Pakistani Sign Language: Grammaticalization and lexicalization processes. In *Perspectives on Classifier Constructions in Sign Languages*, K. Emmorey (ed.), 113–141. Mahwah: Lawrence Erlbaum.

2004   Interrogative constructions in signed languages: Crosslinguistic perspectives. *Language* 80: 7–39.

Topical outline

Erin Eschenroeder, Sarah Mills and Thao Nguyen

Below is a systematic outline of each chapter. This outline is organized according to subjects discussed and the major arguments presented. It is designed to assist in the book's tutorial function and to be a guide to the state of the art of modality.

Modality: Overview and linguistic issues
Jan Nuyts

I. Introduction
    A. Modality
        1. Hard to define, supercategory loosely structured, belongs at higher level of abstraction
        2. Synonymous with *tense-aspect-modality* (TAM) categories or *qualifications of states of affairs*
        3. No unanimity on how modal categories should be characterized
            a. Outer borders – which semantic notions do and do not belong?
            b. Internal organization – how should modals be divided into categories?

II. The basic categories
    A. Dynamic modality (AKA *facultative modality* and *inherent modality*) – ascription of a capacity/ability to the subject-participant of the clause
        1. Modifications
            a. Property of the first argument of the predicate or the controlling participant in the state of affairs
            b. Indicates necessity for the first argument participant

      c. Covers capacity/abilities/potentials and needs/necessities inherent in the first argument participant (*participant-inherent dynamic*) and in participant circumstances (*participant-imposed dynamic*)

      d. Possibly needs to characterize a potential or a necessity/inevitability inherent in the situation described (*situational dynamic*)

B. Deontic modality – notions of permission and obligation; indication of the degree of moral desirability of the state of affairs expressed in the utterance

    1. Notion of morality should be defined widely: can relate to societal norms and/or personal ethical criteria

    2. Degree suggests scale, but strong trend to describe it in discrete values

    3. Negation as a separate operator

    4. Rendered in the most direct way by the modal auxiliaries (expressing respectively moral desirability and necessity), and the predicative adjective (expressing moral desirability)

C. Epistemic modality – an indication of the estimation of the probability that the state of affairs in the clause applies to the real world

    1. Degree suggests scale and polarity

    2. Negation as a separate operator

D. Alternative divisions of the semantic domains

    1. Situational dynamic – some consider not to belong under dynamic modality

      a. Called *participant-external modality*

      b. May be more closely related to deontic modality

      c. Ascription to the first argument participant is the dividing criterion

    2. Root modality – used as the only counterpart of epistemic modality; related to deontic and dynamic modality

    3. Event modality – covers deontic and dynamic modality

    4. Propositional modality – covers epistemic and evidentiality

    5. Epistemic modality

      a. Agent oriented modality – covers meanings which predicate condition on an agent with regard to completion of action referred to by the main predicate

      b. Speaker oriented modality – covers markers of directives representing speech acts through which a speaker attempts to move an addressee to action

  6. Subordinating modality – formal category covering modalities and moods in subordinate clauses

III. Categories on the margins of modality

  A. Mood – inventory of basic utterance types in a language used to refer to distinctions such as indicative vs. subjunctive and realis vs. irrealis

    1. Illocutions – some assign mood and exclude them from the modal category

    2. Modality is semantic whereas mood is grammatical

  B. Alethic modality – concerns the necessary or contingent truth of propositions (modes of truth)

    1. Considered close to but distinct from epistemic modality (which concerns the state of a proposition in terms of knowledge and belief (modes of knowing))

    2. No formal distinction between alethic and epistemic in English

  C. Volition/intention

    1. Considered a subcategory of deontic modality, others include them in dynamic, and others exclude them from modality

    2. Intention – related to the concepts of obligation and permission; relates to action terms

    3. Volition – refers to desires; questionable as a modal notion

  D. Evidentiality – indication of the nature of the speaker's sources of information

    1. Experiential – directly perceived by issuer

    2. Inferential – indirectly deduced

    3. Hearsay/reportative – received from others

    4. Debate over whether it is part of epistemic (inferred certainty) or its own modal category

    5. Semantically not a tight category

E. Boulomaic modality/emotional attitude – indication of the degree
   of the speaker's (dis)liking of the state of affairs
   1. Volition may fall under this category
   2. Difficult to distinguish between boulomaic (disliking) and de-
      ontic (disproving)
   3. Scalar

IV. Dimensions of subcategorizing (expressions of) modal categories
   A. Subjectivity vs. objectivity/intersubjectivity
      1. Objective (expresses an objectively measurable chance that
         the state of affairs under consideration is true or not) vs. sub-
         jective (involves guess regarding truth)
      2. Subjective (issuer's own responsibility) vs. intersubjective
         (shared by a wider group of people)
      3. Present in all evaluative/attitudinal modal categories and under
         inferential and boulomaic modality/attitude
      4. Semantically close to evidentiality
   B. Performativity vs. descriptivity
      1. Pertains to speaker's commitment to the evaluation
      2. Performative – speaker is fully committed to the attitude
      3. Descriptive – reporting on someone else's attitude or attitude
         formerly held by speaker

V. Dimensions relating to modal categories
   A. Modal auxiliaries
      1. Evolve cross-linguistically along fixed path (dynamic > deontic
         > epistemic)
   B. Shared semantic characteristics
      1. Semantic categories of modality share fundamental character-
         istics
         a. Discrete values – possibility and necessity
            i. Scalar view – involves assumption that all categories
               have a strong and weak value and thus volition/inten-
               tion, boulomaic modality/attitude, and inferential evi-
               dentiality could be classified as modalities
         b. Other categories, such as force dynamics

C. Shared status as attitudinal categories
   1. Attitudinal categories – concerned with commitment of speaking subject to the state of affairs
      a. Includes deontic and epistemic, boulomic attitude, evidentiality, but not dynamic

VI. The relationship of modal categories to other TAM categories
   A. Positioning of modal categories
      1. Tendency of TAM markers to be ordered by recurrent semantic pattern
      2. Modal categories have wider semantic scope than TAM
   B. Categories of time and aspect with modality under TAM are misleading: modality is a label of higher level of abstraction

Typological approaches to modality
Ferdinand de Haan

I. Introduction
   A. Concerned with semantic aspects
   B. Focuses on meanings and relative strength of morphemes

II. Terminology
   A. Traditional classification
      1. Epistemic modality – refers to speaker's degree of certainty that what he or she is saying is true
      2. Deontic modality – deals with the degree of force exerted on the subject of the sentence
      3. Dynamic modality – encodes ability, sometimes volition
      4. Root modality – covers both deontic and dynamic modality
         a. Modals have both core and peripheral meanings; *deontic* and *dynamic* refer only to the core meanings while *root* is a neutral term
   B. Diachronic divisions of modality
      1. Epistemic – includes possibility and probability
         a. Inferred certainty – speaker has good reason to believe the statement is true

    2. Subordinating moods – use of modality in subordinating clause

    3. Agent oriented – agent is influenced in performing the action in the clause

       a. Participant oriented modality – used in cases in which the subject is not actually an agent

       b. Root possibility – related to ability, takes external factors into account

    4. Speaker oriented modality – cases in which the speaker gives someone an order or permission

  C. Other classifications

    1. Participant-internal – similar to dynamic modality; deals with ability and need

    2. Participant-external

       a. Deontic modality – encompasses permission and obligation

       b. Non-deontic modality – deals with possibility and necessity; refers to circumstances external to the situation

    3. No need for subject oriented modality; considered part of deontic; does not occur cross-linguistically

    4. Participant oriented modality is too vague

III. Expressions of modality

  A. Modal auxiliary verbs – *must/may* are strong/weak verbs that are ambiguous between deontic and epistemic modality

  B. Mood – morphological verbal category which expresses the modal value of the sentence; grammaticalized version of modality

  C. Modal affixes – can be separated from a verb; different from mood because mood is an obligatory category and cannot be separated from a verb

  D. Lexical means – less grammaticalized means of expressing modality

  E. Modal adverbs and adjectives – have become more grammaticalized

  F. Modal tags – epistemic modality can be expressed with *I think, I guess, I believe*

  G. Modal particles – occur between verbal elements

  H. Modal case – modality marked on noun as a case marker

IV. Realis and irrealis
   A. Divides world into real and unreal events
   B. Two ways to encode irrealis
      1. Joint system – irrealis morphemes co-occur with another morpheme which encodes actual type of irrealis
      2. Non-joint system – irrealis morphemes that function by themselves
         a. It is grammatical to omit the realis/irrealis morphemes without impacting modal status of sentence
   C. Problems with realis/irrealis distinction
      1. Term *irrealis* is vague and the semantic content differs across languages
      2. Future can be used with either realis or irrealis

V.   Semantic map of modality
   A. Used to chart synchronic and diachronic changes in meaning
   B. Pathways are universal and unidirectional
   C. Pathway of morpheme meaning ability > root possibility > epistemic (gram)
   D. Overall developmental path is from agent oriented to subordinate modality (less to more grammaticalization)
      1. Agent oriented modal grams least likely to be bound; subordinate modal grams most likely to be bound
   E. Map has three parts
      1. Premodal – contains lexical sources for modal domain
      2. Modal
      3. Postmodal – contains further grammaticalization paths for modal grams; not part of modal domain

VI. Modality and tense
   A. Tense – grammaticalized expression of time; relates to modality through future (epistemic) and past (irrealis)

VII. Modality and negation
   A. Negation refers to a nonexistent state; hence events not real (irrealis)

B. No language in which a lexical distinction is made between weak modals that express possibility and contingency

C. No language with a weak modal that is made up of a strong modal and double negation

D. *Modal suppletion strategy* for disambiguation

    1. Narrow scope of negation – negation is in scope of modal

    2. Wide scope of negation – modal is in scope of negation

E. *Negation placement strategy* – shows scope relation in Russian; modal verb stays same but place of negation changes

    1. Narrow scope – negation precedes main verb

    2. Wide scope – negation precedes modal verb

VIII. Evidentiality

A. Evidentiality – deals with source of evidence speaker has for statement (either directly or indirectly: quotative or inferential evidentiality)

B. Considered modal category typologically

C. Propositional modality – encompasses evidentiality and epistemic modality

D. Recent proposal to categorize evidentiality as modal/propositional deixis

E. Mirativity – speaker received information from unexpected source

    1. Expressed by same morphemes as evidentiality in languages with both categories

Formal approaches to modality

Stefan Kaufmann, Cleo Condoravdi and Valentina Harizanov

I.   Modal logic

A. General introduction to modal logic

    1. Modals as operators

    2. Representations of modality

B. Propositional modal logic: syntactic approach
1. Language L_A
2. Classical logic defined as axiomatic system
    a. Modus Ponens (inference rule)
3. Derivation
    a. Finite sequence of sentences that are either axioms or are obtained by inference rules
4. Derived rule – rule whose conclusion has derivation from hypotheses
5. Proof – for sentence φ is a derivation sequence whose last member is φ
6. Theorem – sentence that has a proof
7. Formal system K (Kripke)
    a. Contains axiom (K) and *Necessitation Rule*
8. Set Φ is *syntactically consistent* if no contradiction can be derived from Φ
C. Propositional modal logic: semantic approach
1. Possible worlds
2. Models
    a. Set W
    b. Assignment function V
3. Semantic relationships between sentences can be defined in terms of propositions they denote
4. Semantic consistency
5. Semantic consequence
6. Soundness and completeness

II. Modal bases
A. Conversational background
B. Modal force
1. Integral part of lexical meaning of all modals
C. Accessibility relations between possible worlds
1. Frames

D. Properties of modal bases
1. Consistency
2. Realism
3. Introspection
   a. Modal base encodes speaker's beliefs about facts and beliefs about own beliefs: positive and negative introspection
E. Ordering sources
1. Parameter used to characterize gradable notions of modality and avoid inconsistencies
2. May be used to represent normality and plausibility assumptions and hierarchy of laws (Kratzer)

III. Modality and time
A. English present tense
1. Future differs from past in non-determinacy
2. Two notions of truth
   a. Ockhamist: upholds Excluded Middle and Non-Contradiction
   b. Peircean: invokes the force of necessity
B. Temporal dimension
1. Time as a linearly ordered set $(T, <)$
2. Modal/temporal two-dimensional semantics
   a. Change over time
   b. Accessibility relations link world-time pairs whose time coordinate is constant
3. Temporal relations link world-time pairs
4. Truth and settledness
   a. Settledness as historical necessity with respect to accessibility relations
C. Objective and subjective uncertainty
1. Historical necessity model

D. Settledness and scheduling
  1. Present on felicitous scheduling reading
  2. Only future reference gives rise to settledness condition
  3. Sentences carry strong modal force because they are asserted
      a. Listener may react with an accommodation of the information that truth value is objectively settled

Historical aspects of modality
Elizabeth Traugott

I. Introduction
  A. Expressions of modality are derived from non-modal expressions
  B. Morphosyntactic findings
    1. Modal auxiliary and affixes derived from main verbs
    2. Source of tags found in main clauses with first person subjects and verbs of cognition
    3. Adverbial and modal particles have varied sources
  C. Semantic scales
    1. Possession/intention > deontic > epistemic conclusion
    2. Ability > root possibility > epistemic possibility

II. Some basic issues in historical work
  A. Functional and formal approaches
    1. Functionally oriented views concentrate on grammaticalization
    2. Points of disagreement
      a. Theory of change
        i. Functionalist perspective – change in use
        ii. Formalist perspective – differences in individual grammars
      b. Search for universals in language
        i. Functionalist perspective – strong tendencies which allow for exceptions
        ii. Formalist perspective – absolute universals; don't allow for exceptions

      3. Further debates about morphosyntactic change

          a. Semantic change forcing syntactic change

          b. Terminology for significant change

          c. Hypothesis of unidirectionality

          d. Role of frequency in determining change

  B. Grammaticalization – change whereby lexical items serve grammatical functions

      1. Unidirectional path: main verbs > modal auxiliaries > affixes (mood and tense markers)

          a. Bleaching – loss of concrete, referential, and content meaning; retention of modal content

      2. Unidirectionality closely related to scope increase

          a. Syntatic – shifts of epistemic modals and moods to outer position

          b. Semantic – major factor in development of deontic and epistemic modality

      3. Modality goes through periods of indeterminacy and vagueness

  C. Invited inferencing and subjectification

      1. Metonymic inferencing – plays leading role as speakers and hearers negotiate meaning and adopt innovations

      2. Metaphoric mapping – way to conceptualize the relationship between root/obligation and epistemic modality

      3. Invited inferencing – change occurs in strategic interaction: speakers/writers invite hearers/readers to infer meanings beyond what is said

      4. Subjectification – emerges metonymically from inferences that arise in act of communication between speaker and hearer

          a. Intersubjectification – paying attention to the hearer

III. Cross-linguistic typological studies

  A. Work of Bybee and associates

      1. Studies of grammaticalization of TAM in 76 languages

IV. Corpora and frequency studies of English

A. Corpora have allowed researchers to correlate various factors with change, including sex, age, text type, spoken vs. written medium, and variety

B. Modal adverbials

1. Class of essential adverbs and adverbials with at least partially modal meaning has existed since Old English

C. Auxiliary system

1. The use of *may* instead of *might*; modal perfects like *would have* are changes in auxiliary system

2. Core modals replaced by semi-modals

V. Conclusion

A. Modality is a gradient notion, both semantically and morphosyntactically, that can be represented in a variety of morphosyntactic ways

Acquisition of modality
Soonja Choi

I. Introduction

A. Modality – speakers add their own or others' psychological or mental states to the proposition

B. Agent oriented modality – refers to conditions imposed on agent; includes dynamic, deontic, and root possibility

C. Epistemic – refers to the degree of certainty on part of speaker about truth of proposition

1. Evidentials – refers to speaker's source of information; part of epistemic because speaker is conveying varying degrees of certainty of proposition

II. Developmental pattern of agent oriented and epistemic modalities

A. General developmental pattern

1. Children acquire agent oriented modality before epistemic because they start out with non-epistemic acts

a. Finding is consistent with frequency data

B. Acquisition of modality and syntax

    1. Production of modal auxiliary forms seems more lexically than syntactically driven

        a. Motivated by relations of lexical meanings to discourse functions rather than syntax

        b. Limited range of subjecthood

            i. In agent oriented modality, children use 1st person as subject before 3rd person

            ii. Most modals used in the affirmative

            iii. Negative modals used only to express constraints on actions

            iv. Children use epistemic modals with 3rd person as subject to express events and states

C. Epistemic modality: spontaneous speech data

    1. Children express certainty before uncertainty

D. Epistemic modality: experimental data

    1. Epistemic modality acquired later due to unnaturalness of tasks

    2. Children learn modal extremes before points on continuum

III. Modal expression and cognitive development

A. Development of modality and *theory of mind*

    1. Theory of mind – refers to ability to assess others' beliefs about affairs

    2. Linguistic and representational abilities come from general development of representational theory of mind

B. Relation between modal expression and cognitive development

    1. Link between early language development and later-occurring theory of mind

        a. Relationship between language and cognition is bidirectional

        b. Nonlinguistic reasoning ability related to and a prerequisite for comprehension of epistemic modal meanings

        c. In agent oriented modality, no significant relation between nonlinguistic and linguistic tasks

IV.   Discourse-pragmatic meanings of modality in children's speech

    A.   Children are very sensitive to discourse functional aspects of modal forms

V.   Sentence-ending suffixes as modal expressions

    A.   Epistemic modality emerges later than agent oriented modalities when modality is expressed lexically

    B.   Bound modals

        1.   Evidentials – verbal suffixes assessing the source of information; epistemic due to degree of certainty involved

    C.   Children attend to semantic and pragmatic contexts of modal forms as well as morphological properties

VI.   Caregiver input and acquisition of modality

    A.   Evidence for both influence of input and universal cognitive development

        1.   Agent oriented modals acquired earlier than epistemic modals related to frequency of input

        2.   Early acquisition of modals despite low frequency of input explained by salience in here-and-now and interest of child

    B.   Input, universal cognitive processing strategies, and discourse contexts play interactive role in acquisition of TAM

VII.   Conclusion

    A.   Agent oriented modality acquired earlier than epistemic

    B.   Children use agent-oriented modality to express 1st person before 3rd person

    C.   Certainty acquired before uncertainty and inferences

    D.   Early modals more semantically and pragmatically than syntactically based

    E.   No tie of syntactic growth to growth in children's modals

Modal expression in Valley Zapotec
Pamela Munro

I.   Introduction
    A. Valley Zapotec (VZ)
       1. Expresses basic modal concepts through verb inflection, auxiliary verbs, and second-position adverbial clitic
       2. Deontic and epistemic modality expressed with separate grammatical mechanism
       3. No single isolable category of core modal morphemes
    B. Mood – compares real world events to those of reference world; concerned with different types of non-actuality
       1. Negative sentences can be included
    C. Independent modality – non-actuality expressed without any overt operator to determine that modality
       1. Negated clauses are not independent modality
    D. Deontic modality includes dynamic modality

II. Expressions of modality in VZ
    A. Modality in VZ "aspect" system
       1. Verbs consist of base plus and inflectional prefix (aspect prefix) – indicates TAM
    B. Modals vs. non-modals in VZ
       1. Non-modal aspects – describe events taken to occur in actual world of speaker and listener
          a. Habitual – ongoing or regularly repeated states or event
          b. Progressive – immediately ongoing events or states
          c. Perfective – completed actions
          d. Neutral – state resulting from the action; used with restricted number of verbs
       2. Modal aspects – express relationship between events and actual world (include irrealis, subjunctive and definite)
          a. Do not distinguish between modal and non-modal uses of irrealis aspect in VZ because both concern non-actual events

C. Irrealis in VZ

    1. Used in complements of intentional verbs, modal verbs, formal and negative imperatives

D. Definite in VZ

    1. Used in matrix clauses to specify futures that speaker is certain will occur

    2. Licensed by mood features defining events as necessarily true; encodes necessity rather than possibility

    3. Does not allow subjects or objects to be contrastively focused

    4. Often degraded or ungrammatical when negated or when positive response is expected

E. Subjunctive in VZ

    1. Non-actual modal reference

    2. Most common use in negative past statements; also synonymous with negative perfective

    3. Simple conditional sentences use hypothetical 'if' and irrealis with non-present reference in both 'if' and 'then' clauses

    4. Counterfactual conditionals use hypothetical 'if' with subjunctive in both 'if' and 'then' clauses

      a. Counterfactuals may also have perfective in 'then' clause

    5. Used in complements of intentional verbs and certain modal auxiliaries with past reference

    6. Past tense analogue to irrealis past negatives and counterfactual conditionals present alternatives between subjunctive and usual past expressed by perfective

F. Deontic vs. epistemic in VZ

    1. Perfective and irrealis aspects that express imperatives and irrealis in wishes are deontic

    2. More difficult to classify the future uses of definite and irrealis on a deontic-epistemic scale

    3. Definite futures express speaker's assessment of necessity or certainty of future event; epistemic use

    4. Irrealis future does not represent wish or expression of capability but weaker degree of epistemic modality; possibility rather than necessity

5. No case in which any of aspects is ambiguous between epistemic and deontic readings
G. Expression of deontic modality with VZ auxiliary verbs
   1. Expressed through auxiliary verbs
H. Auxiliary status
   1. Two different classes of auxiliaries – between modal necessity and modal possibility
      a. Necessity auxiliaries
         i. Used with irrealis and subjunctive complement
         ii. May be used in a past sense with complement in subjunctive
         iii. Use of subjunctive complement locates reference of modal verb in past
         iv. Many have non-modal uses; modal use metaphorically or lexically derived
         v. Have meanings that are aspectual rather than modal
      b. Possibility auxiliaries
         i. Have meanings that are aspectual rather than modal
         ii. All express deontic modality
         iii. Complements of possibility auxiliaries are rarely non-actual
   2. Necessity and possibility are deontic modal operators
I. Epistemic modality in VZ
   1. Some coded by adverbs
   2. Only one auxiliary with epistemic content
   3. Most common means of epistemic is by second position clitic; indicates the speaker's evaluative comment on reaction to situation
      a. Clitics are simple and special
J. Core modality
   1. Core modality in English
      a. Use of auxiliary verbs
      b. Often same form can express both deontic and epistemic
      c. Dialectal variants allow double modals

        d. Occasional uses to refer to non-actual events

    2. Core modality in Mojave

        a. Bound morphology as markers of modality

        b. Indicate both deontic and epistemic

        c. Support path of grammaticalization from separate to bound forms

    3. Core modality in Chickasaw

        a. Expressed by modal suffixes and tense-aspect morphemes

        b. Appears to support grammaticalization path from free-standing to bound

        c. Epistemic and deontic can be in same form

        d. Can look like English double modal

K. Status of VZ in typology of modality

    1. VZ does not have core set of modal morphemes

        a. Modality expressed morphologically within system of verbal aspect, lexically with modal auxiliary verbs, syntactically with second position clitic

    2. Expression of deontic and epistemic modality is completely distinct

        a. Aspect prefixes have both deontic and epistemic uses; distinguished by construction type

        b. Necessity and possibility auxiliary have only deontic uses

        c. One epistemic auxiliary; no deontic uses

        d. Main expression of epistemic modality is with the second position clitic; no deontic use

Modality in American Sign Language
Sherman Wilcox and Barbara Shaffer

I.   Signed languages

    A. Gestural – visual modality of signed languages reflected in linguistic structure

II.   A brief sketch of ASL

    A. Phonology

       1. Chereme – analyzable unit of structure within a sign

       2. Parameters

          a. Handshape

          b. Location

          c. Movement

          d. Orientation

  B. Morphology

       1. Highly synthetic with tendencies toward polysynthesis

  C. Syntax

       1. Characterized by high degree of topic-comment structure

  D. Grammaticization

       1. Grammatical material develops out of lexical material

       2. Occurs in development of modal auxiliaries and of agentive suffix

  E. Fingerspelling

       1. Used for proper names, technical terms, and loan words

  F. Class of articulators

       1. Manual – produces lexical or grammatical signs

       2. Non-manual – used to code grammatical functions

          a. Forms across language are similar

          b. Facial markers are expressions of modality due to relation to subjectivity

          c. Asymmetry of facial vs. manual articulators in signed languages mirrors semantic subjectivity

III. Modality in ASL

  A. Gestures become lexicalized as ASL modals and exhibit strong and weak forms

  B. Two routes lead from gestural sources to modal forms

       1. Manual gestural forms > lexical signs > modal verbs

       2. Manual markers > prosodic markers > modal strength markers

  C. Necessity

       1. Modal notion of necessity is expressed with *must/should*

       a. Weak and strong variants construed by physical force

  2. Participant-external

       a. Participant-external advisability – speaker offers advice; does not include self in situation

       b. Participant-external root necessity – general circumstances compel action in proposition

  3. Participant-internal

       a. Participant-internal advisability – speaker is participant in situation and is imposing self- limiting condition

  4. Gestural sources of necessity

       a. Grammaticalization leads from lexical morphemes to grammatical morphemes

D. Possibility

  1. Includes notions of physical and mental abilities, skills, root possibility, permission, and epistemic possibility

  2. Participant-internal – physical ability

       a. Root possibility – enabling condition present in the situation

       b. Participant-external

          i. Permission – type of deontic possibility; counterpart to deontic obligation; granted by external source

         ii. Root possibility – condition inherent in situation is external to main clause agent

  3. Gestural sources of possibility

  4. Epistemic modality

       a. Expressed by combination of manual signs and manual and non-manual markers

       b. Specific combinations indicate degree of speaker certainty

       c. Position of modal in utterance corresponds to its scope and degree of grammaticalization

       d. Inferential evidentials – overlaps between epistemic modality and evidentiality

       e. Expressed in ASL with future (distinguished by constellation of manual and non-manual gestures)

IV.   Modality and intensification

   A. Modal strength is specialized expression of general notion of intensification

      1. Indicates degree of ability in participant-internal possibility

      2. Indicates degree of deontic obligation in participant-external necessity

   B. Intensification expressed by phonetic variations in gestural strength

   C. Intensification in ASL

      1. Indicated by change in manner of movement of sign

      2. Markers of intensity show great semantic range, from lexical to grammatical uses

   D. Second route

      1. Facial and manner of movement markers are prosodic; derived from gestural sources

         a.   Manner of movement mirrors spoken languages' intonation

      2. Applies to non-manual markers associated with intensification of modal strength

V.   Conclusion

   A. Two routes leading from gesture to grammar

      3. Manual gestures > lexical signs > grammatical forms

      4. Manual gestures > prosodic device > grammatical forms

Index

List of contributors

William Frawley
Depts. of Anthropology and Psychology

George Washington University
Phillips Hall 212
Washington, DC 20052

frawley@gwu.edu

Soonja Choi
Dept. of Linguistics and Oriental
Languages

San Diego State University
5500 Campanile Dr.
San Diego, CA 92182-7727

schoi@mail.sdsu.edu

Cleo Condoravdi

Palo Alto Research Center
3333 Coyote Hill Road
Palo Alto, CA 94304

condorav@csli.stanford.edu

Erin Eschenroeder & Thao Nguyen
Dept. of Anthropology

George Washington University
Washington, DC 20052

erinesch@yahoo.com
tpnguyen@gwu.edu

Ferdinand de Haan
Department of Linguistics

University of Arizona
P.O. Box 210028
Tucson, AZ 85721

fdehaan@u.arizona.edu

Valentina Harizanov
Dept. of Mathematics

George Washington University
Washington, DC 20052

harizanv@gwu.edu

Stefan Kaufmann
Dept. of Linguistics

Northwestern University
2016 Sheridan Road
Evanston, IL 60208-4090

Kaufmann@northwestern.edu

Sarah Mills
Dept. of Physics

George Washington University
Washington, DC 20052

smills@gwu.edu

Pamela Munro
Department of Linguistics

UCLA Box 951543
Los Angeles, CA 90095-1543

munro@ucla.edu

Elizabeth Traugott
Dept. of Linguistics

Stanford University
Margaret Jacks Hall
Building 460, Room 103
Stanford, CA 94305-2150

traugott@stanford.edu

Jan Nuyts
Dept. of Linguistics

Universiteit Antwerpen (UIA)
Universiteitplein 1
2610 Wilrijk / Belgium

Jan.nuyts@ua.ac.be

Sherman Wilcox & Barbara Shaffer
Department of Linguistics

University of New Mexico
Humanities Bldg. Rm. 526
Albuquerque, NM 87131

wilcox@unm.edu
bshaffer@unm.edu

www.ingramcontent.com/pod-product-compliance
Lightning Source LLC
Chambersburg PA
CBHW070410100426
42812CB00005B/1696